To

_____

From

_____

Date

_____

I will thank the Lord with all my heart;
I will declare all Your wonderful works.
I will rejoice and boast about You;
I will sing about Your name, Most High.
Psalm 9:1-2 HCSB

A DAILY JOURNEY

THROUGH PSALMS

for Women

Freeman-Smith, a division of Worthy Media, Inc.

134 Franklin Road, Suite 200, Brentwood, Tennessee 37027

The quoted ideas expressed in this book (but not Scripture verses) are not, in all cases, exact quotations, as some have been edited for clarity and brevity. In all cases, the author has attempted to maintain the speaker's original intent. In some cases, quoted material for this book was obtained from secondary sources, primarily print media. While every effort was made to ensure the accuracy of these sources, the accuracy cannot be guaranteed. For additions, deletions, corrections, or clarifications in future editions of this text, please write Freeman-Smith.

Scripture quotations are taken from:

The Holy Bible, King James Version (KJV)

The Holy Bible, New International Version (NIV) Copyright © 1973, 1978, 1984, by International Bible Society. Used by permission of Zondervan Publishing House. All rights reserved.

The Holy Bible, New King James Version (NKJV) Copyright © 1982 by Thomas Nelson, Inc. Used by permission.

Holy Bible, New Living Translation, (NLT) copyright © 1996. Used by permission of Tyndale House Publishers, Inc., Wheaton, Illinois 60189. All rights reserved.

The Message (MSG)- This edition issued by contractual arrangement with NavPress, a division of The Navigators, U.S.A. Originally published by NavPress in English as THE MESSAGE: The Bible in Contemporary Language copyright 2002-2003 by Eugene Peterson. All rights reserved.

New Century Version®. (NCV) Copyright © 1987, 1988, 1991 by Word Publishing, a division of Thomas Nelson, Inc. All rights reserved. Used by permission.

The New American Standard Bible®, (NASB) Copyright © 1960, 1962, 1963, 1968, 1971, 1972, 1973, 1975, 1977, 1995 by The Lockman Foundation. Used by permission.

The Holman Christian Standard Bible™ (HCSB) Copyright © 1999, 2000, 2001 by Holman Bible Publishers. Used by permission.

Cover Design by Scott Williams/ Richmond & Williams
Page Layout by Bart Dawson

ISBN 978-1-60587-451-7

Printed in the United States of America

A DAILY JOURNEY

THROUGH PSALMS

for Women

Introduction

Every day is a good day to praise God, but when it comes to the privilege (and the responsibility) of praising Him, some days are easier than others. After all, it isn't easy being a godly woman in today's troubled world. Never have expectations been higher, never have temptations been stronger, never have distractions been so plentiful, and never have demands been greater. Thankfully, God stands ready, willing, and able to help you in every facet of your life if you ask Him. But it's important to remember that the best way to ask God for His help—and the best time to praise Him—is early and often.

The fabric of daily life is woven together with the threads of habit, and no habit is more important than that of consistent prayer and daily devotion to the Creator. And this book is intended to help. This text contains 365 chapters, each of which contains a passage from Psalms. During the next year, please try this experiment: read a chapter each day. If you're already committed to a daily worship time, this book will enrich that experience. If you are not, the simple act of giving God a few minutes each morning will change the direction and the quality of your life.

This text addresses topics of particular interest to you, a Christian woman living in an uncertain world. If you take the time to meditate upon these devotional readings, you will be reminded of God's love, of His Son, and of His promises. May these pages be a blessing to you, and may you, in turn, be a blessing to your family, to your friends, and to the world.

The Book of Psalms and You

It has been called the most widely-used book of the Old Testament; it is, of course, the book of Psalms. In the Hebrew version of the Old Testament, the title of the book is translated "Hymns of Praise," and with good reason. Much of the book is a breathtakingly beautiful celebration of God's power, God's love, and God's creation.

The psalmist writes, "Let everything that has breath praise the Lord. Praise the Lord" (150:6). As Christians, we should continually praise God for all that He has done and all that He will do. For believers who have accepted the transforming love of Jesus Christ, there is simply no other way.

When is the best time to praise God? In church? Before dinner is served? When we tuck little children into bed? None of the above. The best time to praise God is all day, every day, to the greatest extent we can, with thanksgiving in our hearts.

Mrs. Charles E. Cowman, the author of the classic devotional text, *Streams in the Desert*, wrote, "Two wings are necessary to lift our souls toward God: prayer and praise. Prayer asks. Praise accepts the answer." That's why we should find the time to lift our concerns to God in prayer, and to praise Him for all that He has done.

Today, as you travel to work or school, as you hug your loved ones, or marvel at a glorious sunset, think of what God has done for you, for yours, and for all of us. And, every time you notice a gift from the Giver of all things good, praise Him. His works are marvelous, His gifts are beyond understanding, and His love endures forever.

Prayers and Praise

Is anyone cheerful? He should sing praises.

James 5:13 HCSB

Because we have been saved by God's only Son, we must never lose hope in the priceless gifts of eternal love and eternal life. And, because we are so richly blessed, we must approach our Heavenly Father with reverence and thanksgiving.

Sometimes, in our rush "to get things done," we simply don't stop long enough to pause and thank our Creator for the countless blessings He has bestowed upon us. But when we slow down and express our gratitude to the One who made us, we enrich our own lives and the lives of those around us.

Thanksgiving should become a habit, a regular part of our daily routines. God has blessed us beyond measure, and we owe Him everything, including our prayers and our praise.

Preoccupy my thoughts with your praise beginning today.

Joni Eareckson Tada

– Your Daily Journey Through Psalms –

O come, let us sing unto the LORD: let us make a joyful noise to the rock of our salvation. Let us come before his presence with thanksgiving, and make a joyful noise unto him with psalms.

Psalm 95:1-2 KJV

Celebrating His Gifts

Rejoice, and be exceeding glad: for great is your reward in heaven . . . .

Matthew 5:12 KJV

The 100th Psalm reminds us that the entire earth should "Shout for joy to the Lord" (NIV). As God's children, we are blessed beyond measure, but sometimes, as busy women living in a demanding world, we are slow to count our gifts and even slower to give thanks to the Giver.

Our blessings include faith, life, and family—for starters. And, the gifts we receive from God are multiplied when we share them. May we always give thanks to the Creator for His blessings, and may we always demonstrate our gratitude by sharing our gifts with others.

The 118th Psalm reminds us that, "This is the day which the LORD has made; let us rejoice and be glad in it" (v. 24, NASB). May we celebrate this day and the One who created it.

The highest and most desirable state of the soul is to praise God in celebration for being alive.

Luci Swindol

– Your Daily Journey Through Psalms –

This is the day the LORD has made; we will rejoice and be glad in it.

Psalm 118:24 NKJV

Your Growing Faith

I want their hearts to be encouraged and joined together in love, so that they may have all the riches of assured understanding, and have the knowledge of God's mystery— Christ.

Colossians 2:2 HCSB

Your relationship with God is ongoing; it unfolds day by day, and it offers countless opportunities to grow closer to Him . . . or not. As each new day unfolds, you are confronted with a wide range of decisions: how you will behave, where you will direct your thoughts, with whom you will associate, and what you will choose to worship. These choices, along with many others like them, are yours and yours alone. How you choose determines how your relationship with God will unfold.

Are you continuing to grow in your love and knowledge of the Lord, or are you "satisfied" with the current state of your spiritual health? Hopefully, you're determined make yourself a growing Christian. Your Savior deserves no less, and neither, by the way, do you.

– Your Daily Journey Through Psalms –

For You, O God, have tested us; You have refined us as silver is refined. You brought us into the net; You laid affliction on our backs. You have caused men to ride over our heads; we went through fire and through water; but You brought us out to rich fulfillment.

Psalm 66:10-12 NKJV

A Book Unlike Any Other

You will be a good servant of Christ Jesus, nourished by the words of the faith and of the good teaching that you have followed.

1 Timothy 4:6 HCSB

God's Word is unlike any other book. The words of Matthew 4:4 remind us that, "Man shall not live by bread alone but by every word that proceedeth out of the mouth of God" (KJV). As believers, we are instructed to study the Bible and meditate upon its meaning for our lives, yet far too many Bibles are laid aside by well-intentioned believers who would like to study the Bible if they could "just find the time."

Warren Wiersbe observed, "When the child of God looks into the Word of God, he sees the Son of God. And, he is transformed by the Spirit of God to share in the glory of God." God's Holy Word is, indeed, a transforming, life-changing, one-of-a-kind treasure. And it's up to you—and only you—to use it that way.

Study the Bible and observe how the persons behaved and how God dealt with them. There is explicit teaching on every condition of life.

Corrie ten Boom

– Your Daily Journey Through Psalms –
Your word is a lamp for my feet and a light on my path.
Psalm 119:105 HCSB

Accepting His Gifts

I have spoken these things to you so that My joy may be in you and your joy may be complete.

John 15:11 HCSB

God sent His Son so that mankind might enjoy the abundant life that Jesus describes in the familiar words of John 10:10. But, God's gifts are not guaranteed; His gifts must be claimed by those who choose to follow Christ.

Do you sincerely seek the riches that our Savior offers to those who give themselves to Him? Then follow Him completely and obey Him without reservation. When you do, you will receive the love and the abundance that He has promised. Seek first the salvation that is available through a personal, passionate relationship with Christ, and then claim the joy, the peace, and the spiritual abundance that the Shepherd offers His sheep.

Today, as you organize your day and care for your family, accept God's promise of spiritual abundance . . . you may be certain that when you do your part, God will do His part.

– Your Daily Journey Through Psalms –

My cup runneth over. Surely goodness and mercy shall follow me all the days of my life: and I will dwell in the house of the LORD for ever.

Psalm 23:5-6 KJV

Eternal and Unchanging

For I am the Lord, I do not change.

Malachi 3:6 NKJV

God is eternal and unchanging. Before He laid the foundations of our universe, He was a being of infinite power and love, and He will remain so throughout all eternity.

We humans are in a state of constant change. We are born, we grow, we mature, and we die. Along the way, we experience the inevitable joys and hardships of life. And we face the inevitable changes that are the result of our own mortality.

But God never changes. His love never ceases, His wisdom never fails, and His promises endure, unbroken, forever.

There is not one God for the Old Testament, another God for the New Testament, another God for today, and still another God for the future. He is enduringly the same yesterday, today, and forever.

Anne Graham Lotz

– Your Daily Journey Through Psalms –
Your righteousness reaches heaven, God, You who have done great things; God, who is like You?

Psalm 71:19 HCSB

A Clear Conscience

I will cling to my righteousness and never let it go. My conscience will not accuse [me] as long as I live!

Job 27:6 HCSB

A clear conscience is one of the many rewards you earn when you obey God's Word and follow His will. Whenever you know that you've done the right thing, you feel better about yourself, your life, and your future. A guilty conscience, on the other hand, is, for most people, it's own punishment.

In order to keep your conscience clear, you should study God's Word and obey it—you should seek God's will and follow it—you should honor God's Son and walk with Him. When you do, your earthly rewards are never-ceasing, and your heavenly rewards will be everlasting.

There is no pillow so soft as a clear conscience.

French Proverb

To go against one's conscience is neither safe nor right. Here I stand. I cannot do otherwise.

Martin Luther

– Your Daily Journey Through Psalms –
God, create a clean heart for me and renew a steadfast spirit within me.

Psalm 51:10 HCSB

The Futility of Worry

Anxiety in a man's heart weighs it down, but a good word cheers it up.

Proverbs 12:25 HCSB

If you are like most women, it is simply a fact of life: from time to time, you worry. You worry about family, about health, about finances, about safety, and about countless other challenges of life, some great and some small. Where is the best place to take your worries? Take them to God. Take your troubles to Him, and your fears, and your sorrows.

Barbara Johnson correctly observed, "Worry is the senseless process of cluttering up tomorrow's opportunities with leftover problems from today." So if you'd like to make the most out of this day (and every one hereafter), turn your worries over to a Power greater than yourself . . . and spend your valuable time and energy solving the problems you can fix . . . while trusting God to do the rest.

Worship and worry cannot live in the same heart; they are mutually exclusive.

Ruth Bell Graham

– Your Daily Journey Through Psalms –

Cast your burden on the Lord, and He will support you; He will never allow the righteous to be shaken.

Psalm 55:22 HCSB

Your Response to His Love

For God so loved the world that He gave His only begotten Son, that whoever believes in Him should not perish but have everlasting life.

John 3:16 NKJV

God made you in His own image and gave you salvation through the person of His Son Jesus Christ. And now, precisely because you are a wondrous creation treasured by God, a question presents itself: What will you do in response to the Creator's love? Will you ignore it or embrace it? Will you return it or neglect it? That decision, of course, is yours and yours alone.

When you embrace God's love, you are forever changed. When you embrace God's love, you feel differently about yourself, your neighbors, your family, and your world. More importantly, you share God's message—and His love—with others.

Your Heavenly Father—a God of infinite love and mercy—is waiting to embrace you with open arms. Accept His love today and forever.

– Your Daily Journey Through Psalms –

Give thanks to Him and praise His name. For the Lord is good, and His love is eternal; His faithfulness endures through all generations.

Psalm 100:4-5 HCSB

His Will Be Done

Our Father which art in heaven, Hallowed be thy name. Thy kingdom come, Thy will be done in earth, as it is in heaven.

Matthew 6:9-10 KJV

When Jesus went to the Mount of Olives, as described in Luke 22, He poured out His heart to God. Jesus knew of the agony that He was destined to endure, but He also knew that God's will must be done. We, like our Savior, face trials that bring fear and trembling to the very depths of our souls, but like Christ, we, too, must ultimately seek God's will, not our own.

God has a plan for all our lives, but He will not force His plans upon us. To the contrary, He only makes His plans clear to those who genuinely and humbly seek His will. As this day unfolds, let us seek God's will and obey His Word. When we entrust our lives to Him completely and without reservation, He gives us the strength to meet any challenge, the courage to face any trial, and the wisdom to live in His righteousness and in His peace.

Jesus told us that only in God's will would we have real freedom.

Catherine Marshall

– Your Daily Journey Through Psalms –

Teach me to do thy will; for thou art my God: thy Spirit is good; lead me into the land of uprightness.

Psalm 143:10 KJV

We Belong to Him

For He is gracious and compassionate, slow to anger, rich in faithful love.

Joel 2:13 HCSB

The line from the children's song is reassuring and familiar: "Little ones to Him belong. We are weak but He is strong." That message applies to kids of all ages: we are all indeed weak, but we worship a mighty God who meets our needs and answers our prayers.

Are you in the midst of adversity or in the grips of temptation? If so, turn to God for strength. The Bible promises that you can do all things through the power of our risen Savior, Jesus Christ. Your challenge, then, is clear: you must place Christ where He belongs: at the very center of your life. When you do, you will discover that, yes, Jesus loves you and that, yes, He will give you direction and strength if you ask it in His name.

– Your Daily Journey Through Psalms –

O God, You are my God; early will I seek You; my soul thirsts for You; my flesh longs for You in a dry and thirsty land where there is no water. So I have looked for You in the sanctuary, to see Your power and Your glory. Because Your lovingkindness is better than life, my lips shall praise You.

Psalm 63:1-3 NKJV

He Cares for You

And God is able to make every grace overflow to you, so that in every way, always having everything you need, you may excel in every good work.

2 Corinthians 9:8 HCSB

The Bible makes this promise: God will care for you and protect you. In the 6th Chapter of Matthew, Jesus made this point clear when He said, "Do not worry about your life, what you will eat or what you will drink; nor about your body, what you will put on. Is not life more than food and the body more than clothing? Look at the birds of the air, for they neither sow nor reap nor gather into barns; yet your heavenly Father feeds them. Are you not of more value than they? Which of you by worrying can add one cubit to his stature? . . . Therefore do not worry about tomorrow, for tomorrow will worry about its own things. Sufficient for the day is its own trouble" (25-27, 34 NKJV).

This beautiful passage reminds you that God still sits in His heaven and you are His beloved child. Simply put, you are protected.

The Rock of Ages is the great sheltering encirclement.

Oswald Chambers

– Your Daily Journey Through Psalms –
The Lord is for me; I will not be afraid. What can man do to me?

Psalm 118:6 HCSB

Seeking His Will

Blessed are those servants whom the master, when he comes, will find watching.

Luke 12:37 NKJV

The Book of Judges tells the story of Deborah, the fearless woman who helped lead the army of Israel to victory over the Canaanites. Deborah was a judge and a prophetess, a woman called by God to lead her people. And when she answered God's call, she was rewarded with one of the great victories of Old Testament times.

Like Deborah, all of us are called to serve our Creator. And, like Deborah, we may sometimes find ourselves facing trials that can bring trembling to the very depths of our souls. As believers, we must seek God's will and follow it. When we do, we are rewarded with victories, some great and some small. When we entrust our lives to Him completely and without reservation, He gives us the strength to meet any challenge, the courage to face any trial, and the wisdom to live in His righteousness and in His peace.

– Your Daily Journey Through Psalms –

Teach me to do Your will, for You are my God; Your Spirit is good. Lead me in the land of uprightness.

Psalm 143:10 NKJV

Embracing God's Love

We love him, because he first loved us.

1 John 4:19 KJV

God made you in His own image and gave you salvation through the person of His Son Jesus Christ. And now, precisely because you are a wondrous creation treasured by God, a question presents itself: What will you do in response to the Creator's love? Will you ignore it or embrace it? Will you return it or neglect it? That decision, of course, is yours and yours alone.

When you embrace God's love, your life's purpose is forever changed. When you embrace God's love, you feel differently about yourself, your neighbors, your family, and your world. More importantly, you share God's message—and His love—with others.

Your Heavenly Father—a God of infinite love and mercy—is waiting to embrace you with open arms. Accept His love today and forever.

The Christian life is motivated, not by a list of do's and don'ts, but by the gracious outpouring of God's love and blessing.

Anne Graham Lotz

– Your Daily Journey Through Psalms –

A righteous man may have many troubles, but the LORD delivers him from them all . . . .

Psalm 34:19 NIV

Receiving His Joy

I have spoken these things to you so that My joy may be in you and your joy may be complete.

John 15:11 HCSB

Few things in life are more sad, or, for that matter, more absurd, than a grumpy Christian. Christ promises us lives of abundance and joy, but He does not force His joy upon us. We must claim His joy for ourselves, and when we do, Jesus, in turn, fills our spirits with His power and His love.

How can we receive from Christ the joy that is rightfully ours? By giving Him what is rightfully His: our hearts and our souls.

When we earnestly commit ourselves to the Savior of mankind, when we place Jesus at the center of our lives and trust Him as our personal Savior, He will transform us, not just for today, but for all eternity. Then we, as God's children, can share Christ's joy and His message with a world that needs both.

Those who are God's without reserve are, in every sense, content.

Hannah Whitall Smith

– Your Daily Journey Through Psalms –
Make me hear joy and gladness.

Psalm 51:8 NKJV

Beyond Jealousy

Where jealousy and selfishness are, there will be confusion and every kind of evil.

James 3:14 NCV

Are you too wise to be consumed with feelings of jealousy? Hopefully so. After all, Jesus clearly taught us to love our neighbors, not to envy them. But sometimes, despite our best intentions, we fall prey to feelings of resentfulness, jealousy, bitterness, and envy. Why? Because we are human, and because we live in a world that places great importance on material possessions (possessions which, by the way, are totally unimportant to God).

The next time you feel pangs of envy invading your thoughts, remind yourself of two things: 1. Envy is a sin, and 2. God has already showered you with so many blessings that if you're a thoughtful, thankful believer, you have no right to ever be envious of any other person on earth.

What God asks, does, or requires of others is not my business; it is His.

Kay Arthur

– Your Daily Journey Through Psalms –

This is my comfort in my affliction, for Your word has given me life.

Psalm 119:50 NKJV

The Medicine of Laughter

A joyful heart is good medicine, but a broken spirit dries up the bones.

Proverbs 17:22 HCSB

L aughter is medicine for the soul, but sometimes, amid the stresses of the day, we forget to take our medicine. Instead of viewing our world with a mixture of optimism and humor, we allow worries and distractions to rob us of the joy that God intends for our lives.

If your heart is heavy, open the door of your soul to Christ. He will give you peace and joy. And, if you already have the joy of Christ in your heart, share it freely, just as Christ freely shared His joy with you. As you go about your daily activities, approach life with a smile on your lips and hope in your heart. And laugh every chance you get. After all, God created laughter for a reason . . . and Father indeed knows best.

Laughter dulls the sharpest pain and flattens out the greatest stress. To share it is to give a gift of health.

Barbara Johnson

– Your Daily Journey Through Psalms –

Oh, clap your hands, all you peoples! Shout to God with the voice of triumph!

Psalm 47:1 NKJV

The Wisdom of Moderation

Patience is better than power, and controlling one's temper, than capturing a city.

Proverbs 16:32 HCSB

Moderation and wisdom are traveling companions. If we are wise, we must learn to temper our appetites, our desires, and our impulses. When we do, we are blessed, in part, because God has created a world in which temperance is rewarded and intemperance is inevitably punished.

Would you like to improve your life? Then harness your appetites and restrain your impulses. Moderation is difficult, of course; it is especially difficult in a prosperous society such as ours. But the rewards of moderation are numerous and long-lasting. Claim those rewards today.

No one can force you to moderate your appetites. The decision to live temperately (and wisely) is yours and yours alone. And so are the consequences.

Virtue—even attempted virtue—brings light; indulgence brings fog.

C. S. Lewis

– Your Daily Journey Through Psalms –

He only is my rock and my salvation; he is my defence; I shall not be greatly moved.

Psalm 62:2 KJV

The Path He Walked

Therefore as you have received Christ Jesus the Lord, walk in Him.

Colossians 2:6 HCSB

Today, you will take one more step on your life's journey. Today offers one more opportunity to seek God's will and to follow it. Today has the potential to be a time of praise, a time of thanksgiving, and a time of spiritual abundance. The coming day is a canvas upon which you can compose a beautiful work of art if you choose to do so.

If you choose to follow in the footsteps of the One from Galilee, you will continue to mature every day of your life. If you choose to walk along the path that was first walked by Jesus, your life will become a masterpiece, a powerful work of art, and a tribute to your Savior. So today, as a gift to yourself, to your loved ones, and to your God, walk the path that Jesus walked.

The Christian faith is meant to be lived moment by moment. It isn't some broad, general outline—it's a long walk with a real Person. Details count: passing thoughts, small sacrifices, a few encouraging words, little acts of kindness, brief victories over nagging sins.

Joni Eareckson Tada

– Your Daily Journey Through Psalms –
Your word is a lamp for my feet and a light on my path.
Psalm 119:105 HCSB

His Promises to You

Because God wanted to show His unchangeable purpose even more clearly to the heirs of the promise, He guaranteed it with an oath, so that through two unchangeable things, in which it is impossible for God to lie, we who have fled for refuge might have strong encouragement to seize the hope set before us.

Hebrews 6:17-18 HCSB

God's promises are found in a book like no other: the Holy Bible. The Bible is a roadmap for life here on earth and for life eternal. As Christians, we are called upon to trust its promises, to follow its commandments, and to share its Good News.

As believers, we must study the Bible daily and meditate upon its meaning for our lives. Otherwise, we deprive ourselves of a priceless gift from our Creator. God's Holy Word is, indeed, a transforming, life-changing, one-of-a-kind treasure. And, a passing acquaintance with the Good Book is insufficient for Christians who seek to obey God's Word and to understand His will.

God has made promises to mankind and to you. God's promises never fail and they never grow old. You must trust those promises and share them with your family, with your friends, and with the world.

– Your Daily Journey Through Psalms –

This is my comfort in my affliction: Your promise has given me life.

Psalm 119:50 HCSB

Asking for His Guidance

Keep asking, and it will be given to you. Keep searching, and you will find. Keep knocking, and the door will be opened to you. For everyone who asks receives, and the one who searches finds, and to the one who knocks, the door will be opened.

Matthew 7:7-8 HCSB

Have you fervently asked God for His guidance in every aspect of your life? If so, then you're continually inviting your Creator to reveal Himself in a variety of ways. As a follower of Christ, you must do no less.

Jesus made it clear to His disciples: they should pray always. So should we. Genuine, heartfelt prayer produces powerful changes in us and in our world. When we lift our hearts to God, we open ourselves to a never-ending source of divine wisdom and infinite love.

Do you have questions about your future that you simply can't answer? Ask for the guidance of your Heavenly Father. Do you sincerely seek to know God's purpose for your life? Then ask Him for direction—and keep asking Him every day that you live. Whatever your need, no matter how great or small, pray about it and never lose hope. God is not just near; He is here, and He's ready to talk with you. Now!

– Your Daily Journey Through Psalms –
May my prayer reach Your presence; listen to my cry.
Psalm 88:2 HCSB

What Now, Lord?

For we are His making, created in Christ Jesus for good works, which God prepared ahead of time so that we should walk in them.

Ephesians 2:10 HCSB

God has things He wants you to do and places He wants you to go. The most important decision of your life is, of course, your commitment to accept Jesus Christ as your personal Lord and Savior. And, once your eternal destiny is secured, you will undoubtedly ask yourself the question "What now, Lord?" If you earnestly seek God's will for your life, you will find it . . . in time.

As you prayerfully consider God's path for your life, you should study His Word and be ever watchful for His signs. You should associate with fellow believers who will encourage your spiritual growth, and you should listen to that inner voice that speaks to you in the quiet moments of your daily devotionals.

Rest assured: God is here, and He intends to use you in wonderful, unexpected ways. He desires to lead you along a path of His choosing. Your challenge is to watch, to listen . . . and to follow.

– Your Daily Journey Through Psalms –

Every day will I bless thee; and I will praise thy name for ever and ever.

Psalm 145:2 KJV

Respecting Your Talents

Every good gift and every perfect gift is from above, and cometh down from the Father of lights.

James 1:17 KJV

Do you place a high value on your talents, your time, your capabilities, and your opportunities? If so, congratulations. But if you've acquired the insidious habit of devaluing your time, your work, or yourself, it's now time for a change.

Pearl Bailey correctly observed, "The first and worst of all frauds is to cheat one's self. All sin is easy after that."

If you've been squandering opportunities or selling yourself short, it's time to rethink the way that you think about yourself and your opportunities. No one can seize those opportunities for you, and no one can build up your self-confidence if you're unwilling to believe in yourself. So if you've been talking yourself down, stop. You deserve better. And if you don't give yourself healthy respect, who will?

– Your Daily Journey Through Psalms –

For You formed my inward parts; You covered me in my mother's womb. I will praise You, for I am fearfully and wonderfully made; Marvelous are Your works.

Psalm 139:13-14 NKJV

When the Seas Aren't Calm

But He said to them, "Why are you fearful, you of little faith?" Then He got up and rebuked the winds and the sea. And there was a great calm.

Matthew 8:26 HCSB

As every woman knows, some days are just plain difficult. Every woman faces days when the baby is sick, when the laundry is piled high, and the bills are piled even higher.

When we find ourselves overtaken by the inevitable frustrations of life, we must catch ourselves, take a deep breath, and lift our thoughts upward. Although we are here on earth struggling to rise above the distractions of the day, we need never struggle alone. God is here—eternal and faithful—and, if we reach out to Him, He will restore perspective and peace to our souls.

If you find yourself enduring difficult circumstances, remember that God remains in His heaven. If you become discouraged with the direction of your day or your life, take a moment to offer your thoughts and prayers to Him. He is a God of possibility, not negativity. He will guide you through your difficulties and beyond them.

– Your Daily Journey Through Psalms –

I will say to God, my rock, "Why have You forgotten me? Why must I go about in sorrow because of the enemy's oppression?"

Psalm 42:9 HCSB

Encouraging Words for Family and Friends

No rotten talk should come from your mouth, but only what is good for the building up of someone in need, in order to give grace to those who hear.

Ephesians 4.29 HCSB

Life is a team sport, and all of us need occasional pats on the back from our teammates. As Christians, we are called upon to spread the Good News of Christ, and we are also called to spread a message of encouragement and hope to the world.

Whether you realize it or not, many people with whom you come in contact every day are in desperate need of a smile or an encouraging word. The world can be a difficult place, and countless friends and family members may be troubled by the challenges of everyday life. Since you don't always know who needs your help, the best strategy is to try to encourage all the people who cross your path. So today, be a world-class source of encouragement to everyone you meet. Never has the need been greater.

– Your Daily Journey Through Psalms –

Blessed is every one who fears the Lord, who walks in His ways.

Psalm 128:1 NKJV

Faith for the Future

For we walk by faith, not by sight.

2 Corinthians 5:7 NKJV

The first element of a successful life is faith: faith in God, faith in His Son, and faith in His promises. If we place our lives in God's hands, our faith is rewarded in ways that we—as human beings with clouded vision and limited understanding—can scarcely comprehend. But, if we seek to rely solely upon our own resources, or if we seek earthly success outside the boundaries of God's commandments, we reap a bitter harvest for ourselves and for our loved ones.

Do you desire the abundance and success that God has promised? Then trust Him today and every day that you live. Trust Him with every aspect of your life. Trust His promises, and trust in the saving grace of His only begotten Son. Then, when you have entrusted your future to the Giver of all things good, rest assured that your future is secure, not only for today, but also for all eternity.

Faith is strengthened only when we ourselves exercise it.

Catherine Marshall

– Your Daily Journey Through Psalms –

For the Lord watches over the way of the righteous, but the way of the wicked leads to ruin.

Psalm 1:6 HCSB

He Forgave His Enemies

You have heard that it was said, You shall love your neighbor and hate your enemy. But I tell you, love your enemies, and pray for those who persecute you.

Matthew 5:43-44 HCSB

Christ forgave those who hurt Him, and we should do likewise. When we forgive others, we bring ourselves closer to the Savior; when we harbor bitterness in our hearts, we distance ourselves from Him.

Your life is a series of thoughts and actions. Each day, your thoughts and actions can bring you closer to God . . . or not. When you live according to God's commandments, you reap bountiful rewards: abundance, hope, and peace, for starters. But, if you turn your back upon God by disobeying Him, you invite bitter consequences.

Do you seek to walk in the footsteps of the One from Galilee, or will you choose another path? If you sincerely seek Christ's peace and His blessings, you must strive to imitate Him. Your Savior offered forgiveness to His enemies . . . now it's your turn.

When God tells us to love our enemies, He gives, along with the command, the love itself.

Corrie ten Boom

– Your Daily Journey Through Psalms –

"Lord Help!" they cried in their trouble, and he saved them from their distress.

Psalm 107:28 NLT

God's Comfort

Blessed be the God and Father of our Lord Jesus Christ, the Father of mercies and the God of all comfort. He comforts us in all our affliction, so that we may be able to comfort those who are in any kind of affliction, through the comfort we ourselves receive from God.

2 Corinthians 1:3-4 HCSB

We live in a world that is, at times, a frightening place. We live in a world that is, at times, a discouraging place. We live in a world where life-changing losses can be so painful and so profound that it seems we will never recover. But with God's help, and with the help of encouraging family members and friends, we can recover.

During the darker days of life, we are wise to remember that God is with us always and that He offers us comfort, assurance, and peace—our task, of course, is to accept these gifts.

When we trust in God's promises, the world becomes a less frightening place. With God's comfort and His love in our hearts, we can tackle our problems with courage, determination, and faith.

– Your Daily Journey Through Psalms –

This is my comfort in my affliction, for Your word has given me life.

Psalm 119:50 NKJV

Giving Your Thanks
to the Creator

*In everything give thanks; for this is the will of God in Christ
Jesus for you.*

1 Thessalonians 5:18 NKJV

As believing Christians, we are blessed beyond measure. God sent His only Son to die for our sins. And, God has given us the priceless gifts of eternal love and eternal life. We, in turn, are instructed to approach our Heavenly Father with reverence and thanksgiving. But, as busy women caught up in the inevitable demands of everyday life, we sometimes fail to pause and thank our Creator for the countless blessings He has bestowed upon us.

When we slow down and express our gratitude to the One who made us, we enrich our own lives and the lives of our loved ones. Thanksgiving should become a habit, a regular part of our daily routines. Yes, God has blessed us beyond measure, and we owe Him everything, including our eternal praise.

– Your Daily Journey Through Psalms –
Give thanks to Him and praise His name. For the Lord is good, and His love is eternal; His faithfulness endures through all generations.

Psalm 100:4-5 HCSB

God Sees

For am I now trying to win the favor of people, or God? Or am I striving to please people? If I were still trying to please people, I would not be a slave of Christ.

Galatians 1:10 HCSB

The world sees you as you appear to be; God sees you as you really are . . . He sees your heart, and He understands your intentions. The opinions of others should be relatively unimportant to you; however, God's view of you—His understanding of your actions, your thoughts, and your motivations—should be vitally important.

Few things in life are more futile than "keeping up appearances" for the sake of neighbors. What is important, of course, is pleasing your Father in heaven. You please Him when your intentions are pure and your actions are just.

Are you trying to keep up with the Joneses? Don't even try . . . you've got better things to do—far better things—like pleasing your Father in heaven.

You must never sacrifice your relationship with God for the sake of a relationship with another person.

Charles Stanley

– Your Daily Journey Through Psalms –

Commit everything you do to the Lord. Trust him, and he will help you.

Psalm 37:5 NLT

Finding Contentment

I am able to do all things through Him who strengthens me.
Philippians 4:13 HCSB

The preoccupation with happiness and contentment is an ever-present theme in the modern world. We are bombarded with messages that tell us where to find peace and pleasure in a world that worships materialism and wealth. But, lasting contentment is not found in material possessions; genuine contentment is a spiritual gift from God to those who trust in Him and follow His commandments.

Where do we find contentment? If we don't find it in God, we will never find it anywhere else. But, if we put our faith and our trust in Him, we will be blessed with an inner peace that is beyond human understanding. When God dwells at the center of our lives, peace and contentment will belong to us just as surely as we belong to God.

I believe that in every time and place it is within our power to acquiesce in the will of God—and what peace it brings to do so!

Elisabeth Elliot

– Your Daily Journey Through Psalms –
The LORD will give strength to His people; The LORD will bless His people with peace.

Psalm 29:11 NKJV

God Rewards Discipline

Apply yourself to instruction and listen to words of knowledge.
Proverbs 23:12 HCSB

God's Word reminds us again and again that our Creator expects us to lead disciplined lives. God doesn't reward laziness, misbehavior, or apathy. To the contrary, He expects believers to behave with dignity and discipline.

We live in a world in which leisure is glorified and indifference is often glamorized. But God has other plans. He did not create us for lives of mediocrity; He created us for far greater things.

Life's greatest rewards seldom fall into our laps; to the contrary, our greatest accomplishments usually require lots of work, which is perfectly fine with God. After all, He knows that we're up to the task, and He has big plans for us; may we, as disciplined believers, always be worthy of those plans.

The goal of any discipline is to result in greater freedom. Gal. 5:1.

Anonymous

– Your Daily Journey Through Psalms –
Let integrity and uprightness preserve me, for I wait for You.
Psalm 25:21 NKJV

The Power of Encouragement

Blessed be the God and Father of our Lord Jesus Christ, the Father of mercies and the God of all comfort. He comforts us in all our affliction, so that we may be able to comfort those who are in any kind of affliction, through the comfort we ourselves receive from God.

2 Corinthians 1:3-4 HCSB

Do you delight in the victories of others? You should. Each day provides countless opportunities to encourage others and to praise their good works. When you do so, you spread seeds of joy and happiness.

American poet Ella Wheeler Wilcox advised, "Talk happiness. The world is sad enough without your woe." Her words still apply.

Life is a team sport, and all of us need occasional pats on the back from our teammates. So, let us be cheerful with smiles on our faces and encouraging words on our lips. By blessing others, we also bless ourselves, and, when we do, the Creator smiles.

A single word, if spoken in a friendly spirit, may be sufficient to turn one from dangerous error.

Fanny Crosby

– Your Daily Journey Through Psalms –

As for God, His way is perfect; the word of the Lord is proven; He is a shield to all who trust in Him.

Psalm 18:30 NKJV

What to Do?

You have already heard about this hope in the message of truth, the gospel that has come to you. It is bearing fruit and growing all over the world, just as it has among you since the day you heard it and recognized God's grace in the truth.

Colossians 1:5-6 HCSB

"What on earth does God intend for me to do with my life?" It's an easy question to ask but, for many of us, a difficult question to answer. Why? Because God's purposes aren't always clear to us. Sometimes we wander aimlessly in a wilderness of our own making. And sometimes, we struggle mightily against God in an unsuccessful attempt to find success and happiness through our own means, not His.

Sometimes, God's intentions will be clear to you; other times, God's plan will seem uncertain at best. But even on those difficult days when you are unsure of which way to turn, you must never lose sight of these overriding facts: God created you for a reason; He has important work for you to do; and He's waiting patiently for you to do it. And the next step is up to you.

– Your Daily Journey Through Psalms –

Be strong and courageous, all you who put your hope in the Lord.

Psalm 31:24 HCSB

The Power of Habits

Do not be deceived: "Evil company corrupts good habits."
1 Corinthians 15:33 NKJV

It's an old saying and a true one: First, you make your habits, and then your habits make you. Some habits will inevitably bring you closer to God; other habits will lead you away from the path He has chosen for you. If you sincerely desire to improve your spiritual health, you must honestly examine the habits that make up the fabric of your day. And you must abandon those habits that are displeasing to God.

If you trust God, and if you keep asking for His help, He can transform your life. If you sincerely ask Him to help you, the same God who created the universe will help you defeat the harmful habits that have heretofore defeated you. So, if at first you don't succeed, keep praying. God is listening, and He's ready to help you become a better person if you ask Him . . . so ask today.

Prayer is a habit. Worship is a habit. Kindness is a habit. And if you want to please God, you'd better make sure that these habits are your habits.

Marie T. Freeman

– Your Daily Journey Through Psalms –
The counsel of the LORD standeth for ever, the thoughts of his heart to all generations.

Psalm 33:11 KJV

The Abundant Life

I have come that they may have life, and that they may have it more abundantly.

John 10:10 NKJV

When Jesus talks of the abundant life, is He talking about material riches or earthly fame? Hardly. The Son of God came to this world, not to give it prosperity, but to give it salvation. Thankfully for Christians, our Savior's abundance is both spiritual and eternal; it never falters—even if we do—and it never dies. We need only to open our hearts to Him, and His grace becomes ours.

God's gifts are available to all, but they are not guaranteed; those gifts must be claimed by those who choose to follow Christ. As believers, we are free to accept God's gifts, or not; that choice, and the consequences that result from it, are ours and ours alone.

As we go about our daily lives, may we accept God's promise of spiritual abundance, and may we share it with a world in desperate need of the Master's healing touch.

God loves you and wants you to experience peace and life—abundant and eternal.

Billy Graham

– Your Daily Journey Through Psalms –
But it is good for me to draw near to God: I have put my trust in the Lord GOD.

Psalm 73:28 KJV

The Tapestry of Life

Let not your heart be troubled; you believe in God, believe also in Me. In My Father's house are many mansions; if it were not so, I would have told you. I go to prepare a place for you. And if I go and prepare a place for you, I will come again and receive you to Myself; that where I am, there you may be also.

John 14:1-3 NKJV

From time to time, all of us face adversity, hardship, disappointment, and loss. Old Man Trouble pays periodic visits to each of us; none of our families are exempt. When we are troubled, God stands ready and willing to protect us. Our responsibility, of course, is to ask Him for protection. When we call upon Him in heartfelt prayer, He will answer—in His own time and in accordance with His own perfect plan.

Life is often challenging, but as Christian women, we must not be afraid. God loves us, and He will protect us. In times of hardship, He will comfort us; in times of sorrow, He will dry our tears. When we are troubled, or weak, or sorrowful, God is always with us and our families. We must build our lives on the rock that cannot be shaken . . . we must trust in God always. And we must encourage our loved ones to do the same.

– Your Daily Journey Through Psalms –

Consider my affliction and rescue me, for I have not forgotten Your instruction.

Psalm 119:153 HCSB

Your Beliefs and Your Life

For the kingdom of God is not in talk but in power.
1 Corinthians 4:20 HCSB

Do you weave your beliefs into the very fabric of your day? If you do, God will honor your good works, and your good works will honor God.

If you seek to be a responsible believer, you must realize that it is never enough to hear the instructions of God; you must also live by them. And it is never enough to wait idly by while others do God's work here on earth. You, too, must act.

Doing God's work is a responsibility that every Christian (including you) should bear. And when you do, your loving Heavenly Father will reward your efforts with a bountiful harvest.

Jesus taught that the evidence that confirms our leaps of faith comes after we risk believing, not before.

Gloria Gaither

The value and purpose of following God's ways are not in seeing, but in believing, what God wants to say to us.

Franklin Graham

– Your Daily Journey Through Psalms –
The fool hath said in his heart, There is no God.

Psalm 14:1 KJV

Beyond the Status Quo

You are being renewed in the spirit of your minds; you put on the new man, the one created according to God's likeness in righteousness and purity of the truth.

Ephesians 4:23-24 HCSB

I t has been said that a rut is nothing more than a grave with both ends kicked out. That's a thought worth pondering. Have you made your life an exciting adventure, or have you allowed the distractions of everyday life to rob you of a sense of God's purpose?

As a believing Christian, you have every reason to celebrate. So if you find yourself feeling as if you're stuck in a rut, or in an unfortunate circumstance, or in a difficult relationship, abandon the status quo by making the changes that your heart tells you are right. After all, in God's glorious kingdom, there should be no place for disciples who are dejected, discouraged, or disheartened. God has a far better plan than that, and so should you.

There is not a single thing that Jesus cannot change, control, and conquer because He is the living Lord.

Franklin Graham

– Your Daily Journey Through Psalms –

All Your works shall give thanks to You, O LORD, And Your godly ones shall bless You.

Psalm 145:10 NASB

Feed the Church of God

Take heed therefore unto yourselves, and to all the flock, over the which the Holy Ghost hath made you overseers, to feed the church of God.

Acts 20:28 KJV

In the Book of Acts, Luke reminds us to "feed the church of God." As Christians who have been saved by a loving, compassionate Creator, we are compelled not only to worship Him in our hearts but also to worship Him in the presence of fellow believers.

The church belongs to God; it is His just as certainly as we are His. When we help build God's church, we bear witness to the changes that He has made in our lives.

Today and every day, let us worship God with grateful hearts and helping hands as we support the church that He has created. Let us witness to our friends, to our families, and to the world. When we do so, we bless others and we are blessed by the One who sent His Son to die so that we might have eternal life.

The church needs people who are doers of the Word and not just hearers.

Warren Wiersbe

– Your Daily Journey Through Psalms –
All the earth shall worship thee, and shall sing unto thee; and shall sing to thy name . . . .

Psalm 66:4 KJV

Solving Life's Riddles

But the wisdom from above is first pure, then peace-loving, gentle, compliant, full of mercy and good fruits, without favoritism and hypocrisy.

James 3:17 HCSB

Life presents each of us with countless questions, conundrums, doubts, and problems. Thankfully, the riddles of everyday living are not too difficult to solve if we look for answers in the right places. When we have questions, we should consult God's Word, we should seek the guidance of the Holy Spirit, and we should trust the counsel of God-fearing friends and family members.

Are you facing a difficult decision? Take your concerns to God and avail yourself of the messages and mentors that He has placed along your path. When you do, God will speak to you in His own way and in His own time, and when He does, you can most certainly trust the answers that He gives.

God always gives His best to those who leave the choice with Him.

Jim Elliot

– Your Daily Journey Through Psalms –

Lord, I turn my hope to You. My God, I trust in You. Do not let me be disgraced; do not let my enemies gloat over me.

Psalm 25:1-2 HCSB

Your Great Expectations

Delayed hope makes the heart sick.

Proverbs 13:12 HCSB

D o you expect your future to be bright? Are you willing to dream king-sized dreams . . . and are you willing to work diligently to make those dreams happen? Hopefully so—after all, God promises that we can do "all things" through Him. Yet most of us, even the most devout among us, live far below our potential. We take half measures; we dream small dreams; we waste precious time and energy on the distractions of the world. But God has other plans for us.

Our Creator intends that we live faithfully, hopefully, courageously, and abundantly. He knows that we are capable of so much more; and He wants us to do the things we're capable of doing; and He wants us to begin doing those things today.

Always stay connected to people and seek out things that bring you joy. Dream with abandon. Pray confidently.

Barbara Johnson

– Your Daily Journey Through Psalms –
Those who are blessed by Him will inherit the land.

Psalm 37:22 HCSB

What Kind of Example?

You are the light of the world. A city situated on a hill cannot be hidden. No one lights a lamp and puts it under a basket, but rather on a lampstand, and it gives light for all who are in the house. In the same way, let your light shine before men, so that they may see your good works and give glory to your Father in heaven.

Matthew 5:14-16 HCSB

Whether we like it or not, all of us are examples. The question is not whether we will be examples to our families and friends; the question is simply what kind of examples will we be.

What kind of example are you? Are you the kind of woman whose life serves as a powerful example of righteousness? Are you a woman whose behavior serves as a positive role model for young people? Are you the kind of woman whose actions, day in and day out, are based upon integrity, fidelity, and a love for the Lord? If so, you are not only blessed by God, you are also a powerful force for good in a world that desperately needs positive influences such as yours.

Corrie ten Boom advised, "Don't worry about what you do not understand. Worry about what you do understand in the Bible but do not live by." And that's sound advice because our families and friends are watching.

– Your Daily Journey Through Psalms –
But let all who take refuge in You rejoice.

Psalm 5:11 HCSB

As the World Grows Louder

Be silent before Me.

Isaiah 41:1 HCSB

The world seems to grow louder day by day, and our senses seem to be invaded at every turn. If we allow the distractions of a clamorous society to separate us from God's peace, we do ourselves a profound disservice. Our task, as dutiful believers, is to carve out moments of silence in a world filled with noise.

If we are to maintain righteous minds and compassionate hearts, we must take time each day for prayer and for meditation. We must make ourselves still in the presence of our Creator. We must quiet our minds and our hearts so that we might sense God's will and His love.

Has the hectic pace of life robbed you of God's peace? If so, it's time to reorder your priorities and your life. Nothing is more important than the time you spend with your Heavenly Father. So be still and claim the genuine peace that is found in the silent moments you spend with God.

Silence is as fit a garment for devotion as any other language.

C. H. Spurgeon

– Your Daily Journey Through Psalms –
Be silent before the Lord and wait expectantly for Him.
Psalm 37:7 HCSB

He Preserves Us

He will wipe away every tear from their eyes. Death will exist no longer; grief, crying, and pain will exist no longer, because the previous things have passed away.

Revelation 21:4 HCSB

Women of every generation have experienced adversity, and this generation is no different. But, today's women face challenges that previous generations could have scarcely imagined. Thankfully, although the world continues to change, God's love remains constant. And, He remains ready to comfort us and strengthen us whenever we turn to Him.

Paula Rinehart advised, "If you want to know real joy in life, then be willing to let pain tutor your soul." These words remind us that when we face up to suffering, we grow spiritually and emotionally.

When we encounter troubles of whatever kind, we should call upon God, and in time, He will heal us. And until He does, we may be comforted in the knowledge that we never suffer alone.

He screens the suffering, filtering it through fingers of love.

Joni Eareckson Tada and Steve Estes

– Your Daily Journey Through Psalms –
Weeping may endure for a night, but joy cometh in the morning.

Psalm 30:5 KJV

Expecting the Best

Let us hold fast the confession of our hope without wavering, for He who promised is faithful.

Hebrews 10:23 NKJV

What do you expect from the day ahead? Are you expecting God to do wonderful things, or are you living beneath a cloud of apprehension and doubt? Throughout the Bible, we are reminded of a profound yet simple truth: God made this day and gave it to us as a gift. We, in response to that gift, should be grateful.

For Christian believers, every day begins and ends with God and His Son. Christ came to this earth to give us abundant life and eternal salvation. We give thanks to our Maker when we treasure each day and use it to the fullest.

Today, let us give thanks for the gift of life and for the One who created it. And then, let's use this day—a precious gift from the Father above—to serve our Savior faithfully, courageously, and joyfully.

Submit each day to God, knowing that He is God over all your tomorrows.

Kay Arthur

– Your Daily Journey Through Psalms –
This is the day the LORD has made; we will rejoice and be glad in it.

Psalm 118:24 NKJV

Touched by the Savior

For the mind-set of the flesh is death, but the mind-set of the Spirit is life and peace.

Romans 8:6 HCSB

Until we have been touched by the Savior, we can never be completely whole. Until we have placed our hearts and our lives firmly in the hands of the living Christ, we are incomplete. Until we come to know Jesus, we long for a sense of peace that continues to elude us no matter how diligently we search.

It is only through God that we discover genuine peace. We can search far and wide for worldly substitutes, but when we seek peace apart from God, we will find neither peace nor God.

As believers, we are invited to accept the "peace that passes all understanding" (Philippians 4:7 NIV). That peace, of course, is God's peace. Let us accept His peace, and let us share it today, tomorrow, and every day that we live.

We will never be happy until we make God the source of our fulfillment and the answer to our longings.

Stormie Omartian

– Your Daily Journey Through Psalms –
As for me, I will call upon God; and the LORD shall save me.

Psalm 55:16 KJV

How Will You Worship?

For it is written, "You shall worship the Lord your God, and Him only you shall serve."

Matthew 4:10 NKJV

All of mankind is engaged in the practice of worship. Some choose to worship God and, as a result, reap the joy that He intends for His children. Others distance themselves from God by worshiping such things as earthly possessions or personal gratification . . . and when they do so, they suffer.

Today, as one way of worshipping God, make every aspect of your life a cause for celebration and praise. Praise God for the blessings and opportunities that He has given you, and live according to the beautiful words found in the 5th chapter of 1 Thessalonians: "Rejoice evermore. Pray without ceasing. In every thing give thanks: for this is the will of God in Christ Jesus concerning you" (16-18 KJV).

God deserves your worship, your prayers, your praise, and your thanks. And you deserve the joy that is yours when you worship Him with your prayers, with your deeds, and with your life.

– Your Daily Journey Through Psalms –

Shout triumphantly to the Lord, all the earth. Serve the Lord with gladness; come before Him with joyful songs.

Psalm 100:1-2 HCSB

Choose Friends Wisely

Iron sharpens iron, and one man sharpens another.
Proverbs 27:17 HCSB

If you'd like to build a positive life, find positive friends. If you'd like to live a godly life, seek the fellowship of godly friends. If you'd like to live passionately, prayerfully, and purposefully, spend time with people who are already living passionate, prayerful, purposeful lives. Soon, you'll soon discover that you will inevitably become more and more like the people who surround you day in and day out.

In choosing your friends, you set your course for the future. So choose carefully . . . very carefully.

Perhaps the greatest treasure on earth and one of the only things that will survive this life is human relationships: old friends. We are indeed rich if we have friends. Friends who have loved us through the problems and heartaches of life. Deep, true, joyful friendships. Life is too short and eternity too long to live without old friends.

Gloria Gaither

– Your Daily Journey Through Psalms –

Blessed is the man who walks not in the counsel of the ungodly, nor stands in the path of sinners, nor sits in the seat of the scornful; but his delight is in the law of the Lord, and in His law he meditates day and night.

Psalm 1:1-2 NKJV

Holiness Before Happiness

If they serve Him obediently, they will end their days in prosperity and their years in happiness.

Job 36:11 HCSB

Because you are an imperfect human being, you are not "perfectly" happy—and that's perfectly okay with God. He is far less concerned with your happiness than He is with your holiness.

God continuously reveals Himself in everyday life, but He does not do so in order to make you contented; He does so in order to lead you to His Son. So don't be overly concerned with your current level of happiness: it will change. Be more concerned with the current state of your relationship with Christ: He does not change. And because your Savior transcends time and space, you can be comforted in the knowledge that in the end, His joy will become your joy . . . for all eternity.

Perfect obedience would be perfect happiness, if only we had perfect confidence in the power we were obeying.

Corrie ten Boom

– Your Daily Journey Through Psalms –
But I will hope continually and will praise You more and more.

Psalm 71:14 HCSB

Living in Our Material World

There is one who makes himself rich, yet has nothing; And one who makes himself poor, yet has great riches.

Proverbs 13:7 NKJV

On the grand stage of a well-lived life, material possessions should play a rather small role. Of course, we all need the basic necessities of life, but once we meet those needs for ourselves and for our families, the piling up of possessions creates more problems than it solves. Our real riches, of course, are not of this world. We are never really rich until we are rich in spirit.

Do you find yourself wrapped up in the concerns of the material world? If so, it's time to reorder your priorities by turning your thoughts and your prayers to more important matters. And, it's time to begin storing up riches that will endure throughout eternity: the spiritual kind.

I've learned to hold everything loosely because it hurts when God pries my fingers from it.

Corrie ten Boom

– Your Daily Journey Through Psalms –

The Lord is my shepherd; I shall not want. He makes me to lie down in green pastures; He leads me beside the still waters. He restores my soul.

Psalm 23:1-3 NKJV

Trusting His Answers

Trust in the Lord with all your heart, and do not rely on your own understanding; think about Him in all your ways, and He will guide you on the right paths.

Proverbs 3:5-6 HCSB

God answers our prayers. What God does not do is this: He does not always answer our prayers as soon as we might like, and He does not always answer our prayers by saying "Yes." God isn't an order-taker, and He's not some sort of cosmic vending machine. Sometimes—even when we want something very badly—our loving Heavenly Father responds to our requests by saying "No," and we must accept His answer, even if we don't understand it.

God answers prayers not only according to our wishes but also according to His master plan. We cannot know that plan, but we can know the Planner . . . and we must trust His wisdom, His righteousness, and His love. Always.

We are not to have faith in prayer, but in God who answers prayer.

Anonymous

– Your Daily Journey Through Psalms –

Let the words of my mouth and the meditation of my heart be acceptable in Your sight, O Lord, my strength and my Redeemer.

Psalm 19:14 NKJV

The Merry-Go-Round

I will give you a new heart and put a new spirit within you.
Ezekiel 36:26 HCSB

God intends that His children lead joyous lives filled with abundance and peace. But sometimes, abundance and peace seem very far away. It is then that we must turn to God for renewal, and when we do, He will restore us.

Have you "tapped in" to the power of God, or are you muddling along under your own power? If you are weary, worried, fretful or fearful, then it is time to turn to a strength much greater than your own.

The Bible tells us that we can do all things through the power of our risen Savior, Jesus Christ. Our challenge, then, is clear: we must place Christ where He belongs: at the very center of our lives.

Are you tired or troubled? Turn your heart toward God in prayer. Are you weak or worried? Make the time to delve deeply into God's Holy Word. When you do, you'll discover that the Creator of the universe stands ready and able to create a new sense of wonderment and joy in you.

– Your Daily Journey Through Psalms –

Return unto thy rest, O my soul; for the LORD hath dealt bountifully with thee.

Psalm 116:7 KJV

When Your Courage Is Tested

Do not rebel against the LORD, and don't be afraid of the people of the land.

Numbers 14:9 NLT

Even the most dedicated Christian woman may find her courage tested by the inevitable disappointments and tragedies of life. After all, we live in a world filled with uncertainty, hardship, sickness, and danger. Old Man Trouble, it seems, is never too far from the front door.

When we focus upon our fears and our doubts, we may find many reasons to lie awake at night and fret about the uncertainties of the coming day. A better strategy, of course, is to focus not upon our fears, but instead upon our God.

God is as near as your next breath, and He is in control. He offers salvation to all His children, including you. God is your shield and your strength; you are His forever. So don't focus your thoughts upon the fears of the day. Instead, trust God's plan and His eternal love for you. And remember: whatever the size of your challenge, God is bigger.

– Your Daily Journey Through Psalms –

Be strong and courageous, all you who put your hope in the Lord.

Psalm 31:24 HCSB

Praying About Forgiveness

The intense prayer of the righteous is very powerful.

James 5:16 HCSB

Have you been unable to forgive someone? Talk to God about it. Do you have questions that you simply can't answer? Ask for the guidance of your Father in heaven. Have you been unable to forgive yourself for something you did long ago? God has forgiven you; now it's your turn to forgive yourself. Do you sincerely seek the gift of peace and wholeness that only God can give? Then obey His commandments and accept the grace of His only begotten Son.

Whatever your need, no matter how great or small, pray about it. Instead of waiting for mealtimes or bedtimes, follow the instruction of your Savior: pray always and never lose heart. And remember: God is not just near; He is here, and He's ready to talk with you. Now.

As you forgive others, winter will soon make way for springtime as fresh joy pushes up through the soil of your heart.

Barbara Johnson

– Your Daily Journey Through Psalms –

The Lord is gracious and compassionate, slow to anger and great in faithful love. The Lord is good to everyone; His compassion [rests] on all He has made.

Psalm 145:8-9 HCSB

How Has He Blessed You?

I will make them and the area around My hill a blessing: I will send down showers in their season—showers of blessing.
Ezekiel 34:26 HCSB

Have you counted your blessings lately? If you sincerely wish to follow in Christ's footsteps, you should make thanksgiving a habit, a regular part of your daily routine.

How has God blessed you? First and foremost, He has given you the gift of eternal life through the sacrifice of His only begotten Son, but the blessings don't stop there. Today, take time to make a partial list of God's gifts to you: the talents, the opportunities, the possessions, and the relationships that you may, on occasion, take for granted. And then, when you've spent sufficient time listing your blessings, offer a prayer gratitude to the Giver of all things good . . . and, to the best of your ability, use your gifts for the glory of His kingdom.

We do not need to beg Him to bless us; He simply cannot help it.

Hannah Whitall Smith

– Your Daily Journey Through Psalms –
For thou, LORD, wilt bless the righteous . . . .
Psalm 5:12 KJV

Accepting His Will

Should we accept only good from God and not adversity?
Job 2:10 HCSB

All of us must, from time to time, endure days filled with suffering and pain. And as people with limited understanding, we can never fully understand the plans of our Father in Heaven. But as believers in a benevolent God, we must always trust Him.

When Jesus went to the Mount of Olives, He poured out His heart to God (Luke 22). Jesus knew of the agony that He was destined to endure, but He also knew that God's will must be done.

We, like our Savior, face trials that bring fear and trembling to the very depths of our souls, but like Christ, we, too, must seek God's will, not our own. When we learn to accept God's will without reservation, we experience the peace that He offers to wise believers who trust Him completely.

Acceptance says: True, this is my situation at the moment. I'll look unblinkingly at the reality of it. But, I'll also open my hands to accept willingly whatever a loving Father sends me.

Catherine Marshall

– Your Daily Journey Through Psalms –
Give thanks to the Lord, for He is good; His faithful love endures forever.

Psalm 106:1 HCSB

When Your Faith Is Tested

Blessed be the God and Father of our Lord Jesus Christ, the Father of mercies and the God of all comfort. He comforts us in all our affliction, so that we may be able to comfort those who are in any kind of affliction, through the comfort we ourselves receive from God.

2 Corinthians 1:3-4 HCSB

When the sun is shining and all is well, it is easy to have faith. But, when life takes an unexpected turn for the worse, as it will from time to time, your faith will be tested. In times of trouble and doubt, God remains faithful to you—and you must retain faith in yourself.

Social activist Jane Addams observed, "You do not know what life means when all the difficulties are removed. It's like eating a sweet dessert the first thing in the morning." And so it is with your own life.

So the next time you spot storm clouds on the horizon, remind yourself that every difficult day must come to an end . . . and when times are tough, tough women (like you) are tougher.

Faith is strengthened only when we ourselves exercise it.
Catherine Marshall

– Your Daily Journey Through Psalms –
Then they cried out to the Lord in their trouble; He saved them from their distress.

Psalm 107:13 HCSB

A Spiritual Sickness

But if you harbor bitter envy and selfish ambition in your hearts, do not boast about it or deny the truth. Such "wisdom" does not come down from heaven but is earthly, unspiritual, of the devil.

James 3:14-16 NIV

Bitterness is a spiritual sickness. It will consume your soul; it is dangerous to your emotional health. It can destroy you if you let it . . . so don't let it!

If you are caught up in intense feelings of anger or resentment, you know all too well the destructive power of these emotions. How can you rid yourself of these feelings? First, you must prayerfully ask God to cleanse your heart. Then, you must learn to catch yourself whenever thoughts of bitterness or hatred begin to attack you. Your challenge is this: You must learn to resist negative thoughts before they hijack your emotions.

Matthew 5:22 teaches us that if we judge our brothers and sisters, we, too, will be subject to judgement. Let us refrain, then, from judging our neighbors. Instead, let us forgive them and love them, while leaving their judgement to a far more capable authority: the One who sits on His throne in heaven.

– Your Daily Journey Through Psalms –

Stop your anger! Turn from your rage! Do not envy others—it only leads to harm.

Psalm 37:8 NLT

He Does Not Change

One Lord, one faith, one baptism, one God and Father of all, who is above all and through all and in all.

Ephesians 4:5-6 HCSB

We live in a world that is always changing, but we worship a God that never changes—thank goodness! As believers, we can be comforted in the knowledge that our Heavenly Father is the rock that simply cannot be moved: "I am the Lord, I do not change" (Malachi 3:6 NKJV).

Are you facing difficult circumstances or unwelcome changes? If so, please remember that God is far bigger than any problem you may face. So, instead of worrying about life's inevitable challenges, put your faith in the Father and His only begotten Son: "Jesus Christ is the same yesterday, today, and forever" (Hebrews 13:8 HCSB). And rest assured: It is precisely because your Savior does not change that you can face your challenges with courage for this day and hope for the future.

God wants to change our lives—and He will, as we open our hearts to Him.

Billy Graham

– Your Daily Journey Through Psalms –

But I will hope continually and will praise You more and more.

Psalm 71:14 HCSB

Comforting Those in Need

When it is in your power, don't withhold good from the one to whom it is due.

Proverbs 3:27 HCSB

We live in a world that is, on occasion, a frightening place. Sometimes, we sustain life-altering losses that are so profound and so tragic that it seems we could never recover. But, with God's help and with the help of encouraging family members and friends, we can recover.

In times of need, God's Word is clear: as believers, we must offer comfort to those in need by sharing not only our courage but also our faith. In times of adversity, we are wise to remember the words of Jesus, who, when He walked on the waters, reassured His disciples, saying, "Take courage! It is I. Don't be afraid" (Matthew 14:27 NIV). Then, with Christ on His throne—and with trusted friends and loving family members at our sides—we can face our fears with courage and with faith.

Before you can dry another's tears, you too must weep.

Barbara Johnson

– Your Daily Journey Through Psalms –

May Your faithful love comfort me, as You promised Your servant.

Psalm 119:76 HCSB

Finding Time for God

He awakens [Me] each morning; He awakens My ear to listen like those being instructed. The Lord God has opened My ear, and I was not rebellious; I did not turn back.

Isaiah 50:4-5 HCSB

E ach new day is a gift from God, and wise women spend a few quiet moments each morning thanking the Giver. Daily life is woven together with the threads of habit, and no habit is more important to our spiritual health than the discipline of daily prayer and devotion to the Creator.

When we begin each day with heads bowed and hearts lifted, we remind ourselves of God's love, His protection, and His commandments. And if we are wise, we align our priorities for the coming day with the teachings and commandments that God has given us through His Holy Word.

Are you seeking to change some aspect of your life? Then take time out of your hectic schedule to spend time each day with your Creator. Do seek to improve the condition of your spiritual or physical health? If so, ask for God's help and ask for it many times each day . . . starting with your morning devotional.

– Your Daily Journey Through Psalms –

It is good to give thanks to the Lord, And to sing praises to Your name, O Most High; To declare Your lovingkindness in the morning, And Your faithfulness every night.

Psalm 92:1-2 NKJV

Faith Above Feelings

The righteous one will live by his faith.

Habakkuk 2:4 HCSB

Hebrews 10:38 teaches that we should live by faith. Yet sometimes, despite our best intentions, negative feelings can rob us of the peace and abundance that would otherwise be ours through Christ. When anger or anxiety separates us from the spiritual blessings that God has in store, we must rethink our priorities and renew our faith. And we must place faith above feelings. Human emotions are highly variable, decidedly unpredictable, and often unreliable. Our emotions are like the weather, only far more fickle. So we must learn to live by faith, not by the ups and downs of our own emotional roller coasters.

Sometime during this day, you will probably be gripped by a strong negative emotion. Distrust it. Reign it in. Test it. And turn it over to God. Your emotions will inevitably change; God will not. So trust Him completely as you watch your feelings slowly evaporate into thin air—which, of course, they will.

– Your Daily Journey Through Psalms –
The Lord is my rock, my fortress, and my deliverer.

Psalm 18:2 HCSB

Optimistic Christianity

I am able to do all things through Him who strengthens me.
Philippians 4:13 HCSB

A re you an optimistic, hopeful, enthusiastic Christian? You should be. After all, as a believer, you have every reason to be optimistic about life here on earth and life eternal. As C. H. Spurgeon observed, "Our hope in Christ for the future is the mainstream of our joy." But sometimes, you may find yourself pulled down by the inevitable demands and worries of life-here-on-earth. If you find yourself discouraged, exhausted, or both, then it's time to take your concerns to God. When you do, He will lift your spirits and renew your strength.

Today, make this promise to yourself and keep it: vow to be a hope-filled Christian. Think optimistically about your life, your profession, your family, and your future. Trust your hopes, not your fears. Take time to celebrate God's glorious creation. And then, when you've filled your heart with hope and gladness, share your optimism with others. They'll be better for it, and so will you.

– Your Daily Journey Through Psalms –
Make me to hear joy and gladness.

Psalm 51:8 KJV

God Can Help Us Forgive

May mercy, peace, and love be multiplied to you.

Jude 1:2 HCSB

There's no doubt about it: forgiveness is difficult. Being frail, fallible, imperfect human beings, we are quick to anger, quick to blame, slow to forgive, and even slower to forget. Yet as Christians, we are commanded to forgive others, just as we, too, have been forgiven. So even when forgiveness is difficult, we must ask God to help us move beyond the spiritual stumbling blocks of bitterness and hate.

If, in your heart, you hold bitterness against even a single person, forgive. If there exists even one person, alive or dead, whom you have not forgiven, follow God's commandment and His will for your life: forgive. If you are embittered against yourself for some past mistake or shortcoming, forgive. Then, to the best of your abilities, forget. And move on. Bitterness and regret are not part of God's plan for your life. Forgiveness is.

God forgets the past. Imitate him.

Max Lucado

– Your Daily Journey Through Psalms –

I will lift up my eyes to the hills. From whence comes my help? My help comes from the Lord, Who made heaven and earth.

Psalm 121:1-2 NKJV

God First

You shall have no other gods before Me.

Exodus 20:3 NKJV

As you think about the nature of your relationship with God, remember this: you will always have some type of relationship with Him—it is inevitable that your life must be lived in relationship to God. The question is not if you will have a relationship with Him; the burning question is whether or not that relationship will be one that seeks to honor Him.

Are you willing to place God first in your life? And, are you willing to welcome God's Son into your heart? Unless you can honestly answer these questions with a resounding yes, then your relationship with God isn't what it could be or should be. Thankfully, God is always available, He's always ready to forgive, and He's waiting to hear from you now. The rest, of course, is up to you.

Jesus challenges you and me to keep our focus daily on the cross of His will if we want to be His disciples.

Anne Graham Lotz

– Your Daily Journey Through Psalms –
Be still, and know that I am God.

Psalm 46:10 NKJV

A Gift Beyond Comprehension

Therefore, since we are receiving a kingdom that cannot be shaken, let us hold on to grace. By it, we may serve God acceptably, with reverence and awe.

Hebrews 12:28 HCSB

The grace of God overflows from His heart. And if we open our hearts to Him, we receive His grace, and we are blessed with joy, abundance, peace, and eternal life.

The familiar words of Ephesians 2:8 make God's promise perfectly clear: "For by grace you have been saved through faith, and that not of yourselves; it is the gift of God" (NKJV). In other words, we are saved, not by our actions, but by God's mercy. We are saved, not because of our good deeds, but because of our faith in Christ.

God's grace is the ultimate gift, a gift beyond comprehension and beyond compare. And because it is the ultimate gift, we owe God the ultimate in thanksgiving.

God's grace is indeed a gift from the heart—God's heart. And as believers, we must accept God's precious gift thankfully, humbly, and, immediately—today is never too soon because tomorrow may be too late.

– Your Daily Journey Through Psalms –

But let all who take refuge in You rejoice.

Psalm 5:11 HCSB

His Surprising Plans

But as it is written: What no eye has seen and no ear has heard, and what has never come into a man's heart, is what God has prepared for those who love Him.

1 Corinthians 2:9 HCSB

God has big plans for your life, wonderful, surprising plans . . . but He won't force those plans upon you. To the contrary, He has given you free will, the ability to make decisions on your own. Now, it's up to you to make those decisions wisely.

If you seek to live in accordance with God's plan for your life, you will carefully study His Word, you will be attentive to His instructions, and you will be watchful for His signs. You will associate with fellow believers who, by their words and actions, will encourage your spiritual growth. You will assiduously avoid those two terrible temptations: the temptation to sin and the temptation squander time. And finally, you will listen carefully, even reverently, to the conscience that God has placed in your heart.

God intends to use you in wonderful, unexpected ways if you let Him. Let Him. When you do, you'll be thoroughly surprised by the creativity and the beauty of His plans.

– Your Daily Journey Through Psalms –
Unless the Lord builds a house, its builders labor over it in vain.

Psalm 127:1 HCSB

His Strength

But the Lord is faithful; He will strengthen and guard you from the evil one.

2 Thessalonians 3:3 HCSB

Have you made God the cornerstone of your life, or is He relegated to a few hours on Sunday morning? Have you genuinely allowed God to reign over every corner of your heart, or have you attempted to place Him in a spiritual compartment? The answer to these questions will determine the direction of your day and your life.

God loves you. In times of trouble, He will comfort you; in times of sorrow, He will dry your tears. When you are or weak or sorrowful, God is as near as your next breath. He stands at the door of your heart and waits. Welcome Him in and allow Him to rule. And then, accept the peace, and the strength, and the protection, and the abundance that only God can give.

He goes before us, follows behind us, and hems us safe inside the realm of His protection.

Beth Moore

– Your Daily Journey Through Psalms –
The Lord is the strength of my life.

Psalm 27:1 KJV

Honoring God

Honor the Lord with your possessions, and with the firstfruits of all your increase; so your barns will be filled with plenty.

Proverbs 3:9-10 NKJV

Whom will you choose to honor today? If you honor God and place Him at the center of your life, every day is a cause for celebration. But if you fail to honor your Heavenly Father, you're asking for trouble, and lots of it.

At times, your life is probably hectic, demanding, and complicated. When the demands of life leave you rushing from place to place with scarcely a moment to spare, you may fail to pause and thank your Creator for the blessings He has bestowed upon you. But that's a big mistake.

Do you sincerely seek to be a worthy servant of the One who has given you eternal love and eternal life? Then honor Him for who He is and for what He has done for you. And don't just honor Him on Sunday morning. Praise Him all day long, every day, for as long as you live . . . and then for all eternity.

– Your Daily Journey Through Psalms –

Call upon me in the day of trouble: I will deliver thee, and thou shall glorify me.

Psalm 50:15 KJV

Prayer Changes Things

And everything—whatever you ask in prayer, believing—you will receive.

Matthew 21:22 HCSB

I s prayer an integral part of your daily life or is it a hit-or-miss habit? Do you "pray without ceasing," or is your prayer life an afterthought? As you consider the role that prayer currently plays in your life—and the role that you think it should play—remember that the quality of your spiritual life is inevitably related to the quality of your prayer life.

Prayer changes things and it changes you. So today, instead of turning things over in your mind, turn them over to God in prayer. Instead of worrying about your next decision, pray about it. Don't limit your prayers to meals or to bedtime. Pray often about things great and small. God is listening, and He wants to hear from you.

I pray women will choose the only way to true liberation by placing their faith in Jesus Christ as their own personal Savior, surrendering to Him as Lord, and serving Him as King.

Anne Graham Lotz

– Your Daily Journey Through Psalms –

Let the words of my mouth and the meditation of my heart be acceptable in Your sight, O Lord, my strength and my Redeemer.

Psalm 19:14 NKJV

The Glorious Gift of Life

Seek the Lord, and ye shall live . . . .

Amos 5:6 KJV

Life is a glorious gift from God. Treat it that way.
This day, like every other, is filled to the brim with opportunities, challenges, and choices. But, no choice that you make is more important than the choice you make concerning God. Today, you will either place Him at the center of your life—or not—and the consequences of that choice have implications that are both temporal and eternal.

Sometimes, without our even realizing it, we gradually drift away from the One we need most. Thankfully, God never drifts away from us. He remains always present, always steadfast, always loving.

As you begin this day, place God and His Son where they belong: in your head, in your prayers, on your lips, and in your heart. And then, with God as your guide and companion, let the journey begin.

You have a glorious future in Christ! Live every moment in His power and love.

Vonette Bright

– Your Daily Journey Through Psalms –

So teach us to number our days, that we may gain a heart of wisdom.

Psalm 90:12 NKJV

Critics Beware

Do not judge, and you will not be judged. Do not condemn,
and you will not be condemned. Forgive, and you will be
forgiven.

Luke 6:37 HCSB

From experience, we know that it is easier to criticize than to correct. And we know that it is easier to find faults than solutions. Yet the urge to criticize others remains a powerful temptation for most of us. Our task, as obedient believers, is to break the twin habits of negative thinking and critical speech.

Negativity is highly contagious: we give it to others who, in turn, give it back to us. This cycle can be broken by positive thoughts, heartfelt prayers, and encouraging words. As thoughtful servants of a loving God, we can use the transforming power of Christ's love to break the chains of negativity. And we should.

Winners see an answer for every problem; losers see a problem in every answer.

Barbara Johnson

– Your Daily Journey Through Psalms –
Before I was afflicted I went astray, but now I keep Your
word.

Psalm 119:67 HCSB

Claim the Inner Peace

Peace I leave with you. My peace I give to you. I do not give to you as the world gives. Your heart must not be troubled or fearful.

John 14:27 HCSB

A re you at peace with the direction of your life? Or are you still rushing after the illusion of "peace and happiness" that our world promises but cannot deliver? The answer to this simple question will determine, to a surprising extent, the direction and the quality of your day and your life.

Joyce Meyer observes, "We need to be at peace with our past, content with our present, and sure about our future, knowing they are all in God's hands."

Today, as a gift to yourself, to your family, and to your friends, claim the inner peace that is your spiritual birthright. It is offered freely; it is yours for the asking. So ask. And then share.

Prayer guards hearts and minds and causes God to bring peace out of chaos.

Beth Moore

– Your Daily Journey Through Psalms –
Abundant peace belongs to those who love Your instruction; nothing makes them stumble.

Psalm 119:165 HCSB

Whose Expectations?

The one who has My commandments and keeps them is the one who loves Me. And the one who loves Me will be loved by My Father. I also will love him and will reveal Myself to him.

John 14:21 HCSB

Here's a quick quiz: Whose expectations are you trying to meet? A. Your friends' expectations, B. Society's expectations, C. God's expectations.

If you're a Christian, the correct answer is C., but if you're overly concerned with either A. or B., you're not alone. Plenty of people invest too much energy trying to meet society's expectations and too little energy trying to please God.

A better strategy, of course, is to try to please God first. To do so, you must prioritize your day according to God's commandments, and you must seek His will and His wisdom in all matters.

Are you having trouble choosing between God's priorities and society's priorities? If so, turn the concerns over to God—prayerfully, earnestly, and often.

– Your Daily Journey Through Psalms –

Proclaim the power of God, whose majesty is over Israel, whose power is in the skies. You are awesome, O God, in your sanctuary; the God of Israel gives power and strength to his people. Praise be to God!

Psalm 68:34-35 NIV

Trusting His Timing

Therefore humble yourselves under the mighty hand of God,
that He may exalt you in due time.

1 Peter 5:6 NKJV

I f you sincerely seek to be a woman of faith, then you must learn to trust God's timing. You will be sorely tempted, however, to do otherwise. Because you are a fallible human being, you are impatient for things to happen. But, God knows better.

God has created a world that unfolds according to His own timetable, not ours . . . thank goodness! We mortals might make a terrible mess of things. God does not.

God's plan does not always happen in the way that we would like or at the time of our own choosing. Our task—as believing Christians who trust in a benevolent, all-knowing Father—is to wait patiently for God to reveal Himself. And reveal Himself He will. Always. But until God's perfect plan is made known, we must walk in faith and never lose hope. And we must continue to trust Him. Always.

Our challenge is to wait in faith for the day of God's favor and salvation.

Jim Cymbala

– Your Daily Journey Through Psalms –
I wait for the Lord; I wait, and put my hope in His word.
Psalm 130:5 HCSB

Making Time for God

The plans of the diligent certainly lead to profit, but anyone who is reckless only becomes poor.

Proverbs 21:5 HCSB

I f you're a woman with too many responsibilities and too few hours in which to fulfill them, you are not alone. Life is so demanding that sometimes you may feel as if you have no time for yourself . . . and no time for God.

Has the busy pace of life robbed you of the peace that might otherwise be yours through Jesus Christ? If so, you are simply too busy for your own good. Through His Son Jesus, God offers you a peace that surpasses human understanding, but He won't force His peace upon you; in order to experience it, you must slow down long enough to sense His presence and His love.

Today, as a gift to yourself, to your family, and to the world, slow down long enough to claim the inner peace that is your spiritual birthright: the peace of Jesus Christ. It is offered freely; it has been paid for in full; it is yours for the asking. So ask. And then share.

– Your Daily Journey Through Psalms –

Happy are those who hear the joyful call to worship, for they will walk in the light of your presence, Lord.

Psalm 89:15 NLT

The Gift of Cheerfulness

A cheerful heart has a continual feast.

Proverbs 15:15 HCSB

Cheerfulness is a gift that we give to others and to ourselves. And, as believers who have been saved by a risen Christ, why shouldn't we be cheerful? The answer, of course, is that we have every reason to honor our Savior with joy in our hearts, smiles on our faces, and words of celebration on our lips.

Few things in life are more sad, or, for that matter, more absurd, than grumpy Christians. Christ promises us lives of abundance and joy if we accept His love and His grace. Yet sometimes, even the most righteous among us are beset by fits of ill temper and frustration. During these moments, we may not feel like turning our thoughts and prayers to Christ, but if we seek to gain perspective and peace, that's precisely what we must do.

Are you a cheerful Christian? You should be! And what is the best way to attain the joy that is rightfully yours? By giving Christ what is rightfully His: your heart, your soul, and your life.

– Your Daily Journey Through Psalms –

From the rising of the sun to its going down the Lord's name is to be praised.

Psalm 113:3 NKJV

Beyond Discouragement

Watch, stand fast in the faith, be brave, be strong.
1 Corinthians 16:13 NKJV

Life can be difficult and discouraging at times. During our darkest moments, we can depend upon our friends and family, and upon God. When we do, we find the courage to face even the darkest days with hopeful hearts and willing hands.

Eleanor Roosevelt advised, "You gain strength, courage, and confidence by every great experience in which you really stop to look fear in the face. You are able to say to yourself, 'I lived through this horror. I can take the next thing that comes along.' You must do the thing you think you cannot do."

So the next time you find your courage tested to the limit, remember that you're probably stronger than you think. And remember—with you, your friends, your family, and your God all working together, you have nothing to fear.

If a person fears God, he or she has no reason to fear anything else. On the other hand, if a person does not fear God, then fear becomes a way of life.

Beth Moore

– Your Daily Journey Through Psalms –
The Lord is my light and my salvation; whom shall I fear?
The Lord is the strength of my life; of whom shall I be afraid?
Psalm 27:1 NKJV

He Does Not Fail

The Lord is my strength and my song; He has become my salvation.

Exodus 15:2 HCSB

When we fail to meet the expectations of others (or, for that matter, the expectations that we have set for ourselves), we may be tempted to abandon hope. Thankfully, on those cloudy days when our strength is sapped and our faith is shaken, there exists One from whom we can draw courage and wisdom.

The words of Isaiah 40:31 teach us that, "Those who wait on the Lord shall renew their strength; They shall mount up with wings like eagles, They shall run and not be weary, They shall walk and not faint" (NKJV).

So if you're feeling defeated or discouraged, think again. And while you're thinking, consider the following advice from Mrs. Charles E. Cowman: "Never yield to gloomy anticipation. Place your hope and confidence in God. He has no record of failure."

Working in the vineyard, / Working all the day, / Never be discouraged, / Only watch and pray.

Fanny Crosby

– Your Daily Journey Through Psalms –

Lord, how long will You continually forget me? How long will You hide Your face from me?

Psalm 13:1 HCSB

Hope Is Contagious

A word spoken at the right time is like golden apples on a silver tray.

Proverbs 25:11 HCSB

Hope, like other human emotions, is contagious. If you associate with hope-filled, enthusiastic people, their enthusiasm will have a tendency to lift your spirits. But if you find yourself spending too much time in the company of naysayers, pessimists, or cynics, your thoughts, like theirs, will tend to be negative.

Are you a hopeful, optimistic Christian? And do you associate with like-minded people? If so, then you're availing yourself of a priceless gift: the encouragement of fellow believers. But, if you find yourself focusing on the negative aspects of life, perhaps it is time to search out a few new friends.

As a faithful follower of the man from Galilee, you have every reason to be hopeful. So today, look for reasons to celebrate God's endless blessings. And while you're at it, look for people who will join with you in the celebration. You'll be better for their company, and they'll be better for yours.

– Your Daily Journey Through Psalms –

Delight thyself also in the LORD; and he shall give thee the desires of thine heart.

Psalm 37:4 KJV

God Protects

I know whom I have believed and am persuaded that He is able to guard what has been entrusted to me until that day.

2 Timothy 1:12 HCSB

G od is willing to protect us. We, in turn, must open ourselves to His protection and His love. This point is illustrated by the familiar story found in the 4th chapter of Mark: When a terrible storm rose quickly on the Sea of Galilee, the disciples were afraid. Although they had witnessed many miracles, the disciples feared for their lives, so they turned to Jesus, and He calmed the waters and the wind.

Sometimes, we, like the disciples, feel threatened by the storms of life. And when we are fearful, we, too, can turn to Christ for comfort and for courage. The next time you find yourself facing a fear-provoking situation, remember that the One who calmed the wind and the waves is also your personal Savior. Then ask yourself which is stronger: your faith or your fear. The answer, friends, should be obvious: Whatever your challenge, God can handle it. Let Him.

There is not only fear, but terrible danger, for the life unguarded by God.

Oswald Chambers

– Your Daily Journey Through Psalms –

He shall not be afraid of evil tidings: his heart is fixed, trusting in the LORD.

Psalm 112:7 KJV

Forgiveness Is Liberating

Blessed are the merciful, because they will be shown mercy.
Matthew 5:7 HCSB

Bitterness is a form of self-punishment; forgiveness is a means of self-liberation. Bitterness focuses on the injustices of the past; forgiveness focuses on the blessings of the present and the opportunities of the future. Bitterness is an emotion that destroys you; forgiveness is a decision that empowers you. Bitterness is folly; forgiveness is wisdom.

Sometimes, amid the demands of daily life, we lose perspective. Life seems out of balance, and the pressures of everyday living seem overwhelming. What's needed is a fresh perspective, a restored sense of balance . . . and God's wisdom.

If we call upon the Lord and seek to see the world through His eyes, He will give us guidance, wisdom, and perspective. When we make God's priorities our priorities, He will lead us according to His plan and according to His commandments. When we study God's Word, we are reminded that God's reality is the ultimate reality. May we live—and forgive—accordingly.

– Your Daily Journey Through Psalms –
The LORD is gracious and full of compassion, slow to anger and great in mercy. The LORD is good to all, and His tender mercies are over all His works.

Psalm 145:8-9 NKJV

His Comforting Hand

No, I will not abandon you as orphans—I will come to you.
John 14:18 NLT

As Christians, we can be assured of this fact: Whether we find ourselves on the pinnacle of the mountain or in the darkest depths of the valley, God is there.

If you have been touched by the transforming hand of Jesus, then you have every reason to live courageously. After all, Christ has already won the ultimate battle—and He won it for you—on the cross at Calvary.

So the next time you find your courage tested to the limit, lean upon God's promises. Trust His Son. Remember that God is always near and that He is your protector and your deliverer. When you are worried, anxious, or afraid, call upon Him and accept the touch of His comforting hand. Remember that God rules both mountaintops and valleys—with limitless wisdom and love—now and forever.

When God allows extraordinary trials for His people, He prepares extraordinary comforts for them.

Corrie ten Boom

– Your Daily Journey Through Psalms –
When I am filled with cares, Your comfort brings me joy.
Psalm 94:19 HCSB

His Gift, Freely Given

For all have sinned, and fall short of the glory of God, being justified freely by His grace through the redemption that is in Christ Jesus . . . .

Romans 3:23-24 NKJV

Romans 3:23 reminds us that all of us fall short of the glory of God. Yet despite our imperfections and despite our shortcomings, God sent His Son so that we might be redeemed from our sins. In doing so, our Heavenly Father demonstrated His infinite mercy and His infinite love.

We have received countless gifts from God, but none can compare with the gift of salvation. God's grace is the ultimate gift, and we owe Him the ultimate in thanksgiving. Let us praise Him for His priceless gift, and let us share the Good News with our families, with our friends, and with the world.

Christ sacrificed His life on the cross so that we might have eternal life. This gift, freely given from God's only begotten Son, is the priceless possession of everyone who accepts Him as Lord and Savior. We return our Savior's love by welcoming Him into our hearts and sharing His message and His love. When we do so, we are blessed here on earth and throughout all eternity.

– Your Daily Journey Through Psalms –

God is my shield, saving those whose hearts are true and right.

Psalm 7:10 NLT

Infinite Possibilities

We know that all things work together for the good of those who love God: those who are called according to His purpose.
Romans 8:28 HCSB

Ours is a God of infinite possibilities. But sometimes, because of limited faith and limited understanding, we wrongly assume that God cannot or will not intervene in the affairs of mankind. Such assumptions are simply wrong.

Are you afraid to ask God to do big things in your life? Is your faith threadbare and worn? If so, it's time to abandon your doubts and reclaim your faith in God's promises.

God's Holy Word makes it clear: absolutely nothing is impossible for the Lord. And since the Bible means what it says, you can be comforted in the knowledge that the Creator of the universe can do miraculous things in your own life and in the lives of your loved ones. Your challenge, as a believer, is to take God at His word, and to expect the miraculous.

He has transforming power. He can change the quality of our lives.

Charles Swindoll

– Your Daily Journey Through Psalms –
For the kingdom is the LORD's: and his is the governor among the nations.

Psalm 22:28 KJV

The Self-fulfilling Prophecy

But if we hope for what we do not see, we eagerly wait for it with patience.

Romans 8:25 HCSB

The self-fulfilling prophecy is alive, well, and living at your house. If you trust God and have faith for the future, your optimistic beliefs will give you direction and motivation. That's one reason that you should never lose hope, but certainly not the only reason. The primary reason that you, as a believer, should never lose hope, is because of God's unfailing promises.

Your thoughts have the power to lift you up or to hold you down. When you acquire the habit of hopeful thinking, you will have acquired a powerful tool for improving your life. So if you find yourself falling into the spiritual traps of worry and discouragement, seek the healing touch of Jesus and the encouraging words of fellow Christians. And if you fall into the terrible habit of negative thinking, think again. After all, God's Word teaches us that Christ can overcome every difficulty (John 16:33). And when God makes a promise, He keeps it.

– Your Daily Journey Through Psalms –

But I will hope continually and will praise You more and more.

Psalm 71:14 HCSB

Kindness Now

Therefore, God's chosen ones, holy and loved, put on heartfelt compassion, kindness, humility, gentleness, and patience.

Colossians 3:12 HCSB

Christ showed His love for us by willingly sacrificing His own life so that we might have eternal life: "But God demonstrates his own love for us in this: While we were still sinners, Christ died for us" (Romans 5:8 NIV). We, as Christ's followers, are challenged to share His love with kind words on our lips and praise in our hearts.

Just as Christ has been—and will always be—the ultimate friend to His flock, so should we be Christlike in the kindness and generosity that we show toward others, especially those who are most in need.

When we walk each day with Jesus—and obey the commandments found in God's Holy Word—we become worthy ambassadors for Christ. When we share the love of Christ, we share a priceless gift with the world. As His servants, we must do no less.

– Your Daily Journey Through Psalms –

How happy are those whose way is blameless, who live according to the law of the Lord! Happy are those who keep His decrees and seek Him with all their heart.

Psalm 119:1-2 HCSB

Do You Believe in Miracles?

With God's power working in us, God can do much, much more than anything we can ask or imagine.

Ephesians 3:20 NCV

D o you believe in an all-powerful God who can do miraculous things in you and through you? You should. But perhaps, as you have faced the inevitable struggles of life-here-on-earth, you have—without realizing it—placed limitations on God. To do so is a profound mistake. God's power has no such limitations, and He can work mighty miracles in your own life if you let Him.

Do you lack a firm faith in God's power to perform miracles for you and your loved ones? If so, you are attempting to place limitations on a God who has none. Instead of doubting your Heavenly Father, you must place yourself in His hands. Instead of doubting God's power, you must trust it. Expect Him to work miracles, and be watchful. With God, absolutely nothing is impossible, including an amazing assortment of miracles that He stands ready, willing, and perfectly able to perform for you and yours.

– Your Daily Journey Through Psalms –

You are the God who works wonders; You revealed Your strength among the peoples.

Psalm 77:14 HCSB

Being Patient with Yourself

Rejoice in hope; be patient in affliction; be persistent in prayer.

Romans 12:12 HCSB

Being patient with other people can be difficult. But sometimes, we find it even more difficult to be patient with ourselves. We have high expectations and lofty goals. We want to accomplish things now, not later. And, of course, we want our lives to unfold according to our own timetables, not God's.

Throughout the Bible, we are instructed that patience is the companion of wisdom. Proverbs 16:32 teaches us that "Patience is better than strength" (NCV). And, in 1 Peter 5:6, we are told to "humble yourselves under the mighty hand of God, that He may exalt you in due time" (NKJV).

God's message, then, is clear: we must be patient with all people, beginning with that particular person who stares back at us each time we gaze into the mirror.

The times we find ourselves having to wait on others may be the perfect opportunities to train ourselves to wait on the Lord.

Joni Eareckson Tada

– Your Daily Journey Through Psalms –

Wait for the Lord; be courageous and let your heart be strong. Wait for the Lord.

Psalm 27:14 HCSB

Embraced by God

[Because of] the Lord's faithful love we do not perish, for His mercies never end.

Lamentations 3:22 HCSB

Every day of your life—indeed, every moment of your life—you are embraced by God. He is always with you, and His love for you is deeper and more profound than you can imagine. And now, precisely because you are a wondrous creation treasured by God, a question presents itself: What will you do in response to God's love? Will you ignore it or return it? Will you return it or neglect it? The decision, of course, is yours and yours alone.

When you open yourself to God's love, you feel differently about yourself, your neighbors, and your world. When you embrace God's love, you share His message and you obey His commandments.

When you accept the Father's grace and share His love, you are blessed here on earth and throughout all eternity. Accept His love today.

– Your Daily Journey Through Psalms –

But the mercy of the LORD is from everlasting to everlasting upon them that fear him, and his righteousness unto children's children . . . .

Psalm 103:17 KJV

Close to the Brokenhearted

For I am the Lord who heals you.

Exodus 15:26 HCSB

In time, tragedy visits all those who live long and love deeply. When our friends or family members encounter life-shattering events, we struggle to find words that might offer them comfort and support. But finding the right words can be difficult, if not impossible. Sometimes, all that we can do is to be with our loved ones and to pray for them, trusting that God will do the rest.

Thankfully, God promises that He is "close to the brokenhearted" (Psalm 34:18 NIV). In times of intense sadness, we must turn to Him, and we must encourage our friends and family members to do likewise. When we do so, our Father comforts us and, in time, He heals us.

Even in long-term grief there is a way to bring closure and to rise above the rage, the guilt, the pain. In Christ this possible.

Barbara Johnson

– Your Daily Journey Through Psalms –

For he satisfieth the longing soul, and filleth the hungry soul with goodness.

Psalm 107:9 KJV

The Bread of Life

I am the bread of life, Jesus told them. "No one who comes to Me will ever be hungry, and no one who believes in Me will ever be thirsty again."

John 6:35 HCSB

He was the Son of God, but He wore a crown of thorns. He was the Savior of mankind, yet He was put to death on a roughhewn cross made of wood. He offered His healing touch to an unsaved world, and yet the same hands that had healed the sick and raised the dead were pierced with nails.

Jesus Christ, the Son of God, was born into humble circumstances. He walked this earth, not as a ruler of men, but as the Savior of mankind. His crucifixion, a torturous punishment that was intended to end His life and His reign, instead became the pivotal event in the history of all humanity.

Jesus is the bread of life. Accept His grace. Share His love. And follow His in footsteps.

When we are in a situation where Jesus is all we have, we soon discover He is all we really need.

Gigi Graham Tchividjian

– Your Daily Journey Through Psalms –

For the Lord is good; His mercy is everlasting, and His truth endures to all generations.

Psalm 100:5 NKJV

Obeying God

So that you may walk worthy of the Lord, fully pleasing to Him, bearing fruit in every good work and growing in the knowledge of God.

Colossians 1:10 HCSB

L ife is a series of decisions and choices. Each day, we make countless decisions that can bring us closer to God. When we live according to God's commandments, we earn for ourselves the abundance and peace that He intends for our lives. But, when we turn our backs upon God by disobeying Him, we bring needless suffering upon ourselves and our families.

Do you seek God's peace and His blessings? Then obey Him. When you're faced with a difficult choice or a powerful temptation, seek God's counsel and trust the counsel He gives. Invite God into your heart and live according to His commandments. When you do, you will be blessed today, and tomorrow, and forever.

Study the Bible and observe how the persons behaved and how God dealt with them. There is explicit teaching on every condition of life.

Corrie ten Boom

– Your Daily Journey Through Psalms –

Blessed is the man that walketh not in the counsel of the ungodly, nor standeth in the way of sinners, nor sitteth in the seat of the scornful.

Psalm 1:1 KJV

Giving Thanks to the Giver

Is anyone among you suffering? He should pray. Is anyone cheerful? He should sing praises.

James 5:13 HCSB

A re you a woman who celebrates life? Hopefully you are! God has richly blessed you, and He wants you to rejoice in His gifts.

God fills each day to the brim with possibilities, and He challenges each of us to use our gifts for the glory of His kingdom. When we honor the Father and place Him at the center of our lives, every day becomes a cause for celebration.

Today is a non-renewable resource—once it's gone, it's gone forever. Our responsibility, as thoughtful believers who have been transformed by God's grace, is to use this day in the service of God's will and in the service of His people. When we do so, we enrich our own lives and the lives of those whom we love. And the Father smiles.

The highest and most desirable state of the soul is to praise God in celebration for being alive.

Luci Swindol

– Your Daily Journey Through Psalms –
O come, let us sing unto the LORD: let us make a joyful noise to the rock of our salvation. Let us come before his presence with thanksgiving, and make a joyful noise unto him with psalms.

Psalm 95:1-2 KJV

Christ's Love

Just as the Father has loved Me, I also have loved you. Remain in My love.

John 15:9 HCSB

How much does Christ love us? More than we, as mere mortals, can comprehend. His love is perfect and steadfast. Even though we are fallible and wayward, the Good Shepherd cares for us still. Even though we have fallen far short of the Father's commandments, Christ loves us with a power and depth that is beyond our understanding. The sacrifice that Jesus made upon the cross was made for each of us, and His love endures to the edge of eternity and beyond.

Christ's love changes everything. When you accept His gift of grace, you are transformed, not only for today, but also for all eternity. If you haven't already done so, accept Jesus Christ as your Savior. He's waiting patiently for you to invite Him into your heart. Please don't make Him wait a single minute longer.

Live your lives in love, the same sort of love which Christ gives us, and which He perfectly expressed when He gave Himself as a sacrifice to God.

Corrie ten Boom

– Your Daily Journey Through Psalms –
But thou, O LORD, art a shield for me . . . .

Psalm 3:3 KJV

Facing Difficult Days

We are pressured in every way but not crushed; we are perplexed but not in despair.

2 Corinthians 4:8 HCSB

All of us face difficult days. Sometimes even the most devout Christian women can become discouraged, and you are no exception. After all, you live in a world where expectations can be high and demands can be even higher.

If you find yourself enduring difficult circumstances, remember that God remains in His heaven. If you become discouraged with the direction of your day or your life, turn your thoughts and prayers to Him. He is a God of possibility, not negativity. He will guide you through your difficulties and beyond them. And then, with a renewed spirit of optimism and hope, you can thank the Giver of all things good for gifts that are simply too numerous to count.

Trials are not enemies of faith but opportunities to reveal God's faithfulness.

Barbara Johnson

– Your Daily Journey Through Psalms –

But the Lord has been my defense, and my God the rock of my refuge.

Psalm 94:22 NKJV

Opportunities to Encourage

Therefore encourage one another and build each other up as you are already doing.

1 Thessalonians 5:11 HCSB

Here's a question only you can answer: During a typical day, how many opportunities will you have to encourage your family and friends? Unless you're living on a deserted island, the answer is "a lot!" And here's a follow-up question: How often do you take advantage of those opportunities? Hopefully, the answer is "more often than not."

Romans 14:19 advises us to "Pursue what promotes peace and what builds up one another" (HCSB). And whenever we do, God smiles.

Whether you realize it or not, you're surrounded by people who need an encouraging word, a helping hand, or a pat on the back. And every time you encourage one of these folks, you'll being doing God's will by obeying God's Word. So with no further ado, let the encouragement begin.

As you're rushing through life, take time to stop a moment, look into people's eyes, say something kind, and try to make them laugh!

Barbara Johnson

– Your Daily Journey Through Psalms –
Happy is he . . . whose hope is in the LORD his God.

Psalm 146:5 KJV

Actions Speak Louder

For the kingdom of God is not in talk but in power.
1 Corinthians 4:20 HCSB

What kind of example are you? Are you the kind of woman whose life serves as a genuine example of patience and righteousness? Are you a woman whose behavior serves as a positive role model for others? Are you the kind of Christian whose actions, day in and day out, are based upon kindness, faithfulness, and a sincere love for the Lord? If so, you are not only blessed by God, but you are also a powerful force for good in a world that desperately needs positive influences such as yours.

We are to leave an impression on all those we meet that communicates whose we are and what kingdom we represent.

Lisa Bevere

– Your Daily Journey Through Psalms –
For the Lord God is a sun and shield. The Lord gives grace and glory; He does not withhold the good from those who live with integrity. Lord of Hosts, happy is the person who trusts in You!

Psalm 84:11-12 HCSB

The Wisdom of Forgiveness

A person's insight gives him patience, and his virtue is to overlook an offense.

Proverbs 19:11 HCSB

Even the most mild-mannered women will, on occasion, have reason to become angry with the inevitable shortcomings of family members and friends. But wise women are quick to forgive others, just as God has forgiven them.

Forgiveness is God's commandment, but oh how difficult a commandment it can be to follow. Being frail, fallible, imperfect human beings, we are quick to anger, quick to blame, slow to forgive, and even slower to forget. No matter. Even when forgiveness is difficult, God's Word is clear.

If, in your heart, you hold bitterness against even a single person, forgive. If there exists even one person, alive or dead, whom you have not forgiven, follow God's commandment and His will for your life: forgive. If you are embittered against yourself for some past mistake or shortcoming, forgive. Then, to the best of your abilities, forget, and move on.

– Your Daily Journey Through Psalms –

My soul, praise the Lord, and do not forget all His benefits. He forgives all your sin; He heals all your diseases. He redeems your life from the Pit; He crowns you with faithful love and compassion.

Psalm 103:2-4 HCSB

Cultivating God's Gifts

I remind you to keep ablaze the gift of God that is in you.
2 Timothy 1:6 HCSB

All women possess special gifts and talents; you are no exception. But, your gift is no guarantee of success; it must be cultivated and nurtured; otherwise, it will go unused . . . and God's gift to you will be squandered. Today, accept this challenge: value the talent that God has given you, nourish it, make it grow, and share it with the world. After all, the best way to say "Thank You" for God's gift is to use it.

The Lord has abundantly blessed me all of my life. I'm not trying to pay Him back for all of His wonderful gifts; I just realize that He gave them to me to give away.

Lisa Whelchel

Let us use the gifts of God lest they be extinguished by our slothfulness.

John Calvin

– Your Daily Journey Through Psalms –

And let the beauty of the Lord our God be upon us, And establish the work of our hands for us; Yes, establish the work of our hands.

Psalm 90:17 NKJV

Moving Past the Past

One thing I do, forgetting those things which are behind and reaching forward to those things which are ahead, I press toward the goal for the prize of the upward call of God in Christ Jesus.

Philippians 3:13-14 NKJV

Our plans are fallible; God's plans are not. Yet whenever life takes an unexpected turn, we are tempted to fall into the spiritual traps of worry, self-pity, or bitterness. God intends that we do otherwise.

The old saying is familiar: "Forgive and forget." But when we have been hurt badly, forgiveness is often difficult and forgetting is downright impossible. Since we can't forget yesterday's troubles, we should learn from them. Yesterday has much to teach us about tomorrow. We may learn from the past, but we should never live in the past.

So if you're trying to forget the past, don't waste your time. Instead, try a different approach: learn to accept the past and live in the present. Then, you can focus your thoughts and your energies, not on the struggles of yesterday, but instead on the profound opportunities that God has placed before you today.

– Your Daily Journey Through Psalms –

Whoever is wise will observe these things, and they will understand the lovingkindness of the Lord.

Psalm 107:43 NKJV

Abundance, Not Anxiety

Therefore don't worry about tomorrow, because tomorrow will worry about itself. Each day has enough trouble of its own.

Matthew 6:34 HCSB

We live in a world that often breeds anxiety and fear. When we come face-to-face with tough times, we may fall prey to discouragement, doubt, or depression. But our Father in Heaven has other plans. God has promised that we may lead lives of abundance, not anxiety. In fact, His Word instructs us to "be anxious for nothing." But how can we put our fears to rest? By taking those fears to God and leaving them there.

As you face the challenges of everyday living, do you find yourself becoming anxious, troubled, discouraged, or fearful? If so, turn every one of your concerns over to your Heavenly Father. The same God who created the universe will comfort you if you ask Him . . . so ask Him and trust Him. And then watch in amazement as your anxieties melt into the warmth of His loving hands.

– Your Daily Journey Through Psalms –

Why am I so depressed? Why this turmoil within me? Put your hope in God, for I will still praise Him, my Savior and my God.

Psalm 42:11 HCSB

He Provides

The Lord is my rock and my fortress and my deliverer; the God of my strength, in whom I will trust.

2 Samuel 22:2-3 NKJV

As a busy woman, you know from firsthand experience that life is not always easy. But as a recipient of God's grace, you also know that you are protected by a loving Heavenly Father.

In times of trouble, God will comfort you; in times of sorrow, He will dry your tears. When you are troubled, or weak, or sorrowful, God is neither distant nor disinterested. To the contrary, God is always present and always vitally engaged in the events of your life. Reach out to Him, and build your future on the rock that cannot be shaken . . . trust in God and rely upon His provisions. He can provide everything you really need . . . and far, far more.

God will never let you sink under your circumstances. He always provide a safety net and His love always encircles.

Barbara Johnson

– Your Daily Journey Through Psalms –

In my distress I called to the Lord, and He answered me.

Psalm 120:1 HCSB

The Best Policy

The one who lives with integrity lives securely, but whoever perverts his ways will be found out.

Proverbs 10:9 HCSB

It has been said on many occasions and in many ways that honesty is the best policy. For believers, it is far more important to note that honesty is God's policy. And if we are to be servants worthy of Jesus Christ, we must be honest and forthright in our communications with others. Sometimes, honesty is difficult; sometimes, honesty is painful; sometimes, honesty is inconvenient; but always, honesty is God's commandment.

In the Book of Proverbs, we read, "The Lord detests lying lips, but he delights in men who are truthful" (12:22 NIV). Clearly, we must strive to be women whose words are pleasing to our Creator. Truth is God's way, and it must be our way, too, even when telling the truth is difficult. As Christians, we must do no less.

A hypocrite is a person who's not himself on Sunday.

Anonymous

– Your Daily Journey Through Psalms –

Light shines on those who do right; joy belongs to those who are honest. Rejoice in the Lord, you who do right. Praise his holy name.

Psalm 97:11-12 NCV

Share His Joy

So now we can rejoice in our wonderful new relationship with God—all because of what our Lord Jesus Christ has done for us in making us friends of God.

Romans 5:11 NLT

Joni Eareckson Tada spoke for Christian women of every generation when she observed, "I wanted the deepest part of me to vibrate with that ancient yet familiar longing—that desire for something that would fill and overflow my soul."

God's plan for our lives includes great joy, but our Heavenly Father will not force His joy upon us. We must accept God's peace by genuinely welcoming His Son into our hearts.

Let us praise the Creator for His priceless gift, and let us share His Good News with the world. Let us share the Father's promises, His love, and His joy. When we do, we are eternally blessed, and so are our families, our friends, and all whom God has chosen to place along our paths.

Each day, each moment is so pregnant with eternity that if we "tune in" to it, we can hardly contain the joy.

Gloria Gaither

– Your Daily Journey Through Psalms –
The Lord reigns; Let the earth rejoice.

Psalm 97:1 NKJV

Quiet Time

In quietness and confidence shall be your strength.

Isaiah 30:15 NKJV

Face it: We live in a noisy world, a world filled with distractions, frustrations, and complications. But if we allow those distractions to separate us from God's peace, we do ourselves a profound disservice.

Are you one of those busy women who rushes through the day with scarcely a single moment for quiet contemplation and prayer? If so, it's time to reorder your priorities.

Nothing is more important than the time you spend with your Savior. Absolutely nothing.

The manifold rewards of a serious, consistent prayer life demonstrate clearly that time with our Lord should be our first priority.

Shirley Dobson

A quiet time is a basic ingredient in a maturing relationship with God.

Charles Stanley

– Your Daily Journey Through Psalms –
Be silent before the Lord and wait expectantly for Him.

Psalm 37:7 HCSB

Self-Acceptance

You're blessed when you're content with just who you are—no more, no less. That's the moment you find yourselves proud owners of everything that can't be bought.

Matthew 5:5 MSG

Being patient with other people can be difficult. But sometimes, we find it even more difficult to be patient with ourselves. We have high expectations and lofty goals. We want to accomplish things now, not later. And, of course, we want our lives to unfold according to our own timetables, not God's.

Throughout the Bible, we are instructed that patience is the companion of wisdom. Proverbs 16:32 teaches us that "Patience is better than strength" (NCV). And, in 1 Peter 5:6, we are told to "humble yourselves under the mighty hand of God, that He may exalt you in due time" (NKJV).

God's message, then, is clear: we must be patient with all people, beginning with that particular person who stares back at us each time we gaze into the mirror.

– Your Daily Journey Through Psalms –

For You formed my inward parts; You covered me in my mother's womb. I will praise You, for I am fearfully and wonderfully made; Marvelous are Your works.

Psalm 139:13-14 NKJV

Spiritual Growth

But grow in the grace and knowledge of our Lord and Savior Jesus Christ. To Him be the glory both now and to the day of eternity.

2 Peter 3:18 HCSB

If we are to grow as Christians and as women, we need both knowledge and wisdom. Knowledge is found in textbooks. Wisdom, on the other hand, is found in God's Holy Word and in the carefully-chosen words of loving parents, family members, and friends. Knowledge is an important building block in a well-lived life, and it pays rich dividends both personally and professionally. But, wisdom is even more important because it refashions not only the mind, but also the heart.

When it comes to your faith, God doesn't intend for you to stand still. As a Christian, you should continue to grow in the love and the knowledge of your Savior as long as you live. How? By studying God's Word every day, by obeying His commandments, and by allowing His Son to reign over your heart.

The Scriptures were not given for our information, but for our transformation.

D. L. Moody

– Your Daily Journey Through Psalms –

He will fulfil the desire of them that fear him: he also will hear their cry, and will save them.

Psalm 145:19 KJV

Focusing on God

Therefore don't worry about tomorrow, because tomorrow will worry about itself. Each day has enough trouble of its own.

Matthew 6:34 HCSB

All of us may find our courage tested by the inevitable disappointments and tragedies of life. After all, ours is a world filled with uncertainty, hardship, sickness, and danger. Trouble, it seems, is never too far from the front door.

When we focus upon our fears and our doubts, we may find many reasons to lie awake at night and fret about the uncertainties of the coming day. A better strategy, of course, is to focus not upon our fears, but instead upon our God.

God is as near as your next breath, and He is in control. He offers salvation to all His children, including you. God is your shield and your strength; you are His forever. So don't focus your thoughts upon the fears of the day. Instead, trust God's plan and His eternal love for you. And remember: God is good, and He has the last word.

– Your Daily Journey Through Psalms –

The Lord is for me; I will not be afraid. What can man do to me?

Psalm 118:6 HCSB

Forgiveness and Spiritual Growth

He who says he is in the light, and hates his brother, is in darkness until now.

1 John 2:9 NKJV

Forgiveness is an exercise in spiritual growth: the more we forgive, the more we grow. Conversely, bitterness makes spiritual growth impossible: when our hearts are filled with resentment and anger, there is no room left for love.

As Christians, we can and should continue to grow in the love and the knowledge of our Savior as long as we live. When we cease to grow, either emotionally or spiritually, we do ourselves and our loved ones a profound disservice. But, if we study God's Word, if we obey His commandments, and if we live in the center of His will, we will not be "stagnant" believers; we will, instead, be growing Christians.

In those quiet moments when we open our hearts to God, the Creator who made us keeps remaking us. He gives us direction, perspective, wisdom, and courage. And the appropriate moment to accept His spiritual gifts is always this one.

– Your Daily Journey Through Psalms –

The Lord is gracious and compassionate, slow to anger and great in faithful love. The Lord is good to everyone; His compassion [rests] on all He has made.

Psalm 145:8-9 HCSB

Heeding His Call

I, therefore, the prisoner in the Lord, urge you to walk worthy of the calling you have received.

Ephesians 4:1 HCSB

It is terribly important that you heed God's calling by discovering and developing your talents and your spiritual gifts. If you seek to make a difference—and if you seek to bear eternal fruit—you must discover your gifts and begin using them for the glory of God.

Every believer has at least one gift. In John 15:16, Jesus says, "You did not choose Me, but I chose you and appointed you that you should go and bear fruit, and that your fruit should remain, that whatever you ask the Father in My name He may give you." Have you found your special calling? If not, keep searching and keep praying until you find it. God has important work for you to do, and the time to begin that work is now.

God never calls without enabling us. In other words, if He calls you to do something, He makes it possible for you to do it.

Luci Swindoll

– Your Daily Journey Through Psalms –

I will instruct you and teach you in the way you should go; I will guide you with My eye.

Psalm 32:8 NKJV

The Plan for Your Life

The plans of the diligent certainly lead to profit, but anyone who is reckless only becomes poor.

Proverbs 21:5 HCSB

Perhaps you have a clearly defined plan for the future, but even if you don't, rest assured that God does. God has a definite plan for every aspect of your life. Your challenge is straightforward: to sincerely pray for God's guidance, and to obediently follow the guidance you receive.

If you're burdened by the demands of everyday life here in the 21st century, you are not alone. Life is difficult at times, and uncertain. But of this you can be sure: God has a plan for you and yours. He will communicate His plans using the Holy Spirit, His Holy Word, and your own conscience. So listen to God's voice and be watchful for His signs: He will send you messages every day of your life, including this one. Your job is to listen, to learn, to trust, and to act.

Plan ahead—it wasn't raining when Noah built the ark.

Anonymous

– Your Daily Journey Through Psalms –

May He give you what your heart desires and fulfill your whole purpose.

Psalm 20:4 HCSB

Making Peace with the Past

Do not remember the past events, pay no attention to things of old. Look, I am about to do something new; even now it is coming. Do you not see it? Indeed, I will make a way in the wilderness, rivers in the desert.

Isaiah 43:18-19 HCSB

Have you made peace with your past? If so, congratulations. But, if you are mired in the quicksand of regret, it's time to plan your escape. How can you do so? By accepting what has been and by trusting God for what will be.

Because you are human, you may be slow to forget yesterday's disappointments; if so you are not alone. But if you sincerely seek to focus your hopes and energies on the future, then you must find ways to accept the past, no matter how difficult it may be to do so.

If you have not yet made peace with the past, today is the day to declare an end to all hostilities. When you do, you can then turn your thoughts to the wondrous promises of God and to the glorious future that He has in store for you.

– Your Daily Journey Through Psalms –

O Lord, you have examined my heart and know everything about me. You know when I sit down or stand up. You know my every thought when far away. You chart the path ahead of me and tell me where to stop and rest.

Psalm 139:1-3 NLT

A World Filled with Temptations

Let your eyes look forward; fix your gaze straight ahead.
Proverbs 4:25 HCSB

I f you stop to think about it, the cold, hard evidence is right in front of your eyes: you live in a temptation-filled world. The devil is out on the street, hard at work, causing pain and heartache in more ways than ever before. Here in the 21st Century, the bad guys are working around the clock to lead you astray. That's why you must remain vigilant.

In a letter to believers, Peter offered a stern warning: "Your adversary, the devil, prowls around like a roaring lion, seeking someone to devour" (1 Peter 5:8 NASB). What was true in New Testament times is equally true in our own. Satan tempts his prey and then devours them. As believing Christians, we must beware. And, if we seek righteousness in our own lives, we must earnestly wrap ourselves in the protection of God's Holy Word. When we do, we are secure.

– Your Daily Journey Through Psalms –

Blessed is the man who walks not in the counsel of the ungodly, nor stands in the path of sinners, nor sits in the seat of the scornful.

Psalm 1:1 NKJV

Acceptance Today

I have learned to be content in whatever circumstances I am.
Philippians 4:11 HCSB

Are you embittered by a personal tragedy that you did not deserve and cannot understand? If so, it's time to accept the unchangeable past and to have faith in the promise of tomorrow. It's time to trust God completely—and it's time to reclaim the peace—His peace—that can and should be yours.

God doesn't explain Himself in ways that we, as mortals with limited insight and clouded vision, can comprehend. So, instead of understanding every aspect of God's unfolding plan for our lives and our universe, we must be satisfied to trust Him completely. We cannot know God's motivations, nor can we understand His actions. We can, however, trust Him, and we must.

Faith is the willingness to receive whatever he wants to give, or the willingness not to have what he does not want to give.

Elisabeth Elliot

– Your Daily Journey Through Psalms –

O God, You are my God; early will I seek You; my soul thirsts for You; my flesh longs for You in a dry and thirsty land where there is no water. So I have looked for You in the sanctuary, to see Your power and Your glory. Because Your lovingkindness is better than life, my lips shall praise You.
Psalm 63:1-3 NKJV

If You Ask, He Answers

Now if any of you lacks wisdom, he should ask God, who gives to all generously and without criticizing, and it will be given to him.

James 1:5 HCSB

Are you a woman whose batteries need recharging? Ask God to recharge them, and He will. Are you worried? Take your concerns to Him in prayer. Are you discouraged? Seek the comfort of God's promises. Do you feel trapped in circumstances that are disheartening, or confusing, or both? Ask God where He wants you to go, and then go there. In all things great and small, seek the transforming power of God's grace. He hears your prayers. And He answers.

By asking in Jesus' name, we're making a request not only in His authority, but also for His interests and His benefit.

Shirley Dobson

God's help is always available, but it is only given to those who seek it.

Max Lucado

– Your Daily Journey Through Psalms –

Call upon me in the day of trouble: I will deliver thee, and thou shall glorify me.

Psalm 50:15 KJV

Beyond Blame

All bitterness, anger and wrath, insult and slander must be removed from you, along with all wickedness. And be kind and compassionate to one another, forgiving one another, just as God also forgave you in Christ.

Ephesians 4:31-32 HCSB

To blame others for our own problems is the height of futility. Yet blaming others is a favorite human pastime. Why? Because blaming is much easier than fixing, and criticizing others is so much easier than improving ourselves. So instead of solving our problems legitimately (by doing the work required to solve them) we are inclined to fret, to blame, and to criticize, while doing precious little else. When we do, our problems, quite predictably, remain unsolved.

Have you acquired the bad habit of blaming others for problems that you could or should solve yourself? If so, you are not only disobeying God's Word, you are also wasting your own precious time. So, instead of looking for someone to blame, look for something to fix, and then get busy fixing it. And as you consider your own situation, remember this: God has a way of helping those who help themselves, but He doesn't spend much time helping those who don't.

– Your Daily Journey Through Psalms –

If riches increase, do not set your heart on them.

Psalm 62:10 NKJV

When Life Is Difficult

Haven't I commanded you: be strong and courageous? Do not be afraid or discouraged, for the Lord your God is with you wherever you go.

Joshua 1:9 HCSB

This world can be a dangerous and daunting place, but Christians have every reason to live courageously. After all, the ultimate battle has already been fought and won on the cross at Calvary. But even the most dedicated Christian woman may find her courage tested by the inevitable disappointments and fears that visit the lives of believers and non-believers alike.

The next time you find your courage tested to the limit, remember to take your fears to God. If you call upon Him, you will be comforted. Whatever your challenge, whatever your trouble, God can handle it. And will.

When once we are assured that God is good, then there can be nothing left to fear.

Hannah Whitall Smith

– Your Daily Journey Through Psalms –

The Lord is my light and my salvation; whom shall I fear? The Lord is the strength of my life; of whom shall I be afraid?

Psalm 27:1 NKJV

The Importance of Discipline

For God has not given us a spirit of fearfulness, but one of power, love, and sound judgment.

3 Timothy 1:7 HCSB

Wise women teach the importance of discipline using their words and their examples. Disciplined women understand that God doesn't reward laziness or misbehavior. To the contrary, God expects His believers to lead lives that are above reproach. And, He punishes those who disobey His commandments.

It has been said that there are no shortcuts to any place worth going. In Proverbs 28:19, God's message is clear: "He who works his land will have abundant food, but the one who chases fantasies will have his fill of poverty" (NIV).

When we work diligently and consistently, we can expect a bountiful harvest. But we must never expect the harvest to precede the labor. First, we must lead lives of discipline and obedience; then, we will reap the never-ending rewards that God has promised.

– Your Daily Journey Through Psalms –

For You, O God, have tested us; You have refined us as silver is refined. You brought us into the net; You laid affliction on our backs. You have caused men to ride over our heads; we went through fire and through water; but You brought us out to rich fulfillment.

Psalm 66:10-12 NKJV

Celebrating Others

And let us be concerned about one another in order to promote love and good works.

Hebrews 10:24 HCSB

Your loved ones need a regular supply of encouraging words and pats on the back. And you need the rewards that God gives to enthusiastic women who are a continual source of encouragement to their families.

The 118th Psalm reminds us, "This is the day which the Lord hath made; we will rejoice and be glad in it" (v. 24 KJV). As we rejoice in this day that the Lord has given us, let us remember that an important part of today's celebration is the time we spend celebrating others. Each day provides countless opportunities to encourage others and to praise their good works. When we do, we not only spread seeds of joy and happiness, we also follow the commandments of God's Holy Word.

Today, look for the good in others—starting with your loved ones. And then, celebrate the good that you find. When you do, you'll be a powerful force of encouragement in your corner of the world . . . and a worthy servant to your God.

– Your Daily Journey Through Psalms –

Thou wilt show me the path of life: in thy presence is fulness of joy; at thy right hand there are pleasures for evermore.

Psalm 16:11 KJV

Working for the Harvest

I have seen that there is nothing better than for a person to enjoy his activities, because that is his reward. For who can enable him to see what will happen after he dies?

Ecclesiastes 3:22 HCSB

Once the season for planting is upon us, the time to plant seeds is when we make time to plant seeds. And when it comes to planting God's seeds in the soil of eternity, the only certain time that we have is now. Yet because we are fallible human beings with limited vision and misplaced priorities, we may be tempted to delay.

If we hope to reap a bountiful harvest for God, for our families, and for ourselves, we must plant now by defeating a dreaded human frailty: the habit of procrastination. Procrastination often results from our shortsighted attempts to postpone temporary discomfort.

A far better strategy is this: Whatever "it" is, do it now. When you do, you won't have to worry about "it" later.

Never fail to do something because you don't feel like it. Sometimes you just have to do it now, and you'll feel like it later.

Marie T. Freeman

– Your Daily Journey Through Psalms –
Now, Lord, what do I wait for? My hope is in You.

Psalm 39:7 HCSB

Real Repentance

Seek the Lord, and ye shall live . . . .

Amos 5:6 KJV

Genuine repentance requires more than simply offering God apologies for our misdeeds. Real repentance may start with feelings of sorrow and remorse, but it ends only when we turn away from the sin that has heretofore distanced us from our Creator. In truth, we offer our most meaningful apologies to God, not with our words, but with our actions. As long as we are still engaged in sin, we may be "repenting," but we have not fully "repented."

Is there an aspect of your life that is distancing you from your God? If so, ask for His forgiveness, and—just as importantly—stop sinning. Then, wrap yourself in the protection of God's Word. When you do, you will be secure.

Real repentance is always accompanied by godly sorrow. Asking God to forgive us for a sin we are not yet sorry we committed is a waste of time.

Beth Moore

– Your Daily Journey Through Psalms –
The Lord is near to those who have a broken heart.

Psalm 34:18 NKJV

Service and Love

This is how we know that we love God's children when we love God and obey His commands.

1 John 5:2 HCSB

The words of 1st Corinthians 13 remind us that faith is important; so, too, is hope. But love is more important still. Christ showed His love for us on the cross, and, as Christians, we are called upon to return Christ's love by sharing it. Sometimes love is easy (puppies and sleeping children come to mind) and sometimes love is hard (fallible human beings come to mind). But God's Word is clear: We are to love our families and our neighbors without reservation or condition.

As a caring Christian, you are not only shaping the lives of your loved ones, you are also, in a very real sense, reshaping eternity. It's a big job, a job so big, in fact, that God saw fit to entrust it to some of the most important people in His kingdom: loving women like you.

Without God, we cannot. Without us, God will not.

St. Augustine

– Your Daily Journey Through Psalms –

I will thank the Lord with all my heart; I will declare all Your wonderful works. I will rejoice and boast about You; I will sing about Your name, Most High.

Psalm 9:1-2 HCSB

The Source of Strength

Have you not known? Have you not heard? The everlasting God, the Lord, the Creator of the ends of the earth, neither faints nor is weary. His understanding is unsearchable. He gives power to the weak, and to those who have no might He increases strength.

Isaiah 40:28-29 NKJV

God is a never-ending source of strength and courage if we call upon Him. When we are weary, He gives us strength. When we see no hope, God reminds us of His promises. When we grieve, God wipes away our tears.

Do you feel overwhelmed by today's responsibilities? Do you feel pressured by the ever-increasing demands of life? Then turn your concerns and your prayers over to God. He knows your needs, and He has promised to meet those needs. Whatever your circumstances, God will protect you and care for you . . . if you let Him. Invite Him into your heart and allow Him to renew your spirits. When you trust Him and Him alone, He will never fail you.

– Your Daily Journey Through Psalms –

Be of good courage, And He shall strengthen your heart, All you who hope in the Lord.

Psalm 31:24 NKJV

Focusing on Your Hopes

This hope we have as an anchor of the soul, both sure and steadfast, and which enters the Presence behind the veil.
Hebrews 6:19 NKJV

Paul Valéry observed, "We hope vaguely but dread precisely." How true. All too often, we allow the worries of everyday life to overwhelm our thoughts and cloud our vision. What's needed is clearer perspective, renewed faith, and a different focus.

When we focus on the frustrations of today or the uncertainties of tomorrow, we rob ourselves of peace in the present moment. But, when we focus on God's grace, and when we trust in the ultimate wisdom of God's plan for our lives, our worries no longer tyrannize us.

Today, remember that God is infinitely greater than the challenges that you face. Remember also that your thoughts are profoundly powerful, so guard them accordingly.

As we have by faith said no to sin, so we should by faith say yes to God and set our minds on things above, where Christ is seated in the heavenlies.

Vonette Bright

– Your Daily Journey Through Psalms –
May the words of my mouth and the meditation of my heart be acceptable to You, Lord, my rock and my Redeemer.
Psalm 19:14 HCSB

Bearing Witness to the Truth

But the natural man does not welcome what comes from God's Spirit, because it is foolishness to him; he is not able to know it since it is evaluated spiritually. The spiritual person, however, can evaluate everything, yet he himself cannot be evaluated by anyone.

1 Corinthians 2:14-15 HCSB

When God's spirit touches our hearts, we are confronted by a powerful force: the awesome, irresistible force of God's Truth. In response to that force, we will either follow God's lead by allowing Him to guide our thoughts and deeds, or we will resist God's calling and accept the consequences of our rebellion.

Today, as you fulfill the responsibilities that God has placed before you, ask yourself this question: "Do my thoughts and actions bear witness to the ultimate Truth that God has placed in my heart, or am I allowing the pressures of everyday life to overwhelm me?" It's a profound question that only you can answer. You be the judge.

– Your Daily Journey Through Psalms –

The entirety of Your word is truth, and all Your righteous judgments endure forever.

Psalm 119:160 HCSB

Beyond Mediocrity

Therefore by their fruits you will know them.

Matthew 7:20 NKJV

P roviding for a family requires work, and lots of it. And whether or not your work carries you outside the home, your good works have earned the gratitude of your loved ones and the praise of your Heavenly Father.

It has been said that there are no shortcuts to any place worth going. Making the grade in today's competitive workplace is not easy. In fact, it can be very difficult indeed. The same can be said for the important work that occurs within the four walls of your home.

God did not create you and your family for lives of mediocrity; He created you for far greater things. Accomplishing God's work is seldom easy. What's required is determination, persistence, patience, and discipline— which is perfectly fine with God. After all, He knows that you're up to the task, and He has big plans for you.

– Your Daily Journey Through Psalms –

And let the beauty of the Lord our God be upon us, And establish the work of our hands for us; Yes, establish the work of our hands.

Psalm 90:17 NKJV

Life Triumphant

I, therefore, the prisoner in the Lord, urge you to walk worthy of the calling you have received.

Ephesians 4:1 HCSB

A re you living the triumphant life that God has promised? Or are you, instead, a spiritual shrinking violet? As you ponder that question, consider this: God does not intend that you live a life that is commonplace or mediocre. And He doesn't want you hide your light "under a basket." Instead, He wants you to "Let your light so shine before men, that they may see your good works and glorify your Father in heaven" (Matthew 5:16 NKJV). In short, God wants you to live a triumphant life so that others might know precisely what it means to be a believer.

The Christian life should be a triumphal celebration, a daily exercise in thanksgiving and praise. Join that celebration today. And while you're at it, make sure that you let others know that you've joined.

When we invite Jesus into our lives, we experience life in the fullest, most vital sense.

Catherine Marshall

– Your Daily Journey Through Psalms –

Shout triumphantly to the Lord, all the earth. Serve the Lord with gladness; come before Him with joyful songs.

Psalm 100:1-2 HCSB

How Important Is Money?

For the love of money is a root of all kinds of evil, and by craving it, some have wandered away from the faith and pierced themselves with many pains.

1 Timothy 6:10 HCSB

Our society holds material possessions in very high regard. Far too many people seem to worship money and the things that money can buy, but such misplaced priorities inevitably lead to disappointments and dissatisfaction. Popular opinion to the contrary, money cannot buy happiness, period.

Money, in and of itself, is not evil; but the worship of money inevitably leads to troublesome behavior. So today, as you prioritize matters of importance for you and yours, remember that God is almighty, but the dollar is not.

When we worship God, we are blessed. But if we dare to worship "the almighty dollar," we are inevitably punished because of our misplaced priorities—and our punishment invariably comes sooner rather than later.

Have you prayed about your resources lately? Find out how God wants you to use your time and your money. No matter what it costs, forsake all that is not of God.

Kay Arthur

– Your Daily Journey Through Psalms –

If riches increase, do not set your heart on them.

Psalm 62:10 NKJV

The Need to Endure

For you need endurance, so that after you have done God's will, you may receive what was promised.

Hebrews 10:36 HCSB

I f you've led a perfect life with absolutely no foul ups, blunders, mistakes, or flops, you can skip this chapter. But if you're like the rest of us, you know that occasional disappointments and failures are an inevitable part of life. These setbacks are simply the price of growing up and learning about life. But even when you experience bitter disappointments, you must never lose faith.

When we encounter the inevitable difficulties of life-here-on-earth, God stands ready to protect us. And, while we are waiting for God's plans to unfold, we can be comforted in the knowledge that our Creator can overcome any obstacle, even if we cannot.

Failure is one of life's most powerful teachers. How we handle our failures determines whether we're going to simply "get by" in life or "press on."

Beth Moore

– Your Daily Journey Through Psalms –

Search for the Lord and for His strength; seek His face always. Remember the wonderful works He has done.

Psalm 105:4-5 HCSB

Prayer and Work

*Be kindly affectionate to one another with brotherly love,
in honor giving preference to one another; not lagging in
diligence, fervent in spirit, serving the Lord; rejoicing in
hope, patient in tribulation, continuing steadfastly in prayer.*
Romans 12:10-12 NKJV

The old adage is both familiar and true: We must
pray as if everything depended upon God, but
work as if everything depended upon us. Yet
sometimes, when we are weary and discouraged, we
may allow our worries to sap our energy and our hope.
God has other intentions. God intends that we pray for
things, and He intends that we be willing to work for the
things that we pray for. More importantly, God intends
that our work should become His work.

Are you willing to work diligently for yourself, for
your family, and for your God? And are you willing to
engage in work that is pleasing to your Creator? If so,
you can expect your Heavenly Father to bring forth a
rich harvest.

– Your Daily Journey Through Psalms –

*And let the beauty of the Lord our God be upon us, And
establish the work of our hands for us; Yes, establish the work
of our hands.*

Psalm 90:17 NKJV

Reaping His Rewards

The good obtain favor from the Lord, but He condemns a man who schemes.

Proverbs 12:2 HCSB

The Bible instructs us that a righteous life has many components: faith, honesty, generosity, love, kindness, humility, gratitude, and worship, to name but a few. And, if we seek to follow the steps of our Savior, Jesus Christ, we must, to the best of our abilities, live according to the principles contained in God's Holy Word.

God has entrusted you with a profound responsibility: caring for the needs of your family and friends, including their spiritual needs. To fulfill that responsibility, you must study God's Word and live by it. When you do, your example will be a blessing not only to your loved ones, but also to generations yet unborn.

As you walk by faith, you live a righteous life, for righteousness is always by faith.

Kay Arthur

– Your Daily Journey Through Psalms –
God, create a clean heart for me and renew a steadfast spirit within me.

Psalm 51:10 HCSB

He Wants Your Attention

Let us lay aside every weight and the sin that so easily ensnares us, and run with endurance the race that lies before us, keeping our eyes on Jesus, the source and perfecter of our faith.

Hebrews 12:1-2 HCSB

Is yours a life of moderation or accumulation? Are you more interested in the possessions you can acquire or in the person you can become? The answers to these questions will determine the direction of your day and, in time, the direction of your life.

Ours is a highly complicated society, a place where people and corporations vie for your attention, for your time, and for your dollars. Don't let them succeed in complicating your life! Keep your eyes focused instead upon God.

If your material possessions are somehow distancing you from God, discard them. If your outside interests leave you too little time for your family or your Creator, slow down the merry-go-round, or better yet, get off the merry-go-round completely. Remember: God wants your full attention, and He wants it today, so don't let anybody or anything get in His way.

– Your Daily Journey Through Psalms –

I was helpless, and He saved me.

Psalm 116:6 HCSB

Using Your Talents

Based on the gift they have received, everyone should use it to serve others, as good managers of the varied grace of God.
1 Peter 4:10 HCSB

Your talents, resources, and opportunities are all gifts from the Giver of all things good. And the best way to say "Thank You" for these gifts is to use them.

Do you have a particular talent? Hone your skill and use it. Do you possess financial resources? Share them. Have you been blessed by a particular opportunity, or have you experienced unusual good fortune? Use your good fortune to help others.

When you share the gifts God has given you—and when you share them freely and without fanfare—you invite God to bless you more and more. So today, do yourself and the world a favor: be a faithful steward of your talents and treasures. And then prepare yourself for even greater blessings that are sure to come.

Not everyone possesses boundless energy or a conspicuous talent. We are not equally blessed with great intellect or physical beauty or emotional strength. But we have all been given the same ability to be faithful.

Gigi Graham Tchividjian

– Your Daily Journey Through Psalms –
I will praise thee with my whole heart . . . .

Psalm 138:1 KJV

The World . . . and You

Do not be conformed to this age, but be transformed by the renewing of your mind, so that you may discern what is the good, pleasing, and perfect will of God.

Romans 12:2 HCSB

We live in the world, but we must not worship it. Our duty is to place God first and everything else second. But because we are fallible beings with imperfect faith, placing God in His rightful place is often difficult. In fact, at every turn, or so it seems, we are tempted to do otherwise.

The 21st-century world is a noisy, distracting place filled with countless opportunities to stray from God's will. The world seems to cry, "Worship me with your time, your money, your energy, and your thoughts!" But God commands otherwise: He commands us to worship Him and Him alone; everything else must be secondary.

All those who look to draw their satisfaction from the wells of the world—pleasure, popularity, position, possessions, politics, power, prestige, finances, fame, fortune, career, clubs, sports, success, recognition, reputation, education, entertainment, exercise, honors, health, hobbies—will soon be thirsty again!

Anne Graham Lotz

– Your Daily Journey Through Psalms –
If riches increase, set not your heart upon them.

Psalm 62:10 KJV

Infinite Possibilities

Everything is possible to the one who believes.

Mark 9:23 HCSB

We live in a world of infinite possibilities. But sometimes, because of limited faith and limited understanding, we wrongly assume that God cannot or will not intervene in the affairs of mankind. Such assumptions are simply wrong.

Are you afraid to ask God to do big things in your life? Is your faith threadbare and worn? If so, it's time to abandon your doubts and reclaim your faith—faith in yourself, faith in your abilities, faith in your future, and faith in your Heavenly Father.

Catherine Marshall notes that, "God specializes in things thought impossible." And make no mistake: God can help you do things you never dreamed possible . . . your job is to let Him.

There is Someone who makes possible what seems completely impossible.

Catherine Marshall

– Your Daily Journey Through Psalms –

The voice of the Lord is upon the waters: the God of glory thundereth: the Lord is upon many waters.

Psalm 29:3 KJV

Countless Opportunities

Love does no harm to a neighbor; therefore love is the fulfillment of the law.

Romans 13:10 NKJV

Each waking moment holds the potential to think a creative thought or offer a heartfelt prayer. So even if you're a person with too many demands and too few hours in which to meet them, don't panic. Instead, be comforted in the knowledge that when you sincerely seek to discover God's priorities for your life, He will provide answers in marvelous and surprising ways.

Remember: this is the day that God has made and that He has filled it with countless opportunities to love, to serve, and to seek His guidance. Seize those opportunities. And as a gift to yourself, to your family, and to the world, slow down and establish clear priorities that are pleasing to God. When you do, you will earn the inner peace that is your spiritual birthright: the peace of Jesus Christ. It is yours for the asking. So ask . . . and be thankful.

– Your Daily Journey Through Psalms –

I will instruct you and show you the way to go; with My eye on you, I will give counsel.

Psalm 32:8 HCSB

Renewal and Celebration

*He will wipe away every tear from their eyes. Death will exist
no longer; grief, crying, and pain will exist no longer, because
the previous things have passed away.*

Revelation 21:4 HCSB

Each new day offers countless opportunities to celebrate life and to serve God's children. But each day also offers countless opportunities to fall prey to the countless distractions of our difficult age.

Gigi Graham Tchividjian spoke for women everywhere when she observed, "How much of our lives are, well, so daily. How often our hours are filled with the mundane, seemingly unimportant things that have to be done, whether at home or work. These very 'daily' tasks could—and should—become a celebration."

Make your life a celebration. After all, your talents are unique, as are your opportunities. So the best time to really live—and really celebrate—is now.

God specializes in things fresh and firsthand. His plans for you this year may outshine those of the past. He's prepared to fill your days with reasons to give Him praise.

Joni Eareckson Tada

– Your Daily Journey Through Psalms –

*For he satisfieth the longing soul, and filleth the hungry soul
with goodness.*

Psalm 107:9 KJV

Serving God . . . With Humility

The greatest among you must be a servant. But those who exalt themselves will be humbled, and those who humble themselves will be exalted.

Matthew 23:11-12 NKJV

If you genuinely seek to discover God's unfolding purpose for your life, you must ask yourself this question: "How does God want me to serve others?"

Whatever your path, whatever your calling, you may be certain of this: service to others is an integral part of God's plan for your life. Christ was the ultimate servant, the Savior who gave His life for mankind. As His followers, we, too, must become humble servants.

Every single day of your life, including this one, God will give you opportunities to serve Him by serving His children. Welcome those opportunities with open arms. They are God's gift to you, His way of allowing you to achieve greatness in His kingdom.

God wants us to serve Him with a willing spirit, one that would choose no other way.

Beth Moore

– Your Daily Journey Through Psalms –

Delight yourself also in the Lord, and He shall give you the desires of your heart.

Psalm 37:4 NKJV

Be Transformed

And do not be conformed to this world, but be transformed by the renewing of your mind, that you may prove what is that good and acceptable and perfect will of God.

Romans 12:2 NKJV

Believers who fashion their days around Jesus are transformed: They see the world differently; they act differently, and they feel differently about themselves and their neighbors.

Thoughtful believers face the inevitable challenges and disappointments of each day armed with the joy of Christ and the promise of salvation. So whatever this day holds for you, begin it and end it with God as your partner and Christ as your Savior. And throughout the day, give thanks to the One who created you and saved you. God's love for you is infinite. Accept it joyously and be thankful.

In the midst of the pressure and the heat, I am confident His hand is on my life, developing my faith until I display His glory, transforming me into a vessel of honor that pleases Him!

Anne Graham Lotz

– Your Daily Journey Through Psalms –

Teach me, O Lord, the way of Your statutes, and I shall keep it to the end.

Psalm 119:33 NKJV

Stillness

Be silent before the Lord and wait expectantly for Him.
Psalm 37:7 HCSB

Are you so busy that you rush through the day with scarcely a single moment for quiet contemplation and prayer? If so, it's time to reorder your priorities.

We live in a noisy world, a world filled with distractions, frustrations, and complications. But if we allow the distractions of a clamorous world to separate us from God's peace, we do ourselves a profound disservice. If we are to maintain righteous minds and compassionate hearts, we must take time each day for prayer and for meditation. We must make ourselves still in the presence of our Creator. We must quiet our minds and our hearts so that we might sense God's will, God's love, and God's Son.

Nothing is more important than the time you spend with your Savior. So be still and claim the inner peace that is your spiritual birthright: the peace of Jesus Christ. It is offered freely; it has been paid for in full; it is yours for the asking. So ask.

– Your Daily Journey Through Psalms –
Be still, and know that I am God.

Psalm 46:10 KJV

A Heart Aflame?

Whatever your hands find to do, do with [all] your strength.
Ecclesiastes 9:10 HCSB

When we feel worried or weary, a few moments spent in quiet conversation with the Creator can calm our fears and restore our perspective.

Mary Lou Retton observed, "Heat is required to forge anything. Every great accomplishment is the story of a flaming heart." Is your heart aflame? Are you fully engaged in life—and in love? If so, keep up the good work! But if you feel the passion slowly draining from your life, it's time to refocus your thoughts, your energies, and your prayers . . . now.

If your heart has grown cold, it is because you have moved away from the fire of His presence.

Beth Moore

– Your Daily Journey Through Psalms –

How happy are those whose way is blameless, who live according to the law of the Lord! Happy are those who keep His decrees and seek Him with all their heart.

Psalm 119:1-2 HCSB

Finding Happiness and Abundance

A joyful heart makes a face cheerful.

Proverbs 15:13 HCSB

Do you seek happiness, abundance, and contentment? If so, here are some things you should do: Love God and His Son; depend upon God for strength; try, to the best of your abilities, to follow God's will; and strive to obey His Holy Word. When you do these things, you'll discover that happiness goes hand-in-hand with righteousness. The happiest people are not those who rebel against God; the happiest people are those who love God and obey His commandments.

What does life have in store for you? A world full of possibilities (of course it's up to you to seize them), and God's promise of abundance (of course it's up to you to accept it). So, as you embark upon the next phase of your journey, remember to celebrate the life that God has given you. Your Creator has blessed you beyond measure. Honor Him with your prayers, your words, your deeds, and your joy.

– Your Daily Journey Through Psalms –

Happy is the man who fears the Lord, taking great delight in His commandments.

Psalm 112:1 HCSB

The Foundation That Cannot Be Shaken

I will show you what someone is like who comes to Me, hears My words, and acts on them: He is like a man building a house, who dug deep and laid the foundation on the rock. When the flood rose, the river crashed against that house and couldn't shake it, because it was well built.

Luke 6:47-48 HCSB

Women know that life is seldom easy. But, godly women also know that they are protected by a loving God. In times of trouble, God comforts us; in times of sorrow, He dries our tears. When we are troubled, or weak, or sorrowful, God is as near as our next breath. Let us build our lives on the rock that cannot be shaken . . . let us trust in God.

Once we recognize our need for Jesus, then the building of our faith begins. It is a daily, moment-by-moment life of absolute dependence upon Him for everything.

Catherine Marshall

– Your Daily Journey Through Psalms –

Search for the Lord and for His strength; seek His face always. Remember the wonderful works He has done.

Psalm 105:4-5 HCSB

The Lessons of Tough Times

No discipline seems enjoyable at the time, but painful. Later on, however, it yields the fruit of peace and righteousness to those who have been trained by it.

Hebrews 12:11 HCSB

The times that try your soul are also the times that build your character. During the darker days of life, you can learn lessons that are impossible to learn during sunny, happier days. Times of adversity can—and should—be times of intense spiritual and personal growth. But God will not force you to learn the lessons of adversity. You must learn them for yourself.

The next time Old Man Trouble knocks on your door, remember that he has lessons to teach. So turn away Mr. Trouble as quickly as you can, but as you're doing so, don't forget to learn his lessons. And remember: the trouble with trouble isn't just the trouble it causes; it's also the trouble we cause ourselves if we ignore the things that trouble has to teach. Got that? Then please don't forget it!

The trials of life can be God's tools for engraving His image on our character.

Warren Wiersbe

– Your Daily Journey Through Psalms –
The Lord lifts the burdens of those bent beneath their loads. The Lord loves the righteous.

Psalm 146:8 NLT

The Gift of Family

But if any widow has children or grandchildren, they should learn to practice their religion toward their own family first and to repay their parents, for this pleases God.

1 Timothy 5:4 HCSB

As every woman knows, family life is a mixture of conversations, mediations, irritations, deliberations, commiserations, frustrations, negotiations and celebrations. In other words, the life of the typical woman is incredibly varied.

Certainly, in the life of every family, there are moments of frustration and disappointment. Lots of them. But, for those who are lucky enough to live in the presence of a close-knit, caring clan, the rewards far outweigh the frustrations.

No family is perfect, and neither is yours. But, despite the inevitable challenges and occasional hurt feelings of family life, your clan is God's gift to you. That little band of men, women, kids, and babies is a priceless treasure on temporary loan from the Father above. Give thanks to the Giver for the gift of family . . . and act accordingly.

– Your Daily Journey Through Psalms –

Unless the Lord builds a house, its builders labor over it in vain.

Psalm 127:1 HCSB

Pray Without Ceasing

Is anyone cheerful? He should sing praises.

James 5:13 HCSB

In his first letter to the Thessalonians, Paul advised members of the new church to "pray without ceasing" (5:16-18). His advice applies to Christians of every generation. When we consult God on an hourly basis, we avail ourselves of His wisdom, His strength, and His love. As Corrie ten Boom observed, "Any concern that is too small to be turned into a prayer is too small to be made into a burden."

Today, instead of turning things over in your mind, turn them over to God in prayer. And leave the rest up to Him. He is big enough and strong enough to manage your life and solve your problems. Your job is to let him.

Prayer is the same as the breathing of air for the lungs. Exhaling makes us get rid of our dirty air. Inhaling gives clean air. To exhale is to confess, to inhale is to be filled with the Holy Spirit.

Corrie ten Boom

– Your Daily Journey Through Psalms –

You are the God who does wonders; You have declared Your strength among the peoples.

Psalm 77:14 NKJV

He Renews

Finally, be strengthened by the Lord and by His vast strength.
Ephesians 6:10 HCSB

God's Word is clear: When we genuinely lift our hearts and prayers to Him, He renews our strength. Are you almost too weary to lift your head? Then bow it. Offer your concerns and your fears to your Father in Heaven. He is always at your side, offering His love and His strength.

Are you troubled or anxious? Take your anxieties to God in prayer. Are you weak or worried? Delve deeply into God's Holy Word and sense His presence in the quiet moments of the early morning. Are you spiritually exhausted? Call upon fellow believers to support you, and call upon Christ to renew your spirit and your life. Your Savior will not let you down. To the contrary, He will lift you up when you ask Him to do so. So what, dear friend, are you waiting for?

He is the God of wholeness and restoration.

Stormie Omartian

– Your Daily Journey Through Psalms –
Give us help from trouble: for vain is the help of man.
Psalm 60:11 KJV

The Joy of Serving God

Shepherd God's flock among you, not overseeing out of compulsion but freely, according to God's will; not for the money but eagerly.

1 Peter 5:2 HCSB

Martha and Mary both loved Jesus, but they showed their love in different ways. Mary sat at the Master's feet, taking in every word. Martha, meanwhile, busied herself with preparations for the meal to come. When Martha asked Jesus if He was concerned about Mary's failure to help, Jesus replied, "Mary has chosen better" (Luke 10:42 NIV). The implication is clear: as believers, we must spend time with Jesus before we spend time for Him. But, once we have placed Christ where He belongs—at the center of our hearts—we must go about the business of serving the One who has saved us.

How can we serve Christ? By sharing His message and by serving those in need. As followers of Jesus, we must make ourselves humble servants to our families, to our neighbors, and to the world. We must help the helpless, love the unloved, protect the vulnerable, and care for the infirm. When we do, our lives will be blessed by the One who sacrificed His life for us.

– Your Daily Journey Through Psalms –

Serve the Lord with gladness.

Psalm 100:2 HCSB

Your Journey Continues

I have spoken these things to you so that My joy may be in you and your joy may be complete.

John 15:11 HCSB

Complete spiritual maturity is never achieved in a day, or a in year, or even in a lifetime. The journey toward spiritual maturity is an ongoing process that continues, day by day, throughout every stage of life. Every stage of life has its opportunities and its challenges, and if we're wise, we continue to seek God's guidance as each new chapter of life unfolds. Norman Vincent Peale advised: "Ask the God who made you to keep remaking you." That counsel is perfectly sound, but easy to ignore.

When we cease to grow, either emotionally or spiritually, we do ourselves a profound disservice. But, if we focus our thoughts—and attune our hearts—to the will of God, we will make each day another stage in the spiritual journey.

You are either becoming more like Christ every day or you're becoming less like Him. There is no neutral position in the Lord.

Stormie Omartian

– Your Daily Journey Through Psalms –

Many sorrows come to the wicked, but unfailing love surrounds those who trust the LORD.

Psalm 32:10 NLT

Thank Him Now

We always thank God, the Father of our Lord Jesus Christ, when we pray for you.

Colossians 1:3 HCSB

Sometimes, life-here-on-earth can be complicated, demanding, and busy. When the demands of life leave us rushing from place to place with scarcely a moment to spare, we may fail to pause and say a word of thanks for all the good things we've received. But when we fail to count our blessings, we rob ourselves of the happiness, the peace, and the gratitude that should rightfully be ours.

Today, even if you're busily engaged in life, slow down long enough to start counting your blessings. You most certainly will not be able to count them all, but take a few moments to jot down as many blessings as you can. Then, give thanks to the Giver of all good things: God. His love for you is eternal, as are His gifts. And it's never too soon—or too late—to offer Him thanks.

It is always possible to be thankful for what is given rather than to complain about what is not given. One or the other becomes a habit of life.

Elisabeth Elliot

– Your Daily Journey Through Psalms –
Bless the LORD, O my soul, and forget not all his benefits.
Psalm 103:2 KJV

Actions Speak Louder

Who is wise and understanding among you? He should show his works by good conduct with wisdom's gentleness.

James 3:13 HCSB

The old saying is both familiar and true: actions speak louder than words. And as believers, we must beware: our actions should always give credence to the changes that Christ can make in the lives of those who walk with Him.

God calls upon each of us to act in accordance with His will and with respect for His commandments. If we are to be responsible believers, we must realize that it is never enough simply to hear the instructions of God; we must also live by them. And it is never enough to wait idly by while others do God's work here on earth; we, too, must act. Doing God's work is a responsibility that each of us must bear, and when we do, our loving Heavenly Father rewards our efforts with a bountiful harvest.

Pray as if it's all up to God, and work as if it's all up to you.

Anonymous

– Your Daily Journey Through Psalms –

You are my hope, O Lord God; You are my trust from my youth.

Psalm 71:5 NKJV

What's Your Attitude?

Set your minds on what is above, not on what is on the earth.
Colossians 3:2 HCSB

The Christian life is a cause for celebration, but sometimes we don't feel much like celebrating. In fact, when the weight of the world bears down upon our shoulders, celebration may be the last thing on our minds . . . but it shouldn't be. As God's children, we have been blessed beyond measure. And we should be quick to acknowledge those blessings.

This day is a non-renewable resource—once it's gone, it's gone forever. So celebrate the life that God has given you by thinking optimistically about yourself, your family, and your future. Give thanks to the One who has showered you with blessings, and trust in your heart that He wants to give you so much more.

Some people complain that God put thorns on roses, while others praise Him for putting roses on thorns.

Anonymous

– Your Daily Journey Through Psalms –
Because your love is better than life, my lips will glorify you. I will praise you as long as I live, and in your name I will lift up my hands. My soul will be satisfied as with the richest of foods; with singing lips my mouth will praise you.
Psalm 63:3-5 NIV

Too Busy

Rejoice in hope; be patient in affliction; be persistent in prayer.

Romans 12:12 HCSB

Has the busy pace of life robbed you of the peace that might otherwise be yours through Jesus Christ? If so, you are simply too busy for your own good. Through His Son Jesus, God offers you a peace that passes human understanding, but He won't force His peace upon you; in order to experience it, you must slow down long enough to sense His presence and His love.

Today, as a gift to yourself, to your family, and to the world, slow down and claim the inner peace that is your spiritual birthright: the peace of Jesus Christ. It is offered freely; it has been paid for in full; it is yours for the asking. So ask. And then share.

In our tense, uptight society where folks are rushing to make appointments they have already missed, a good laugh can be a refreshing as a cup of cold water in the desert.

Barbara Johnson

– Your Daily Journey Through Psalms –

I trust in You, O LORD, I say, "You are my God." My times are in Your hand.

Psalm 31:14-15 NASB

Making Quality Choices

I have set before you life and death, blessing and curse. Choose life so that you and your descendants may live, love the Lord your God, obey Him, and remain faithful to Him. For He is your life, and He will prolong your life in the land the Lord swore to give to your fathers Abraham, Isaac, and Jacob.

Deuteronomy 30:19-20 HCSB

Every life, including yours, is a tapestry of choices. And the quality of your life depends, to a surprising extent, on the quality of the choices you make.

Would you like to enjoy a life of abundance and significance? If so, you must you must make choices that are pleasing to God.

From the instant you wake up in the morning until the moment you nod off to sleep at night, you make lots of decisions: decisions about the things you do, decisions about the words you speak, and decisions about the thoughts you choose to think.

Today and every day, it's up to you (and only you) to make wise choices, choices that enhance your relationship with God. After all, He deserves no less than your best . . . and so do you.

– Your Daily Journey Through Psalms –
Happy are those who deal justly with others and always do what is right.

Psalm 106:3 NLT

Courtesy Matters

Be hospitable to one another without grumbling.

1 Peter 4:9 NKJV

Did Christ instruct us in matters of etiquette and courtesy? Of course He did. Christ's instructions are clear: "In everything, therefore, treat people the same way you want them to treat you, for this is the Law and the Prophets" (Matthew 7:12 NASB). Jesus did not say, "In some things, treat people as you wish to be treated." And, He did not say, "From time to time, treat others with kindness." Christ said that we should treat others as we wish to be treated in every aspect of our daily lives. This, of course, is a tall order indeed, but as Christians, we are commanded to do our best.

Today, be a little kinder than necessary to family members, friends, and total strangers. And, as you consider all the things that Christ has done in your life, honor Him with your words and with your deeds.

Courtesy is contagious.

Marie T. Freeman

– Your Daily Journey Through Psalms –

Lord, set up a guard for my mouth; keep watch at the door of my lips.

Psalm 141:3 HCSB

Beyond Your Hardships

He gives power to the weak, and to those who have no might He increases strength.

Isaiah 40:29 NKJV

We Christians have many reasons to celebrate. God is in His heaven; Christ has risen, and we are the sheep of His flock. Yet sometimes, even the most devout Christian women can become discouraged. After all, we live in a world where expectations can be high and demands can be even higher. If you become discouraged with the direction of your day or your life, turn your thoughts and prayers to God. He is a God of possibility, not negativity. He will help you count your blessings instead of your hardships. And then, with a renewed spirit of optimism and hope, you can properly thank your Father in heaven for His blessings, for His love, and for His Son.

Just as courage is faith in good, so discouragement is faith in evil, and, while courage opens the door to good, discouragement opens it to evil.

Hannah Whitall Smith

– Your Daily Journey Through Psalms –

He shall not be afraid of evil tidings: his heart is fixed, trusting in the LORD.

Psalm 112:7 KJV

Beyond Envy

We must not become conceited, provoking one another, envying one another.

Galatians 5:26 HCSB

Because we are frail, imperfect human beings, we are sometimes envious of others. But God's Word warns us that envy is sin. Thus, we must guard ourselves against the natural tendency to feel resentment and jealousy when other people experience good fortune.

As believers, we have absolutely no reason to be envious of any people on earth. After all, as Christians we are already recipients of the greatest gift in all creation: God's grace. We have been promised the gift of eternal life through God's only begotten Son, and we must count that gift as our most precious possession.

Rather than succumbing to the sin of envy, we should focus on the marvelous things that God has done for us—starting with Christ's sacrifice. And we must refrain from preoccupying ourselves with the blessings that God has chosen to give others.

So here's a surefire formula for a happier, healthier life: Count your own blessings and let your neighbors count theirs. It's the godly way to live.

– Your Daily Journey Through Psalms –

Do not fret because of evil men or be envious of those who do wrong . . . .

Psalm 37:1 NIV

The Importance of Fellowship

I want their hearts to be encouraged and joined together in love, so that they may have all the riches of assured understanding, and have the knowledge of God's mystery—Christ.

Colossians 2:2 HCSB

It is almost impossible to underestimate the importance of Christian fellowship. When you join with fellow believers in worship and praise, you enrich their lives in the same way that they enrich yours.

Christ promised that wherever two or more are gathered together in His name, He is there also (Matthew 18:20). So let us gather together in the presence of Christ and worship Him with thanksgiving in our hearts, praise on our lips, and fellow believers by our sides.

One of the ways God refills us after failure is through the blessing of Christian fellowship. Just experiencing the joy of simple activities shared with other children of God can have a healing effect on us.

Anne Graham Lotz

– Your Daily Journey Through Psalms –
How good and pleasant it is when brothers can live together!

Psalm 133:1 HCSB

Christlike Love and Generosity

Whatever you did for one of the least of these brothers of Mine, you did for Me

Matthew 25:40 HCSB

Hymn writer Fanny Crosby wrote, "To God be the glory; great thing He hath done! So loved He the world that He gave us His son." God's love for us is so complete that He sent Jesus to this earth so that we, His believers, might have eternal life: "But God demonstrates his own love for us in this: While we were still sinners, Christ died for us" (Romans 5:8 NIV).

We, as Christ's followers, are challenged to share His love. We do so, in part, by dealing generously and lovingly with others.

When we walk each day with Christ—and obey the commandments found in God's Holy Word—we are worthy ambassadors for Him. Just as Christ has been—and will always be—the ultimate friend to His flock, so should we be Christlike in our love and generosity to those in pain and to those in need. When we share the love of Christ, we share a priceless gift; may we share it today and every day that we live.

– Your Daily Journey Through Psalms –

He has dispersed abroad, He has given to the poor; His righteousness endures forever; His horn will be exalted with honor.

Psalm 112:9 NKJV

God's Correction

My son, do not despise the chastening of the Lord, nor detest His correction.

Proverbs 3:11 NKJV

The hand of God corrects us when we disobey His commandments. The hand of God guides us when we stray from His chosen path. When our behavior is inconsistent with God's will, our Heavenly Father inevitably disciplines us in the same fashion that a loving parent disciplines a wayward child.

Hebrews 12:5 reminds us that when God chastises us, we should accept His discipline without bitterness or despair. We should, instead, look upon God's instruction as an occasion to repent from our sins, to reorder our priorities, and to realign our lives.

God's correction is purposeful: He intends to guide us back to Him. When we trust God completely and without reservation, He gives us the strength to meet any challenge, the courage to face any trial, and the wisdom to live in His righteousness and in His peace.

God is a God of unconditional, unremitting love, a love that corrects and chastens but never ceases.

Kay Arthur

– Your Daily Journey Through Psalms –

You will show me the path of life; in Your presence is fullness of joy; at Your right hand are pleasures forevermore.

Psalm 16:11 NKJV

Joy Is . . .

Rejoice evermore. Pray without ceasing. In every thing give thanks: for this is the will of God in Christ Jesus concerning you.

1 Thessalonians 5:16-18 KJV

Are you a woman whose joy is evident for all to see? If so, congratulations: your joyful spirit serves as a powerful example to your family and friends. And because of your attitude, you may be assured that your children will indeed "rise up" and call you blessed (Proverbs 31:28).

Psalm 100 reminds us that, as believers, we have every reason to celebrate: "Shout for joy to the LORD, all the earth. Worship the LORD with gladness" (v. 1-2 NIV). Yet sometimes, amid the inevitable hustle and bustle of life here on earth, we can forfeit—albeit temporarily—the joy that God intends for our lives.

God's plan for you and your family includes heaping helpings of abundance and joy. Claim them. And remember that Christ offers you and your family a priceless gift: His abundance, His peace, and His joy. Accept those gifts and share them freely, just as Christ has freely shared Himself with you.

– Your Daily Journey Through Psalms –

Shout triumphantly to the Lord, all the earth. Serve the Lord with gladness; come before Him with joyful songs.

Psalm 100:1-2 HCSB

Light of the World

I have come as a light into the world, so that everyone who believes in Me would not remain in darkness.

John 12:46 HCSB

The Bible says that you are "the light that gives light to the world." The Bible also says that you should live in a way that lets other people understand what it means to be a follower of Jesus.

What kind of light have you been giving off? Hopefully, you've been a good example for everybody to see. Why? Because the world needs all the light it can get, and that includes your light, too!

The old familiar hymn begins, "What a friend we have in Jesus . . . ." No truer words were ever penned. Jesus is the sovereign friend and ultimate Savior of mankind. Christ showed enduring love for you by willingly sacrificing His own life so that you might have eternal life. As a response to His sacrifice, you should love Him, praise Him, and share His message of salvation with your neighbors and with the world.

Do you seek to be an extreme follower of Christ? Then you must let your light shine today and every day.

– Your Daily Journey Through Psalms –

The heavens declare the glory of God; and the firmament showeth his handiwork.

Psalm 19:1 KJV

Demonstrating Our Love

*For this is the love of God, that we keep His commandments.
And His commandments are not burdensome.*

1 John 5:3 NKJV

How can we demonstrate our love for God? By accepting His Son as our personal Savior and by placing Christ squarely at the center of our lives and our hearts. Jesus said that if we are to love Him, we must obey His commandments (John 14:15). Thus, our obedience to the Master is an expression of our love for Him.

In Ephesians 2:10 we read, "For we are His workmanship, created in Christ Jesus for good works" (NKJV). These words are instructive: We are not saved by good works, but for good works. Good works are not the root, but rather the fruit of our salvation.

Today, let the fruits of your stewardship be a clear demonstration of your love for Christ. When you do, your good heart will bring forth many good things for yourself and for God. Christ has given you spiritual abundance and eternal life. You, in turn, owe Him good treasure from a single obedient heart: yours.

– Your Daily Journey Through Psalms –

*Happy is the man who fears the Lord, taking great delight in
His commandments.*

Psalm 112:1 HCSB

What's Really Important

Anyone trusting in his riches will fall, but the righteous will flourish like foliage.

Proverbs 11:28 HCSB

In the demanding world in which we live, financial prosperity can be a good thing, but spiritual prosperity is profoundly more important. Yet our society leads us to believe otherwise. The world glorifies material possessions, personal fame, and physical beauty above all else; these things, of course, are totally unimportant to God. God sees the human heart, and that's what is important to Him.

As you establish your priorities for the coming day, remember this: The world will do everything it can to convince you that "things" are important. The world will tempt you to value fortune above faith and possessions above peace. God, on the other hand, will try to convince you that your relationship with Him is all-important. Trust God.

Greed is enslaving. The more you have, the more you want—until eventually avarice consumes you.

Kay Arthur

– Your Daily Journey Through Psalms –
If wealth increases, pay no attention to it.

Psalm 62:10 HCSB

Spiritual Traps

*So we must not get tired of doing good, for we will reap at the
proper time if we don't give up.*

Galatians 6:9 HCSB

Pessimism and Christianity don't mix. Why? Because Christians have every reason to be optimistic about life here on earth and life eternal.

Sometimes, despite our trust in God, we may fall into the spiritual traps of worry, frustration, anxiety, or sheer exhaustion, and our hearts become heavy. What's needed is plenty of rest, a large dose of perspective, and God's healing touch, but not necessarily in that order.

Today, make this promise to yourself and keep it: vow to be a hope-filled Christian. Think optimistically about your life, your profession, and your future. Trust your hopes, not your fears. Take time to celebrate God's glorious creation. And then, when you've filled your heart with hope and gladness, share your optimism with others. They'll be better for it, and so will you. But not necessarily in that order.

– Your Daily Journey Through Psalms –

*Why are you cast down, O my soul? And why are you
disquieted within me? Hope in God; For I shall yet praise
Him, The help of my countenance and my God.*

Psalm 42:11 NKJV

Recouping Your Losses

Disaster pursues sinners, but good rewards the righteous.
Proverbs 13:21 HCSB

Have you ever made a big-time financial blunder? If so, welcome to a very large club!

When we commit the inevitable missteps of life, we must correct them, learn from them, and pray for the wisdom not to repeat them. When we do, our mistakes become lessons, and our lives become adventures in growth, not stagnation.

So here's the big question: Have you used your mistakes as stumbling blocks or stepping stones? The answer to that question will determine how quickly you gain financial security and peace of mind.

As you place yourself under the sovereign lordship of Jesus Christ, each mistake or failure can lead you right back to the throne.

Barbara Johnson

When all else is gone, God is still left. Nothing changes Him.

Hannah Whitall Smith

– Your Daily Journey Through Psalms –
Be of good courage, And He shall strengthen your heart, All you who hope in the Lord.

Psalm 31:24 NKJV

Your Bible and His Purpose

The Lord has prepared everything for His purpose—even the wicked for the day of disaster.

Proverbs 16:4 HCSB

Are you sincerely seeking to discover God's will and follow it? If so, study His Word and obey His commandments. The words of Matthew 4:4 remind us that, "Man shall not live by bread alone, but by every word that proceeds from the mouth of God" (NKJV). As believers, we must study the Bible and meditate upon its meaning for our lives. Otherwise, we deprive ourselves of a priceless gift from our Creator.

Jonathan Edwards advised, "Be assiduous in reading the Holy Scriptures. This is the fountain whence all knowledge in divinity must be derived. Therefore let not this treasure lie by you neglected." God's Holy Word is, indeed, a priceless, one-of-a-kind treasure, and a passing acquaintance with the Good Book is insufficient for Christians who seek to obey God's Word and to understand His will.

The Holy Scriptures are our letters from home.

St. Augustine

– Your Daily Journey Through Psalms –

The words of the Lord are pure words, like silver tried in a furnace . . . .

Psalm 12:6 NKJV

The Gift of Time

The one who works his land will have plenty of food, but whoever chases fantasies lacks sense.

Proverbs 12:11 HCSB

As every woman knows all too well, there simply isn't enough time to do everything we want—and need—to do. That's why we should be so very careful about the ways that we choose to spend the time that God has given us.

Time is a nonrenewable gift from the Creator. But sometimes, we treat our time here on earth as if it were not a gift at all: We may be tempted to invest our lives in petty diversions or in trivial pursuits. But our Father in heaven beckons each of us to a higher calling.

An important element of our stewardship to God is the way that we choose to spend the time He has entrusted to us. Each waking moment holds the potential to do a good deed, to say a kind word, or to offer a heartfelt prayer. Our challenge, as believers, is to use our time wisely in the service of God's work and in accordance with His plan for our lives.

– Your Daily Journey Through Psalms –

Show me, O LORD, my life's end and the number of my days; let me know how fleeting is my life. You have made my days a mere handbreadth; the span of my years is as nothing before you. Each man's life is but a breath.

Psalm 39:4-5 NIV

Practical Christianity

But be doers of the word and not hearers only.

James 1:22 HCSB

As Christians, we must do our best to ensure that our actions are accurate reflections of our beliefs. Our theology must be demonstrated, not only by our words but, more importantly, by our actions. In short, we should be practical believers, quick to act whenever we see an opportunity to serve God.

Are you the kind of practical Christian who is willing to dig in and do what needs to be done when it needs to be done? If so, congratulations: God acknowledges your service and blesses it. But if you find yourself more interested in the fine points of theology than in the needs of your neighbors, it's time to rearrange your priorities. God needs believers who are willing to roll up their sleeves and go to work for Him. Count yourself among that number. Theology is a good thing unless it interferes with God's work. And it's up to you to make certain that your theology doesn't.

God has lots of folks who intend to go to work for him "some day." What He needs is more people who are willing to work for Him this day.

Marie T. Freeman

– Your Daily Journey Through Psalms –
I will set no wicked thing before mine eyes . . . .

Psalm 101:3 KJV

Your Reasons to Rejoice

Let your eyes look forward; fix your gaze straight ahead.
Proverbs 4:25 HCSB

As a Christian woman, you have every reason to rejoice. God is in His heaven; Christ has risen, and dawn has broken on another day of life. But, when the demands of life seem great, you may find yourself feeling exhausted, discouraged, or both. That's when you need a fresh supply of hope . . . and God is ready, willing, and able to supply it.

The advice contained in Proverbs 4:5 is clear-cut: "Keep your eyes focused on what is right, and look straight ahead to what is good" (NCV). That's why you should strive to maintain a positive, can-do attitude—an attitude that pleases God.

As you face the challenges of the coming day, use God's Word as a tool for directing your thoughts. When you do, your attitude will be pleasing to God, pleasing to your friends, and pleasing to yourself.

Developing a positive attitude means working continually to find what is uplifting and encouraging.

Barbara Johnson

– Your Daily Journey Through Psalms –
Satisfy us in the morning with your unfailing love, that we may sing for joy and be glad all our days.

Psalm 90:14 NIV

Time to Celebrate

Rejoice in the Lord always. I will say it again: Rejoice!
Philippians 4:4 HCSB

Are you living a life of agitation or celebration? If you're a believer, it should most certainly be the latter. With Christ as your Savior, every day should be a time of celebration.

Today, celebrate the life that God has given you. Today, put a smile on your face, kind words on your lips, and a song in your heart. Be generous with your praise and free with your encouragement. And then, when you have celebrated life to the fullest, invite your friends to do likewise. After all, this is God's day, and He has given us clear instructions for its use. We are commanded to rejoice and be glad. So, with no further ado, let the celebration begin . . .

Oh! what a Savior, gracious to all, / Oh! how His blessings round us fall, / Gently to comfort, kindly to cheer, / Sleeping or waking, God is near.

Fanny Crosby

– Your Daily Journey Through Psalms –
This is the day the LORD has made; we will rejoice and be glad in it.

Psalm 118:24 NKJV

Real Christianity

But now in Christ Jesus you who once were far off have been brought near by the blood of Christ. For He Himself is our peace.

Ephesians 2:13-14 NKJV

What is "real" Christianity? Think of it as an ongoing relationship—an all-encompassing relationship with God and with His Son Jesus. It is inevitable that your life must be lived in relationship to God. The question is not if you will have a relationship with Him; the burning question is whether or not that relationship will be one that seeks to honor Him or one that seeks to ignore Him.

We live in a world that discourages heartfelt devotion and obedience to God. Everywhere we turn, or so it seems, we are confronted by a mind-numbing assortment of distractions, temptations, obligations, and frustrations. Yet even on our busiest days, God beckons us to slow down and consult Him. When we do, we avail ourselves of the peace and abundance that only He can give.

– Your Daily Journey Through Psalms –

I waited patiently for the Lord, and He turned to me and heard my cry for help. He brought me up from a desolate pit, out of the muddy clay, and set my feet on a rock, making my steps secure. He put a new song in my mouth, a hymn of praise to our God.

Psalm 40:1-3 HCSB

Beyond the Crises

But the wisdom that is from above is first pure, then peaceable, gentle, willing to yield, full of mercy and good fruits, without partiality and without hypocrisy.

James 3:17 NKJV

Your decision to seek a deeper relationship with God will not remove all problems from your life; to the contrary, it will bring about a series of personal crises as you constantly seek to say "yes" to God although the world encourages you to do otherwise. You live in a world that seeks to snare your attention and lead you away from God. Each time you are tempted to distance yourself from the Creator, you will face a spiritual crisis. A few of these crises may be monumental in scope, but most will be the small, everyday decisions of life. In fact, life can be seen as one test after another—and with each crisis comes yet another opportunity to grow closer to God.

Today, you will face many opportunities to say "yes" to your Creator—and you will also encounter many opportunities to say "no" to Him. Your answers will determine the quality of your day and the direction of your life, so answer carefully.

– Your Daily Journey Through Psalms –

Yea, though I walk through the valley of the shadow of death, I will fear no evil: for thou art with me; thy rod and thy staff they comfort me.

Psalm 23:4 KJV

When Faith Slips Away

Immediately the father of the child cried out and said with tears, "Lord, I believe; help my unbelief!"

Mark 9:24 NKJV

Sometimes we feel threatened by the storms of life. During these moments, when our hearts are flooded with uncertainty, we must remember that God is not simply near, He is here.

Have you ever felt your faith in God slipping away? If so, you are in good company. Even the most faithful Christians are, at times, beset by occasional bouts of discouragement and doubt. But even when you feel far removed from God, God never leaves your side. He is always with you, always willing to calm the storms of life. When you sincerely seek His presence—and when you genuinely seek to establish a deeper, more meaningful relationship with His Son—God will calm your fears, answer your prayers, and restore your soul.

We are most vulnerable to the piercing winds of doubt when we distance ourselves from the mission and fellowship to which Christ has called us.

Joni Eareckson Tada

– Your Daily Journey Through Psalms –

When I am filled with cares, Your comfort brings me joy.

Psalm 94:19 HCSB

Eternal Life:
God's Priceless Gift

Jesus said, "Everyone who drinks from this water will get thirsty again. But whoever drinks from the water that I will give him will never get thirsty again--ever! In fact, the water I will give him will become a well of water springing up within him for eternal life."

John 4:13-14 HCSB

Your ability to envision the future, like your life here on earth, is limited. God's vision, however, is not burdened by any such limitations. He sees all things, He knows all things, and His plans for you endure for all time.

God's plans are not limited to the events of life-here-on-earth. Your Heavenly Father has bigger things in mind for you . . . much bigger things. So praise the Creator for the gift of eternal life and share the Good News with all who cross your path. You have given your heart to the Son, so you belong to the Father—today, tomorrow, and for all eternity.

– Your Daily Journey Through Psalms –

Thy kingdom is an everlasting kingdom, and thy dominion endureth throughout all generations.

Psalm 145:13 KJV

Fitness Matters

Do you not know that your body is a sanctuary of the Holy Spirit who is in you, whom you have from God? You are not your own, for you were bought at a price; therefore glorify God in your body.

1 Corinthians 6:19-20 HCSB

Are you shaping up or spreading out? Do you eat sensibly and exercise regularly, or do you spend most of your time on the couch with a snack in one hand and a clicker in the other? Are you choosing to treat your body like a temple or a trash heap? How you answer these questions will help determine how long you live and how well you live.

Physical fitness is a choice, a choice that requires discipline—it's as simple as that. So, do yourself this favor: treat your body like a one-of-a-kind gift from God . . . because that's precisely what your body is.

Our primary motivation should not be for more energy or to avoid a heart attack but to please God with our bodies.

Carole Lewis

– Your Daily Journey Through Psalms –
I shall yet praise him, who is the health of my countenance, and my God.

Psalm 42:11 KJV

Freely Give

Give, and it will be given to you; a good measure, pressed down, shaken together, and running over will be poured into your lap. For with the measure that you use, it will be measured back to you.

Luke 6:38 HCSB

The words are familiar to those who study God's Word: "Freely you have received, freely give" (Matthew 10:8 NKJV). As followers of Christ, we have been given so much by God. In return, we must give freely of our time, our possessions, our testimonies, and our love.

Your salvation was earned at a terrible price: Christ gave His life for you on the cross at Calvary. Christ's gift is priceless, yet when you accept Jesus as your personal Savior, His gift of eternal life costs you nothing. From those to whom much has been given, much is required. And because you have received the gift of salvation, you are now called by God to be a cheerful, generous steward of the gifts He has placed under your care.

Today and every day, let Christ's words be your guide and let His eternal love fill your heart. When you do, your stewardship will be a reflection of your love for Him, and that's exactly as it should be.

– Your Daily Journey Through Psalms –

Blessed is he that considereth the poor: the LORD will deliver him in time of trouble.

Psalm 41:1 KJV

The Foundations of Friendship

Therefore, putting away lying, "Let each one of you speak truth with his neighbor," for we are members of one another.
Ephesians 4:25 NKJV

Family ties and lasting friendships are built upon a foundation of honesty and trust. It has been said on many occasions that honesty is the best policy. For believers, it is far more important to note that honesty is God's policy. And if we are to be servants worthy of our Savior, Jesus Christ, we must be honest and forthright in all our communications with others.

Sometimes, honesty is difficult; sometimes, honesty is painful; sometimes, honesty makes us feel uncomfortable. Despite these temporary feelings of discomfort, we must make honesty the hallmark of all our relationships; otherwise, we invite needless suffering into our own lives and into the lives of those we love.

Sometime soon, perhaps even today, you will be tempted to bend the truth or perhaps even to break it. Resist that temptation. Truth is God's way . . . and it must be your way, too.

– Your Daily Journey Through Psalms –

Light shines on the godly, and joy on those who do right. May all who are godly be happy in the Lord and praise his holy name.

Psalm 97:11-12 NLT

Serenity

Should we accept only good from God and not adversity?
Job 2:10 HCSB

When you encounter unfortunate circumstances that are beyond your power to control, here's a proven way to retain your sanity: accept those circumstances (no matter how unpleasant), and trust God.

Reinhold Niebuhr composed a profoundly simple verse known as the Serenity Prayer: "God, grant me the serenity to accept the things I cannot change, the courage to change the things I can, and the wisdom to know the difference." Niebuhr's words are far easier to recite than they are to live by. Why? Because most of us want life to unfold in accordance with to our own wishes and timetables. But sometimes God has other plans.

When you trust God, you can be comforted in the knowledge that your Creator is both loving and wise, and that He understands His plans perfectly, even when you do not.

Loving Him means the thankful acceptance of all things that His love has appointed.

Elisabeth Elliot

– Your Daily Journey Through Psalms –
Abundant peace belongs to those who love Your instruction; nothing makes them stumble.

Psalm 119:165 HCSB

Where to Take Your Troubles

Be anxious for nothing, but in everything by prayer and supplication, with thanksgiving, let your requests be made known to God.

Philippians 4:6 NKJV

Sometimes, the world seems to shift beneath our feet. From time to time, all of us face adversity, discouragement, or disappointment. And, throughout life, we must all endure life-changing personal losses that leave us anxiously struggling for breath. When we do, God stands ready to protect us.

The Bible instructs us to, "Be strong and courageous, and do the work. Don't be afraid or discouraged, for the Lord God, my God, is with you. He won't leave you or forsake you" (1 Chronicles 28:20 HCSB). When we are troubled, we must call upon God, and in time He will heal us.

Are you anxious? Take those anxieties to God. Are you troubled? Take your troubles to Him. Does your future seem uncertain? Place your trust in the One who is forever faithful.

– Your Daily Journey Through Psalms –
When I am filled with cares, Your comfort brings me joy.
Psalm 94:19 HCSB

Beyond Bitterness

All bitterness, anger and wrath, insult and slander must be removed from you, along with all wickedness. And be kind and compassionate to one another, forgiving one another, just as God also forgave you in Christ.

Ephesians 4:31-32 HCSB

Are you mired in the quicksand of bitterness or regret? If so, you are not only disobeying God's Word, you are also wasting your time. The world holds few if any rewards for those who remain angrily focused upon the past. Still, the act of forgiveness is difficult for all but the most saintly men and women.

Being frail, fallible, imperfect human beings, most of us are quick to anger, quick to blame, slow to forgive, and even slower to forget. Yet as Christians, we are commanded to forgive others, just as we, too, have been forgiven.

If there exists even one person—alive or dead—against whom you hold bitter feelings, it's time to forgive. Or, if you are embittered against yourself for some past mistake or shortcoming, it's finally time to forgive yourself and move on. Hatred, bitterness, and regret are not part of God's plan for your life. Forgiveness is.

– Your Daily Journey Through Psalms –
He heals the brokenhearted and binds up their wounds.

Psalm 147:3 HCSB

He Rewards Integrity

The integrity of the upright guides them, but the perversity of the treacherous destroys them.

Proverbs 11:3 HCSB

The Bible makes it clear that God rewards integrity just as surely as He punishes duplicity. So, if we seek to earn the kind of lasting rewards that God bestows upon those who obey His commandments, we must make honesty the hallmark of our dealings with others.

Character is built slowly over a lifetime. Character is the sum of every right decision, every honest word, every noble thought, and every heartfelt prayer. It is built upon a foundation of industry, generosity, and humility. Character is a precious thing—difficult to build but easy to tear down. As believers in Christ, we must seek to live each day with discipline, honesty, and faith. When we do, integrity becomes a habit. And God smiles.

God never called us to naïveté. He called us to integrity .... The biblical concept of integrity emphasizes mature innocence not childlike ignorance.

Beth Moore

– Your Daily Journey Through Psalms –

Let integrity and uprightness preserve me, for I wait for You.

Psalm 25:21 NKJV

Peace and Prayer

Rejoice always! Pray constantly. Give thanks in everything,
for this is God's will for you in Christ Jesus.
1 Thessalonians 5:16-18 HCSB

Do you seek a more peaceful life? Then you must lead a prayerful life. Do you have questions that you simply can't answer? Ask for the guidance of your Father in heaven. Do you sincerely seek the gift of everlasting love and eternal life? Accept the grace of God's only begotten Son.

When you weave the habit of prayer into the very fabric of your day, you invite God to become a partner in every aspect of your life. When you consult God on a constant basis, you avail yourself of His wisdom, His strength, and His love. And, because God answers prayers according to His perfect timetable, your petitions to Him will transform your family, your world, and yourself.

Today, turn everything over to your Creator in prayer. Instead of worrying about your next decision, decide to let God lead the way. Don't limit your prayers to meals or to bedtime. Pray constantly about things great and small. God is listening, and He wants to hear from you. Now.

– Your Daily Journey Through Psalms –
Therefore let everyone who is faithful pray to You . . . .
Psalm 32:6 HCSB

Purpose and Service

*Let this mind be in you which was also in Christ Jesus, who
. . . made Himself of no reputation, taking the form of a
bondservant, and coming in the likeness of men.*

Philippians 2:5,7 NKJV

The teachings of Jesus are clear: We achieve greatness through humble service. So, as you seek to discover God's purpose for your life, you may rest assured that His plan for you is centered around service to your family, to your friends, to your church, to your community, and to the world.

Today, you may feel the temptation to build yourself up in the eyes of your neighbors. Resist that temptation. Instead, serve your neighbors quietly and without fanfare. Find a need and fill it . . . humbly. Lend a helping hand and share a word of kindness . . . anonymously, for this is God's way.

As a humble servant, you will glorify yourself not before men, but before God, and that's what God intends. After all, earthly glory is fleeting: here today and soon gone. But, heavenly glory endures throughout eternity. So the choice is yours: Either you can lift yourself up here on earth and be humbled in heaven, or vice versa. Choose vice versa.

– Your Daily Journey Through Psalms –

*Unless the Lord builds a house, its builders labor over it in
vain.*

Psalm 127:1 HCSB

If He Returned Today

But the Day of the Lord will come like a thief; on that day the heavens will pass away with a loud noise, the elements will burn and be dissolved, and the earth and the works on it will be disclosed . . . . Therefore, dear friends, while you wait for these things, make every effort to be found in peace without spot or blemish before Him.

2 Peter 3:10, 14 HCSB

When will our Lord return? The Bible clearly states that the day and the hour of Christ's return is known only to God. Therefore, we must conduct our lives as if He were returning today.

If Jesus were to return this instant, would you be ready? Would you be proud of your actions, your thoughts, your relationships, and your prayers? If not, you must face up to a harsh reality: even if Christ does not return to earth today, He may call you home today! And if He does so, you must be prepared.

Have you given your heart to the resurrected Savior? If the answer to that question is anything other than an unqualified yes, then accept Him as your personal Savior before you close this book.

– Your Daily Journey Through Psalms –
Yet He saved them because of His name, to make His power known.

Psalm 106:8 HCSB

Helpful Words

Careful words make for a careful life; careless talk may ruin everything.

Proverbs 13:3 MSG

This world can be a difficult place, a place where many of our friends and family members are troubled by the inevitable challenges of everyday life. And since we can never be certain who needs our help, we should be careful to speak helpful words to everybody who crosses our paths.

In the book of Ephesians, Paul writes, "Do not let any unwholesome talk come out of your mouths, but only what is helpful for building others up according to their needs, that it may benefit those who listen" (4:29 NIV). Paul reminds us that when we choose our words carefully, we can have a powerful impact on those around us.

Today, let's share kind words, smiles, encouragement, and hugs with family, with friends, and with the world.

– Your Daily Journey Through Psalms –

I will thank the Lord with all my heart; I will declare all Your wonderful works. I will rejoice and boast about You; I will sing about Your name, Most High.

Psalm 9:1-2 HCSB

Your Unique Talents

There are diversities of gifts, but the same Spirit.
1 Corinthians 12:4 NKJV

God has given you an array of talents, and He has given you unique opportunities to share those talents with the world. Your Creator intends for you to use your talents for the glory of His kingdom in the service of His children. Will you honor Him by sharing His gifts? And, will you share His gifts humbly and lovingly? Hopefully you will.

As a woman who has been touched by the transforming love of Jesus Christ, your obligation is clear: You must strive to make the most of your own God-given talents, and you must encourage your family and friends to do likewise.

God has given you special talents—now it's your turn to give them back to God.

Marie T. Freeman

– Your Daily Journey Through Psalms –
Teach us to number our days carefully so that we may develop wisdom in our hearts.

Psalm 90:12 HCSB

Marveling at the Miracle of Nature

Then God saw everything that He had made, and indeed it was very good.

Genesis 1:31 NKJV

When we consider God's glorious universe, we marvel at the miracle of nature. The smallest seedlings and grandest stars are all part of God's infinite creation. God has placed His handiwork on display for all to see, and if we are wise, we will make time each day to celebrate the world that surrounds us.

Today, as you fulfill the demands of everyday life, pause to consider the majesty of heaven and earth. It is as miraculous as it is beautiful, as incomprehensible as it is breathtaking.

The Psalmist reminds us that the heavens are a declaration of God's glory. May we never cease to praise the Father for a universe that stands as an awesome testimony to His presence and His power.

Man was created by God to know and love Him in a permanent, personal relationship.

Anne Graham Lotz

– Your Daily Journey Through Psalms –

When I observe Your heavens, the work of Your fingers, the moon and the stars, which You set in place, what is man that You remember him?

Psalm 8:3-4 HCSB

He Is Love

God is love, and the one who remains in love remains in God, and God remains in him.

1 John 4:16 HCSB

God is love. It's a sweeping statement, a profoundly important description of what God is and how God works. God's love is perfect. When we open our hearts to His perfect love, we are touched by the Creator's hand, and we are transformed.

Barbara Johnson observed, "We cannot protect ourselves from trouble, but we can dance through the puddles of life with a rainbow smile, twirling the only umbrella we need—the umbrella of God's love."

And the English mystical writer Juliana of Norwich noted, "We are so preciously loved by God that we cannot even comprehend it. No created being can ever know how much and how sweetly and tenderly God loves them."

So today, even if you can only carve out a few quiet moments, offer sincere prayers of thanksgiving to your Father. Thank Him for His blessings and His love.

– Your Daily Journey Through Psalms –

Praise the Lord, all you Gentiles! Laud Him, all you peoples! For His merciful kindness is great toward us, and the truth of the Lord endures forever. Praise the Lord!

Psalm 117:1-2 NKJV

Still Growing

When I was a child, I spoke like a child, I thought like a child, I reasoned like a child. When I became a man, I put aside childish things.

1 Corinthians 13:11 HCSB

If we are to grow as women, we need both knowledge and wisdom. Knowledge is found in textbooks. Wisdom, on the other hand, is found through experience, through years of trial and error, and through careful attention to the Word of God. Knowledge is an important building block in a well-lived life, and it pays rich dividends both personally and professionally. But, wisdom is even more important because it refashions not only our minds, but also our hearts.

When it comes to your faith, God doesn't intend for you to stand still. He wants you to keep growing as a woman and as a spiritual being. No matter how "grown-up" you may be, you still have growing to do. And the more you grow, the more beautiful you become, inside and out.

– Your Daily Journey Through Psalms –

When I observe Your heavens, the work of Your fingers, the moon and the stars, which You set in place, what is man that You remember him?

Psalm 8:3-4 HCSB

Sharing the Joy

Honor His holy name; let the hearts of those who seek the Lord rejoice. Search for the Lord and for His strength; seek His face always.

1 Chronicles 16:10-11 HCSB

God's intends that His joy should become our joy. He intends that we, His children, should share His love, His joy, and His peace. Yet sometimes, amid the inevitable hustle and bustle of life-here-on-earth, we don't feel much like sharing. So we forfeit—albeit temporarily—God's joy as we wrestle with the challenges of everyday life.

If, today, your heart is heavy, open the door of your soul to your Heavenly Father. When you do, He will renew your spirit. And, if you already have the joy of Christ in your heart, share it freely with others. When you discover ways to make your joy become their joy, you will have discovered a wonderful way to say, "I love you" to your family, to your friends, and, most especially, to your God.

– Your Daily Journey Through Psalms –

Now I know that the LORD saves His anointed; He will answer him from His holy heaven with the saving strength of His right hand.

Psalm 20:6 NASB

Walking in the Light

I have come as a light into the world, that whoever believes in Me should not abide in darkness.

John 12:46 NKJV

Jesus walks with you. Are you walking with Him? Hopefully, you will choose to walk with Him today and every day of your life. And hopefully, you will encourage your family to do the same.

God's Word is clear: When we genuinely invite Christ to reign over our hearts, and when we accept His transforming love, we are forever changed. When we welcome Christ into our hearts, an old life ends and a new way of living—along with a completely new way of viewing the world—begins.

Each morning offers a fresh opportunity to invite Christ, yet once again, to rule over our hearts and our days. Each morning presents yet another opportunity to take up His cross and follow in His footsteps. Today, let us rejoice in the new life that is ours through Christ, and let us follow Him, step by step, on the path that He first walked.

– Your Daily Journey Through Psalms –

Those long hours of leisure as we walked arm in arm, God a third party to our conversation.

Psalm 55:14 MSG

Obedience Matters

Follow the whole instruction the Lord your God has commanded you, so that you may live, prosper, and have a long life in the land you will possess.

Deuteronomy 5:33 HCSB

Are you living outside the commandments of God? If so, you are inviting untold suffering into your own life and into the lives of your loved ones. God's commandments are not "suggestions," and they are not "helpful hints." They are, instead, immutable laws which, if followed, lead to repentance, salvation, and abundance. But if you disobey the commandments of your Heavenly Father or His Son, you will most surely reap a harvest of bitterness and regret.

Would you like a time-tested formula for successful living? Here is a formula that is proven and true: Study God's Word and obey it. Does this sound too simple? Perhaps it is simple, but it is also the only way to reap the marvelous riches that God has in store for you.

I don't always like His decisions, but when I choose to obey Him, the act of obedience still "counts" with Him even if I'm not thrilled about it.

Beth Moore

– Your Daily Journey Through Psalms –

I have sought You with all my heart; don't let me wander from Your commands.

Psalm 119:10 HCSB

He Persevered and so Must We

If you do nothing in a difficult time, your strength is limited.
Proverbs 24:10 HCSB

Someone once said, "Life is a marathon, not a sprint." Life requires courage, perseverance, determination, and, of course, an unending supply of love. Are you tired? Ask God for strength. Are you discouraged? Believe in His promises. Are you frustrated or fearful? Pray as if everything depended upon God, and work as if everything depended upon you. With God's help, you will find the strength to be the kind of woman who makes her Heavenly Father beam with pride.

Your life is not a boring stretch of highway. It's a straight line to heaven. And just look at the fields ripening along the way. Look at the tenacity and endurance. Look at the grains of righteousness. You'll have quite a crop at harvest . . . so don't give up!

Joni Eareckson Tada

– Your Daily Journey Through Psalms –
The Lord is near all who call out to Him, all who call out to Him with integrity. He fulfills the desires of those who fear Him; He hears their cry for help and saves them.
Psalm 145:18-19 HCSB

Hope and Happiness

But the truly happy people are those who carefully study God's perfect law that makes people free, and they continue to study it. They do not forget what they heard, but they obey what God's teaching says. Those who do this will be made happy.

James 1:25 NCV

Hope and happiness are traveling companions. And if you're a Christian, you have every reason to be hopeful. After all, God is good; His love endures; and He has offered you the priceless gift of eternal life. But sometimes, in life's darker moments, you may lose sight of these blessings, and when you do, it's easy to lose hope.

When a suffering woman sought healing by merely touching the hem of His cloak, Jesus replied, "Daughter, be of good comfort; thy faith hath made thee whole" (Matthew 9:22 KJV). The message to believers is clear: if we are to be made whole by God, we must live by faith.

Are you a hope-filled woman? You should be. God has promised you peace, joy, and eternal life. And, of course, God keeps His promises today, tomorrow, and forever, amen!

– Your Daily Journey Through Psalms –
Happy is he . . . whose hope is in the LORD his God.

Psalm 146:5 KJV

Acceptance Now

A man's heart plans his way, but the Lord determines his steps.

Proverbs 16:9 HCSB

Sometimes, we must accept life on its terms, not our own. Life has a way of unfolding, not as we will, but as it will. And sometimes, there is precious little we can do to change things.

When events transpire that are beyond our control, we have a choice: we can either learn the art of acceptance, or we can make ourselves miserable as we struggle to change the unchangeable.

We must entrust the things we cannot change to God. Once we have done so, we can prayerfully and faithfully tackle the important work that He has placed before us: doing something about the things we can change . . . and doing it sooner rather than later.

Part of waiting upon the Lord is telling God that you want only what He wants—whatever it is.

Kay Arthur

– Your Daily Journey Through Psalms –

Praise the Lord, all you Gentiles! Laud Him, all you peoples! For His merciful kindness is great toward us, and the truth of the Lord endures forever. Praise the Lord!

Psalm 117:1-2 NKJV

Beyond the Frustrations

But now you must also put away all the following: anger,
wrath, malice, slander, and filthy language from your mouth.
Colossians 3:8 HCSB

Your temper is either your master or your servant.
Either you control it, or it controls you. And the
extent to which you allow anger to rule your life
will determine, to a surprising degree, the quality of your
relationships with others and your relationship with
God.

If you've allowed anger to become a regular visitor
at your house, you should pray for wisdom, for patience,
and for a heart that is so filled with forgiveness that it
contains no room for bitterness. God will help you terminate your tantrums if you ask Him to—and that's a
good thing because anger and peace cannot coexist in
the same mind.

So the next time you're tempted to lose your temper
over the minor inconveniences of life, don't. Turn away
from anger, hatred, bitterness and regret. Turn instead to
God. He's waiting with open arms . . . patiently.

– Your Daily Journey Through Psalms –
Don't sin by letting anger gain control over you. Think about
it overnight and remain silent.

Psalm 4:4 NLT

Strength for Today

But those who trust in the Lord will renew their strength;
they will soar on wings like eagles; they will run and not grow
weary; they will walk and not faint.

Isaiah 40:31 HCSB

Where do you go to find strength? The gym? The health food store? The espresso bar? There's a better source of strength, of course, and that source is God. He is a never-ending source of strength and courage if you call upon Him.

Are you an energized Christian woman? You should be. But if you're not, you must seek strength and renewal from the source that will never fail: that source, of course, is your Heavenly Father. And rest assured—when you sincerely petition Him, He will give you all the strength you need to live victoriously for Him.

Have you "tapped in" to the power of God? Have you turned your life and your heart over to Him, or are you muddling along under your own power? The answer to this question will determine the quality of your life here on earth and the destiny of your life throughout all eternity. So start tapping in—and remember that when it comes to strength, God is the Ultimate Source.

– Your Daily Journey Through Psalms –
Give to the Lord the glory due His name; bring an offering,
and come into His courts.

Psalm 96:8 NKJV

The Power of Fellowship

Don't you know that you are God's sanctuary and that the Spirit of God lives in you?

1 Corinthians 3:16 HCSB

Fellowship with other believers should be an integral part of your everyday life. Your association with fellow Christians should be uplifting, enlightening, encouraging, and consistent.

Are you an active member of your own fellowship? Are you a builder of bridges inside the four walls of your church and outside it? Do you contribute to God's glory by contributing your time and your talents to a close-knit band of believers? Hopefully so. The fellowship of believers is intended to be a powerful tool for spreading God's Good News and uplifting His children. And God intends for you to be a fully contributing member of that fellowship. Your intentions should be the same.

Christians are like coals of a fire. Together they glow—apart they grow cold.

Anonymous

– Your Daily Journey Through Psalms –
How good and pleasant it is when brothers can live together!
Psalm 133:1 HCSB

What's Your Grade?

The greatest among you must be a servant. But those who exalt themselves will be humbled, and those who humble themselves will be exalted.

Matthew 23:11-12 NKJV

God's heart overflows with generosity and mercy. And as believers in a loving God, we must, to the best of our abilities, imitate our Heavenly Father. Because God has been so incredibly generous with us, we, in turn must be generous with others.

Jesus has much to teach us about generosity. He teaches that the most esteemed men and women are not the self-congratulatory leaders of society but are, instead, the humblest of servants.

If you were being graded on generosity, how would you score? Would you earn "A"s in philanthropy and humility? Hopefully so. But if your grades could stand a little improvement, today is the perfect day to begin.

Today, you may feel the urge to hoard your blessings. Don't do it. Instead, give generously to your neighbors, and do so without fanfare. Find a need and fill it . . . humbly. Lend a helping hand and share a word of kindness . . . anonymously. This is God's way.

– Your Daily Journey Through Psalms –
The good person is generous and lends lavishly . . . .
Psalm 112:5 MSG

Obey and Be Blessed

Blessings are on the head of the righteous.

Proverbs 10:6 HCSB

God gave us His commandments for a reason: so that we might obey them and be blessed. Elisabeth Elliot advised, "Obedience to God is our job. The results of that obedience are God's." These words should serve to remind us that obedience is imperative. But, we live in a world that presents us with countless temptations to disobey God's laws.

When we stray from God's path, we suffer. So, whenever we are confronted with sin, we have clear instructions: we must walk—or better yet run—in the opposite direction.

Don't worry about what you do not understand. Worry about what you do understand in the Bible but do not live by.

Corrie ten Boom

– Your Daily Journey Through Psalms –

I will instruct you and show you the way to go; with My eye on you, I will give counsel.

Psalm 32:8 HCSB

God's Love, God's Power

The Lord your God in your midst, The Mighty One, will save; He will rejoice over you with gladness, He will quiet you with His love, He will rejoice over you with singing.

Zephaniah 3:17 NKJV

God's power is not burdened by boundaries or by limitations—and neither, for that matter, is His love. The love that flows from the heart of God is infinite—and today offers yet another opportunity to celebrate that love.

God's love for you is deeper and more profound than you can fathom. In times of trouble, He will comfort you; in times of sorrow, He will dry your tears. When you are or weak or sorrowful, God is as near as your next breath. He stands at the door of your heart and waits. Welcome Him in and allow Him to rule. And then, accept the peace, and the power, and the protection, and the abundance that only God can give.

No part of our prayers creates a greater feeling of joy than when we praise God for who He is. He is our Master Creator, our Father, our source of all love.

Shirley Dobson

– Your Daily Journey Through Psalms –
Give thanks to the Lord, for He is good; His faithful love endures forever.

Psalm 106:1 HCSB

Guard Your Heart

Guard your heart above all else, for it is the source of life.
Proverbs 4:23 HCSB

You are near and dear to God. He loves you more than you can imagine, and He wants the very best for you. And one more thing: God wants you to guard your heart.

Every day, you are faced with choices . . . lots of them. You can do the right thing, or not. You can tell the truth, or not. You can be kind, and generous, and obedient. Or not.

Today, the world will offer you countless opportunities to let down your guard and, by doing so, let the devil do his worst. Be watchful and obedient. Guard your heart by giving it to your Heavenly Father; it is safe with Him.

The fruit of our placing all things in God's hands is the presence of His abiding peace in our hearts.
Hannah Whitall Smith

– Your Daily Journey Through Psalms –

I will instruct you and show you the way to go; with My eye on you, I will give counsel.

Psalm 32:8 HCSB

The Cornerstone

For the Son of Man has come to save that which was lost.
Matthew 18:11 NKJV

I s Jesus the cornerstone of your life . . . or have you relegated Him to a far corner of your life? The answer to this question will determine the quality, the direction, the tone, and the ultimate destination of your life here on earth and your life throughout eternity.

Thomas Brooks spoke for believers of every generation when he observed, "Christ is the sun, and all the watches of our lives should be set by the dial of His motion." Christ, indeed, is the ultimate Savior of mankind and the personal Savior of those who believe in Him. As His servants, we should place Him at the very center of our lives. And every day that God gives us breath, we should share Christ's love and His message with a world that needs both.

How awesome that the "Word" that was in the beginning, by which and through which God created everything, was—and is—a living Person with a mind, will, emotions, and intellect.

Anne Graham Lotz

– Your Daily Journey Through Psalms –
God is our refuge and strength, a helper who is always found in times of trouble.

Psalm 46:1 HCSB

Another Day, Countless Opportunities

Therefore, as we have opportunity, we must work for the good of all, especially for those who belong to the household of faith.

Galatians 6:10 HCSB

Each day, as we awaken from sleep and begin the new day, we are confronted with countless opportunities to serve God and to worship Him. When we do, He blesses us. But, if we turn our backs to Him, or, if we are simply too busy to acknowledge His greatness, we do ourselves a profound disservice.

As women in a fast-changing world, we face challenges that sometimes leave us feeling overworked, overcommitted, and overwhelmed. But God has different plans for us. He intends that we take time each day to slow down long enough to praise Him and glorify His Son. When we do, our spirits are calmed and our lives are enriched, as are the lives of our families and friends.

Each day provides a glorious opportunity to place ourselves in the service of the One who is the Giver of all blessings. May we seek His will, trust His Word, and place Him where He belongs: at the center of our lives.

– Your Daily Journey Through Psalms –

He makes me to lie down in green pastures; He leads me beside the still waters. He restores my soul; He leads me in the paths of righteousness for His name's sake.

Psalm 23:2-3 NKJV

Neighbors

Show family affection to one another with brotherly love. Outdo one another in showing honor. Do not lack diligence; be fervent in spirit; serve the Lord. Rejoice in hope; be patient in affliction; be persistent in prayer.

Romans 12:10-12 HCSB

Neighbors. We know that we are instructed to love them, and yet there's so little time . . . and we're so busy. No matter. As Christians, we are commanded by our Lord and Savior Jesus Christ to love our neighbors just as we love ourselves. We are not asked to love our neighbors, nor are we encouraged to do so. We are commanded to love them. Period.

This very day, you will encounter someone who needs a word of encouragement, or a pat on the back, or a helping hand, or a heartfelt prayer. And, if you don't reach out to that person, who will? If you don't take the time to understand the needs of your neighbors, who will? If you don't love your brothers and sisters, who will? So, today, look for a neighbor in need . . . and then do something to help. Father's orders.

If my heart is right with God, every human being is my neighbor.

Oswald Chambers

– Your Daily Journey Through Psalms –
I will sing about the Lord's faithful love forever

Psalm 89:1 HCSB

His Perspective . . . and Yours

So if you have been raised with the Messiah, seek what is above, where the Messiah is, seated at the right hand of God.
Colossians 3:1 HCSB

Even if you're the world's most thoughtful woman, you may, from time to time, lose perspective— it happens on those days when life seems out of balance and the pressures of life seem overwhelming. What's needed is a fresh perspective, a restored sense of balance . . . and God.

If a temporary loss of perspective has left you worried, exhausted, or both, it's time to readjust your thought patterns. Negative thoughts are habit-forming; thankfully, so are positive ones. With practice, you can form the habit of focusing on God's priorities and your possibilities. When you do, you'll spend less time fretting about your challenges and more time praising God for His gifts.

So today and every day hereafter, pray for a sense of balance and perspective. And remember: your thoughts are intensely powerful things, so handle them with care.

– Your Daily Journey Through Psalms –
Surely goodness and mercy shall follow me all the days of my life: and I will dwell in the house of the Lord for ever.
Psalm 23:6 KJV

Pray Always

Watch therefore, and pray always that you may be counted worthy . . . .

Luke 21:36 NKJV

Jesus made it clear to His disciples: they should pray always. And so should we. Genuine, heartfelt prayer changes things and it changes us. When we lift our hearts to our Father in heaven, we open ourselves to a never-ending source of divine wisdom and infinite love.

Do you have questions that you simply can't answer? Ask for the guidance of your Father in heaven. Do you sincerely seek the gift of everlasting love and eternal life? Accept the grace of God's only begotten Son. Whatever your need, no matter how great or small, pray about it. Instead of waiting for mealtimes or bedtimes, follow the instruction of your Savior: pray always and never lose heart. And remember: God is not just near; He is here, and He's ready to talk with you. Are you ready to talk to Him?

Prayer moves the arm that moves the world.

Annie Armstrong

– Your Daily Journey Through Psalms –

In my distress I called upon the LORD; I cried unto my God for help. From his temple, he heard my voice.

Psalm 18:6 NIV

Living on Purpose

For it is God who is working among you both the willing and the working for His good purpose.

Philippians 2:13 HCSB

Life is best lived on purpose. And purpose, like everything else in the universe, begins with God. Whether you realize it or not, God has a plan for your life, a divine calling, a direction in which He is leading you. When you welcome God into your heart and establish a genuine relationship with Him, He will begin, in time, to make His purposes known.

Sometimes, God's intentions will be clear to you; other times, God's plan will seem uncertain at best. But even on those difficult days when you are unsure which way to turn, you must never lose sight of these overriding facts: God created you for a reason; He has important work for you to do; and He's waiting patiently for you to do it. The next step is up to you.

There is something about having endured great loss that brings purity of purpose and strength of character.

Barbara Johnson

– Your Daily Journey Through Psalms –

May He give you what your heart desires and fulfill your whole purpose.

Psalm 20:4 HCSB

Praising the Savior

At the name of Jesus every knee should bow, of those in heaven, and of those on earth, and of those under the earth, and that every tongue should confess that Jesus Christ is Lord, to the glory of God the Father.

Philippians 2:10-11 NKJV

The words by Fanny Crosby are familiar: "This is my story, this is my song, praising my Savior, all the day long." As believers who have been saved by the blood of a risen Christ, we must do exactly as the song instructs: We must praise our Savior time and time again throughout the day. Worship and praise should be a part of everything we do. Otherwise, we quickly lose perspective as we fall prey to the demands of everyday life.

Do you sincerely desire to be a worthy servant of the One who has given you eternal love and eternal life? Then praise Him for who He is and for what He has done for you. And don't just praise Him on Sunday morning. Praise Him all day long, every day, for as long as you live . . . and then for all eternity.

– Your Daily Journey Through Psalms –

Happy are the people who know how to praise you. Lord, let them live in the light of your presence.

Psalm 89:15 NCV

Getting Past the Regrets

However, each one must live his life in the situation the Lord assigned when God called him.

1 Corinthians 7:17 HCSB

Bitterness can destroy you if you let it . . . so don't let it!

If you are caught up in intense feelings of anger or regret, you know all too well the destructive power of these emotions. How can you rid yourself of these feelings? First, you must prayerfully ask God to free you from these feelings. Then, you must learn to catch yourself whenever thoughts of bitterness begin to attack you. Your challenge is this: You must learn to resist negative thoughts before they hijack your emotions.

Christina Rossetti had this sound advice: "Better by far you should forget and smile than you should remember and be sad." And she was right—it's better to forget than regret.

No matter what, don't ever let yesterday use up too much of today.

Barbara Johnson

– Your Daily Journey Through Psalms –
Hold up my goings in thy paths, that my footsteps slip not.
Psalm 17:5 KJV

Repentance and Peace

They should repent, turn to God, and do works befitting repentance.

Acts 26:20 NKJV

Who among us has sinned? All of us. But, the good news is this: When we ask God's forgiveness and turn our hearts to Him, He forgives us absolutely and completely.

Genuine repentance requires more than simply offering God apologies for our misdeeds. Real repentance may start with feelings of sorrow and remorse, but it ends only when we turn away from the sin that has heretofore distanced us from our Creator. As long as we are still engaged in sin, we may be sorry but we have not fully "repented."

Is there an aspect of your life that is distancing you from your God and robbing you of His peace? If so, ask for His forgiveness, and—just as importantly—stop sinning. Then, wrap yourself in the protection of God's Word. When you do, you will be forgiven, you will be secure, and you will know peace.

– Your Daily Journey Through Psalms –

He restoreth my soul: he leadeth me in the paths of righteousness for his name's sake.

Psalm 23:3 KJV

Serving Others

Let each of us please his neighbor for his good, leading to edification.

Romans 15:2 NKJV

We live in a world that glorifies power, prestige, fame, and money. But the words of Jesus teach us that the most esteemed men and women in this world are not the self-congratulatory leaders of society but are instead the humblest of servants.

Today, you may feel the temptation to build yourself up in the eyes of your neighbors. Resist that temptation. Instead, serve your neighbors quietly and without fanfare. Find a need and fill it . . . humbly. Lend a helping hand . . . anonymously. Share a word of kindness . . . with quiet sincerity. As you go about your daily activities, remember that the Savior of all humanity made Himself a servant, and we, as His followers, must do no less.

Jesus never asks us to give Him what we don't have. But He does demand that we give Him all we do have if we want to be a part of what He wishes to do in the lives of those around us!

Anne Graham Lotz

– Your Daily Journey Through Psalms –
I was helpless, and He saved me.

Psalm 116:6 HCSB

Defining Success

If you do not stand firm in your faith, then you will not stand at all.

Isaiah 7:9 HCSB

How do you define success? Do you define it as the accumulation of material possessions or the adulation of your neighbors? If so, you need to reorder your priorities. Genuine success has little to do with fame or fortune; it has everything to do with God's gift of love and His promise of salvation.

If you have accepted Christ as your personal Savior, you are already a towering success in the eyes of God, but there is still more that you can do. Your task—as a believer who has been touched by the Creator's grace— is to accept the spiritual abundance and peace that He offers through the person of His Son. Then, you can share the healing message of God's love and His abundance with a world that desperately needs both. When you do, you will have reached the pinnacle of success.

Success isn't the key. Faithfulness is.

Joni Eareckson Tada

– Your Daily Journey Through Psalms –

And let the beauty of the Lord our God be upon us, And establish the work of our hands for us; Yes, establish the work of our hands.

Psalm 90:17 NKJV

Each Day Is a Gift

This is the day which the LORD hath made; we will rejoice and be glad in it.

Psalm 118:24 KJV

This day is a gift from God. How will you use it? Will you celebrate God's gifts and obey His commandments? Will you share words of encouragement and hope with all who cross your path? Will you share the Good News of the risen Christ? Will you trust in the Father and praise His glorious handiwork? The answer to these questions will determine, to a surprising extent, the direction and the quality of your day.

The familiar words of Psalm 118:24 remind us of a profound yet simple truth: "This is the day which the LORD hath made; we will rejoice and be glad in it" (KJV). For Christian believers, every day begins and ends with God and His Son. Christ came to this earth to give us abundant life and eternal salvation. We give thanks to our Maker when we treasure each day and use it to the fullest.

Today, may we give thanks for this day and for the One who created it.

– Your Daily Journey Through Psalms –
Teach us to number our days carefully so that we may develop wisdom in our hearts.

Psalm 90:12 HCSB

Walking with God

And now, Israel, what does the Lord your God ask of you except to fear the Lord your God by walking in all His ways, to love Him, and to worship the Lord your God with all your heart and all your soul?

Deuteronomy 10:12 HCSB

Are you tired? Discouraged? Fearful? Be comforted. Take a walk with God. Jesus called upon believers to walk with Him, and He promised them that He would teach them how to live freely and lightly (Matthew 11:28-30). Are you worried or anxious? Be confident in God's power. He will never desert you. Do you see no hope for the future? Be courageous and call upon God. He will protect you and then use you according to His purposes. Are you grieving? Know that God hears your suffering. He will comfort you and, in time, He will dry your tears. Are you confused? Listen to the quiet voice of your Heavenly Father. He is not a God of confusion. Talk with Him; listen to Him; follow His commandments. He is steadfast, and He is your Protector . . . forever.

– Your Daily Journey Through Psalms –

How happy is everyone who fears the Lord, who walks in His ways!

Psalm 128:1 HCSB

Mountain-moving Faith

I assure you: If anyone says to this mountain, 'Be lifted up and thrown into the sea,' and does not doubt in his heart, but believes that what he says will happen, it will be done for him.
Mark 11:23 HCSB

Are you a woman whose faith is evident for all to see? Do you trust God's promises without reservation, or do you question His promises without hesitation?

Every life including yours is a series of successes and failures, celebrations and disappointments, joys and sorrows. Every step of the way, through every triumph and tragedy, God will stand by your side and strengthen you . . . if you have faith in Him.

Jesus taught His disciples that if they had faith, they could move mountains. You can too, and so can your family. But you must have faith. So today and every day, trust your Heavenly Father, praise the sacrifice of His Son . . . and then let the mountain-moving begin.

Faith in small things has repercussions that ripple all the way out. In a huge, dark room a little match can light up the place.

Joni Eareckson Tada

– Your Daily Journey Through Psalms –
Happy is he . . . whose hope is in the LORD his God.
Psalm 146:5 KJV

A Smile On Your Face

The one who understands a matter finds success, and the one who trusts in the Lord will be happy.

Proverbs 16:20 HCSB

Okay, it's been a typical day. You've cared for your family, worked your fingers to the bone, rushed from Point A to Point Z, and taken barely a moment for yourself. But have you taken time to smile? If so, you're a very wise woman. If not, it's time to slow down, to take a deep breath, and to recount your blessings!

God has promised all of us the opportunity to experience spiritual abundance and peace. But it's up to each of us to claim the spiritual riches that God has in store. God promises us a life of fulfillment and joy, but He does not force His joy upon us.

Would you like to experience the peace and the joy that God intends for you? Then accept His Son and lay claim to His promises. And then, put a smile on your face that stretches all the way down to your heart. When you do, you'll discover that when you smile at God, He smiles back.

– Your Daily Journey Through Psalms –

Happy is the man who fears the Lord, taking great delight in His commandments.

Psalm 112:1 HCSB

The Rock

Can you search out the deep things of God? Can you find out the limits of the Almighty? They are higher than heaven— what can you do? Deeper than Sheol—what can you know? Their measure is longer than the earth And broader than the sea.

Job 11:7-9 NKJV

God is the Creator of life, the Sustainer of life, and the Rock upon which righteous lives are built. God is a never-ending source of support for those who trust Him, and He is a never-ending source of wisdom for those who study His Holy Word.

Do the demands of this day seem overwhelming? If so, you must rely not only upon your own resources, but more importantly upon the Rock that cannot be shaken. God will hold your hand and walk with you today and every day if you let Him. Even if your circumstances are difficult, trust the Father. His promises remain true; His love is eternal; and His goodness endures. And because He is the One who can never be moved, you can stand firm in the knowledge that you are protected by Him now and forever.

– Your Daily Journey Through Psalms –

The Lord is my rock, my fortress, and my deliverer.

Psalm 18:2 HCSB

Accepting His Love

Love consists in this: not that we loved God, but that He loved us and sent His Son to be the propitiation for our sins.
1 John 4:10 HCSB

Because God's power is limitless, it is far beyond the comprehension of mortal minds. But even though we cannot fully understand the heart of God, we can be open to God's love.

God's ability to love is not burdened by temporal boundaries or by earthly limitations. The love that flows from the heart of God is infinite—and today presents yet another opportunity to celebrate that love.

You are a glorious creation, a unique individual, a beautiful example of God's handiwork. God's love for you is limitless. Accept that love, acknowledge it, and be grateful.

. . . God loves these people too, just because they're unattractive or warped in their thinking doesn't mean the Lord doesn't love them.

Ruth Bell Graham

– Your Daily Journey Through Psalms –
Praise the Lord, all nations! Glorify Him, all peoples! For great is His faithful love to us; the Lord's faithfulness endures forever. Hallelujah!

Psalm 117 HCSB

He Is With Us Always

I am not alone, because the Father is with Me.
John 16:32 HCSB

Where is God? God is eternally with us. He is omnipresent. He is, quite literally, everywhere you have ever been and everywhere you will ever go. He is with you night and day; He knows your every thought; He hears your every heartbeat.

Sometimes, in the crush of your daily duties, God may seem far away. Or sometimes, when the disappointments and sorrows of life leave you brokenhearted, God may seem distant, but He is not. When you earnestly seek God, you will find Him because He is here, waiting patiently for you to reach out to Him . . . right here . . . right now.

God walks with us. He scoops us up in His arms or simply sits with us in silent strength until we cannot avoid the awesome recognition that yes, even now, He is here.
Gloria Gaither

– Your Daily Journey Through Psalms –
He maketh me to lie down in green pastures: he leadeth me beside the still waters. He restoreth my soul.
Psalm 23:2-3 KJV

God's Timing

Therefore humble yourselves under the mighty hand of God, that He may exalt you in due time.

1 Peter 5:6 NKJV

We should learn to trust God's timing, but we are sorely tempted to do otherwise. Why? Because we human beings are usually anxious for things to happen sooner rather than later. But, God knows better.

God has created a world that unfolds according to His own timetable, not ours . . . thank goodness! We mortals might make a terrible mess of things. God does not. God's plan does not always happen in the way that we would like or at the time of our own choosing. Our task is to wait patiently and never lose hope.

In the words of Elisabeth Elliot, "We must learn to move according to the timetable of the Timeless One, and to be at peace." That's advice worth following today, tomorrow, and every day of your life.

Waiting on God brings us to the journey's end quicker than our feet.

Mrs. Charles E. Cowman

– Your Daily Journey Through Psalms –

Wait for the Lord; be courageous and let your heart be strong. Wait for the Lord.

Psalm 27:14 HCSB

He Overcomes the World

God wanted to make known to those among the Gentiles the glorious wealth of this mystery, which is Christ in you, the hope of glory.

Colossians 1:27 HCSB

There are few sadder sights on earth than the sight of a person who has lost all hope. In difficult times, hope can be elusive, but Christians need never lose it. After all, God is good; His love endures; He has promised His children the gift of eternal life.

If you find yourself falling into the spiritual traps of worry and discouragement, consider the words of Jesus. It was Christ who promised, "In the world you will have tribulation; but be of good cheer, I have overcome the world" (John 16:33 NKJV). This world is, indeed, a place of trials and tribulations, but as believers, we are secure. God has promised us peace, joy, and eternal life. And, of course, God always keeps His promises.

– Your Daily Journey Through Psalms –

I wait for the Lord, my soul waits, And in His word I do hope. My soul waits for the Lord More than those who watch for the morning—Yes, more than those who watch for the morning.

Psalm 130:5-6 NKJV

Judging Others

Do not judge, so that you won't be judged.

Matthew 7:1 HCSB

We have all fallen short of God's commandments, and He has forgiven us. We, too, must forgive others. And, we must refrain from judging them.

Are you one of those people who finds it easy to judge others? If so, it's time to change.

God does not need (or, for that matter, want) your help. Why? Because God is perfectly capable of judging the human heart . . . while you are not.

As Christians, we are warned that to judge others is to invite fearful consequences: to the extent we judge others, so, too, will we be judged by God. Let us refrain, then, from judging our neighbors. Instead, let us forgive them and love them in the same way that God has forgiven us.

Judging draws the judgment of others.

Catherine Marshall

– Your Daily Journey Through Psalms –

For he satisfieth the longing soul, and filleth the hungry soul with goodness.

Psalm 107:9 KJV

Looking for Miracles

But Jesus looked at them and said to them, "With men this is impossible, but with God all things are possible."

Matthew 19:26 NKJV

If you haven't seen any of God's miracles lately, you haven't been looking. Throughout history, the Creator has intervened in the course of human events in ways that cannot be explained by science or human rationale. And He's still doing so today.

God's miracles are not limited to special occasions, nor are they witnessed by a select few. God is crafting His wonders all around us: the miracle of the birth of a new baby; the miracle of a world renewing itself with every sunrise; the miracle of lives transformed by God's love and grace. Each day, God's handiwork is evident for all to see and experience.

Today, seize the opportunity to inspect God's hand at work. His miracles come in a variety of shapes and sizes, so keep your eyes and your heart open. Be watchful, and you'll soon be amazed.

– Your Daily Journey Through Psalms –

Search for the Lord and for His strength; seek His face always. Remember the wonderful works He has done.

Psalm 105:4-5 HCSB

During Difficult Days

I called to the Lord in my distress; I called to my God. From His temple He heard my voice.

2 Samuel 22:7 HCSB

All of us face difficult days. Sometimes even the most optimistic women can become discouraged, and you are no exception. If you find yourself enduring difficult circumstances, perhaps it's time for an extreme intellectual makeover—perhaps it's time to focus more on your strengths and opportunities, and less on the challenges that confront you. And one more thing: perhaps it's time to put a little more faith in God.

Your Heavenly Father is a God of possibility, not negativity. He will guide you through your difficulties and beyond them. And then, with a renewed spirit of optimism and hope, you can thank the Giver of all things good for gifts that are simply too numerous to count.

No matter how heavy the burden, daily strength is given, so I expect we need not give ourselves any concern as to what the outcome will be. We must simply go forward.

Annie Armstrong

– Your Daily Journey Through Psalms –

He shall not be afraid of evil tidings: his heart is fixed, trusting in the LORD.

Psalm 112:7 KJV

Managing Change

The sensible see danger and take cover; the foolish keep going and are punished.

Proverbs 27:12 HCSB

There is no doubt. Your world is changing constantly. So today's question is this: How will you manage all those changes? Will you do your best and trust God with the rest, or will you spend fruitless hours worrying about things you can't control, while doing precious little else? The answer to these simple questions will help determine the direction and quality of your life.

The best way to confront change is head-on . . . and with God by your side. The same God who created the universe will protect you if you ask Him, so ask Him—and then serve Him with willing hands and a trusting heart. When you do, you may rest assured that while the world changes moment by moment, God's love endures—unfathomable and unchanging—forever.

Before God changes our circumstances, He wants to change our hearts.

Warren Wiersbe

– Your Daily Journey Through Psalms –
Teach me Your way, O LORD, and lead me in a level path.
Psalm 27:11 NASB

Involved in His Church

The church, you see, is not peripheral to the world; the world is peripheral to the church. The church is Christ's body, in which he speaks and acts, by which he fills everything with his presence.

Ephesians 1:23 MSG

One way that we come to know God is by involving ourselves in His church. In the Book of Acts, Luke reminds us to "feed the church of God" (20:28). As Christians, we are compelled not only to worship Him in our hearts but also to worship Him in the presence of fellow believers.

Do you attend church regularly? And when you attend, are you an active participant, or are you just taking up space? The answer to these questions will have a profound impact on the quality and direction of your spiritual journey.

So do yourself a favor: become actively involved in your church. Don't just go to church out of habit. Go to church out of a sincere desire to know and worship God. When you do, you'll be blessed by the One who sent His Son to die so that you might have everlasting life.

– Your Daily Journey Through Psalms –

O come, let us sing unto the LORD: let us make a joyful noise to the rock of our salvation. Let us come before his presence with thanksgiving, and make a joyful noise unto him with psalms.

Psalm 95:1-2 KJV

When Solutions Aren't Easy

For God has not given us a spirit of fearfulness, but one of power, love, and sound judgment.

2 Timothy 1:7 HCSB

Sometimes, we all face problems that defy easy solutions. If you find yourself facing a difficult decision, here's a simple formula for making the right choice: let God decide. Instead of fretting about your future, pray about it.

When you consult your Heavenly Father early and often, you'll soon discover that the quiet moments you spend with God can be very helpful. Many times, God will quietly lead you along a path of His choosing, a path that is right for you.

So the next time you arrive at one of life's inevitable crossroads, take a moment or two to bow your head and have a chat with the Ultimate Advisor. When you do, you'll never stay lost for long.

When we learn to listen to Christ's voice for the details of our daily decisions, we begin to know Him personally.

Catherine Marshall

– Your Daily Journey Through Psalms –

The fear of the Lord is the beginning of wisdom; A good understanding have all those who do His commandments. His praise endures forever.

Psalm 111:10 NKJV

Meeting the Obligations

Whatever you do, do it enthusiastically, as something done for the Lord and not for men.

Colossians 3:23 HCSB

Nobody needs to tell you the obvious: You have lots of responsibilities—obligations to yourself, to your family, to your community, and to your God. And which of these duties should take priority? The answer can be found in Matthew 6:33: "But seek first the kingdom of God and His righteousness, and all these things will be provided for you" (HCSB).

When you "seek first the kingdom of God," all your other obligations have a way of falling into place. When you obey God's Word and seek His will, your many responsibilities don't seem quite so burdensome. When you honor God with your time, your talents. and your prayers, you'll be much more likely to count your blessings instead of your troubles.

So do yourself and your loved ones a favor: take all your duties seriously, especially your duties to God. When you do, you'll discover that pleasing your Father in heaven isn't just the right thing to do; it's also the best way to live.

– Your Daily Journey Through Psalms –

From the rising of the sun to its going down the Lord's name is to be praised.

Psalm 113:3 NKJV

Beyond Our Obstacles

Though a righteous man falls seven times, he will get up, but the wicked will stumble into ruin.

Proverbs 24:16 HCSB

The occasional disappointments and failures of life are inevitable. Such setbacks are simply the price that we must occasionally pay for our willingness to take risks as we follow our dreams. But even when we encounter bitter disappointments, we must never lose faith.

The reassuring words of Hebrews 10:36 remind us that when we persevere, we will eventually receive that which God has promised. What's required is perseverance, not perfection.

When we encounter the inevitable difficulties of life-here-on-earth, God stands ready to protect us. Our responsibility, of course, is to ask Him for protection. When we call upon Him in heartfelt prayer, He will answer—in His own time and according to His own plan—and He will heal us. And, while we are waiting for God's plans to unfold and for His healing touch to restore us, we can be comforted in the knowledge that our Creator can overcome any obstacle, even if we cannot.

– Your Daily Journey Through Psalms –
For in You, O Lord, I hope; You will hear, O Lord my God.
Psalm 38:15 NKJV

Forgiveness Now

He who says he is in the light, and hates his brother, is in darkness until now.

1 John 2:9 NKJV

Forgiveness is seldom easy, but it is always right. When we forgive those who have hurt us, we honor God by obeying His commandments. But when we harbor bitterness against others, we disobey God—with predictably unhappy results.

Are you easily frustrated by the inevitable shortcomings of others? Are you a prisoner of bitterness or regret? If so, perhaps you need a refresher course in the art of forgiveness.

If there exists even one person, alive or dead, whom you have not forgiven (and that includes yourself), follow God's commandment and His will for your life: forgive that person today. And remember that bitterness, anger, and regret are not part of God's plan for your life. Forgiveness is.

– Your Daily Journey Through Psalms –

Have mercy upon me, O God, according to thy lovingkindness: according unto the multitude of thy tender mercies blot out my transgressions. Wash me thoroughly from mine iniquity, and cleanse me from my sin.

Psalm 51:1-2 KJV

He Is Never Distant

Haven't I commanded you: be strong and courageous? Do not be afraid or discouraged, for the Lord your God is with you wherever you go.

Joshua 1:9 HCSB

I f you are a busy woman with more obligations than you have time to count, you know all too well that the demands of everyday life can, on occasion, seem overwhelming. Thankfully, even on the days when you feel overburdened, overworked, overstressed and under-appreciated, God is trying to get His message through . . . your job is to listen.

Are you tired, discouraged or fearful? Be comforted because God is with you. Are you confused? Listen to the quiet voice of your Heavenly Father. Are you bitter? Talk with God and seek His guidance. In whatever condition you find yourself—whether you are happy or sad, victorious or vanquished, troubled or triumphant—carve out moments of silent solitude to celebrate God's gifts and to experience His presence.

The familiar words of Psalm 46:10 remind us to be still before the Creator. When we do, we encounter the awesome presence of our loving Heavenly Father, and we are comforted in the knowledge that God is not just near. He is here.

– Your Daily Journey Through Psalms –
The fool says in his heart, "God does not exist."

Psalm 14:1 HCSB

How Much Does God Love You?

For God loved the world in this way: He gave His only Son, so that everyone who believes in Him will not perish but have eternal life.

John 3:16 HCSB

How much does God love you? To answer that question, you need only to look at the cross. God's love for you is so great that He sent His only Son to this earth to die for your sins and to offer you the priceless gift of eternal life.

You must decide whether or not to accept God's gift. Will you ignore it or embrace it? Will you return it or neglect it? Will you invite Christ to dwell in the center of your heart, or will you relegate Him to a position of lesser importance? The decision is yours, and so are the consequences. So choose wisely . . . and choose today.

God calls upon the loved not just to love but to be loving. God calls upon the forgiven not just to forgive but to be forgiving.

Beth Moore

– Your Daily Journey Through Psalms –

The LORD is gracious and full of compassion, slow to anger and great in mercy. The LORD is good to all, and His tender mercies are over all His works.

Psalm 145:8-9 NKJV

God Is at Work

Now may the God of peace, who brought up from the dead our Lord Jesus—the great Shepherd of the sheep—with the blood of the everlasting covenant, equip you with all that is good to do His will . . . .

Hebrews 13:20-21 HCSB

Whether you realize it or not, God is busily working in you and through you. He has things He wants you to do and people He wants you to help. Your assignment, should you choose to accept it, is to seek the will of God and to follow it.

Elisabeth Elliot said, "I believe that in every time and place it is within our power to acquiesce in the will of God—and what peace it brings to do so!" And Corrie ten Boom observed, "Surrendering to the Lord is not a tremendous sacrifice, not an agonizing performance. It is the most sensible thing you can do."

So, as you make plans for the future, make sure that your plans conform to God's plans—that's the safest and best way to live.

God has no problems, only plans. There is never panic in heaven.

Corrie ten Boom

– Your Daily Journey Through Psalms –
The Lord will work out his plans for my life—for your faithful love, O Lord, endures forever.

Psalm 138:8 NLT

God's Sufficiency

My grace is sufficient for you, for My strength is made perfect in weakness.

2 Corinthians 12:9 NKJV

Do the demands of life seem overwhelming at times? If so, you must learn to rely not only upon your own resources, but also upon the promises of your Father in heaven. God will hold your hand and walk with you and your family if you let Him. So even if your circumstances are difficult, trust the Father.

The Psalmist writes, "Weeping may endure for a night, but joy comes in the morning" (Psalm 30:5 NKJV). But when we are suffering, the morning may seem very far away. It is not. God promises that He is "near to those who have a broken heart" (Psalm 34:18 NKJV). When we are troubled, we must turn to Him, and we must encourage our friends and family members to do likewise.

If you are discouraged by the inevitable demands of life here on earth, be mindful of this fact: the loving heart of God is sufficient to meet any challenge . . . including yours.

– Your Daily Journey Through Psalms –

I will lift up my eyes to the hills. From whence comes my help? My help comes from the Lord, Who made heaven and earth.

Psalm 121:1-2 NKJV

Hope Now

Let us hold fast the confession of our hope without wavering,
for He who promised is faithful.

Hebrews 10:23 NKJV

A re you a hope-filled woman? You should be. After all, God is good; His love endures; and He
has offered you the priceless gift of eternal life.
And, of course, God has blessed you with a loving family. But sometimes, in life's darker moments, you may
lose sight of those blessings, and when you do, it's easy
to lose hope.

When a suffering woman sought healing by merely
touching the hem of His cloak, Jesus replied, "Daughter,
be of good comfort; thy faith hath made thee whole"
(Matthew 9:22 KJV). The message to believers is clear:
if we are to be made whole by God, we must live by faith.

If you find yourself falling into the spiritual traps of
worry and discouragement, seek the healing touch of Jesus and the encouraging words of fellow Christians. This
world can be a place of trials and tribulations, but as believers, we are secure. Our hope is in God; He has promised us peace, joy, and eternal life. And, of course, God
keeps His promises today, tomorrow, and forever, amen!

– Your Daily Journey Through Psalms –

Sustain me as You promised, and I will live; do not let me be
ashamed of my hope.

Psalm 119:116 HCSB

Kindness in Action

If you really carry out the royal law prescribed in Scripture,
You shall love your neighbor as yourself, you are doing well.
James 2:8 HCSB

The words of Matthew 7:12 remind us that, as believers in Christ, we are commanded to treat others as we wish to be treated. This commandment is, indeed, the Golden Rule for Christians of every generation.

Kindness is a choice. Sometimes, when we feel happy or prosperous, we find it easy to be kind. Other times, when we are discouraged or tired, we can scarcely summon the energy to utter a single kind word. But, God's commandment is clear: we must observe the Golden Rule "in everything." God intends that we make the conscious choice to treat others with kindness and respect, no matter our circumstances, no matter our emotions. Kindness, therefore, is a choice that we, as Christians must make many times each day.

When we weave the thread of kindness into the very fabric of our lives, we give a priceless gift to others, and we give glory to the One who gave His life for us. As believers, we must do no less.

– Your Daily Journey Through Psalms –
For thou, LORD, wilt bless the righteous . . . .
Psalm 5:12 KJV

Speech and the Golden Rule

A good man produces good things from his storeroom of good, and an evil man produces evil things from his storeroom of evil.

Matthew 12:35 HCSB

The words of Matthew 7:12 are clear: "In everything, do to others what you would have them do to you, for this sums up the Law and the Prophets" (NIV). This commandment is, indeed, the Golden Rule for Christians of every generation. And if we are to observe the Golden Rule, we must be careful to speak words of encouragement, hope, and truth to all who cross our paths.

Sometimes, when we feel uplifted and secure, it is easy to speak kind words. Other times, when we are discouraged or tired, we can scarcely summon the energy to uplift ourselves, much less anyone else. But, God's commandment is clear: we must observe the Golden Rule "in everything."

God intends that we speak words of kindness, wisdom, and truth, no matter our circumstances, no matter our emotions. When we do, we share a priceless gift with the world, and we give glory to the One who gave His life for us.

– Your Daily Journey Through Psalms –

Lord, set up a guard for my mouth; keep watch at the door of my lips.

Psalm 141:3 HCSB

Beyond the Temptations

Then Jesus told him, "Go away, Satan! For it is written: You must worship the Lord your God, and you must serve Him only."

Matthew 4:10 HCSB

After fasting forty days and nights in the desert, Jesus was tempted by Satan. Christ used scripture to rebuke the devil (Matthew 4:1-11). We must do likewise. The Holy Bible provides us with a perfect blueprint for righteous living. If we consult that blueprint daily and follow it carefully, we build our lives according to God's plan.

We live in a world that is brimming with opportunities to stray from God's will. Ours is a society filled with temptations, a place where it is all too easy to disobey God. We, like our Savior, must guard ourselves against these temptations. We do so, in part, through prayer and through a careful reading of God's Word.

The battle against Satan is ongoing. Be vigilant, and call upon your Heavenly Father to protect you. When you petition Him with a sincere heart, God will be your shield, now and forever.

– Your Daily Journey Through Psalms –

For the Lord watches over the way of the righteous, but the way of the wicked leads to ruin.

Psalm 1:6 HCSB

He Changes You

I have baptized you with water, but He will baptize you with the Holy Spirit.

Mark 1:8 HCSB

God has the power to transform your life if you invite Him to do so. Your decision is straight-forward: whether or not to allow the Father's transforming power to work in you and through you. God stands at the door and waits; all you must do is knock. When you do, God always answers.

God's work is not in buildings, but in transformed lives.

Ruth Bell Graham

In the midst of the pressure and the heat, I am confident His hand is on my life, developing my faith until I display His glory, transforming me into a vessel of honor that pleases Him!

Anne Graham Lotz

– Your Daily Journey Through Psalms –

Then I will praise God's name with singing, and I will honor him with thanksgiving.

Psalm 69:30 NLT

Seeking His Wisdom

Does not wisdom cry out, And understanding lift up her voice?

Proverbs 8:1 NKJV

D o you seek wisdom for yourself and for your family? Of course you do. But, as a thoughtful woman living in a society that is filled with temptations and distractions, you know that it's all too easy for parents and children alike to stray far from the source of the ultimate wisdom: God's Holy Word.

When you commit yourself to daily study of God's Word—and when you live according to His commandments—you will become wise . . . in time. But don't expect to open your Bible today and be wise tomorrow. Acquiring wisdom takes time.

Today and every day, as a way of understanding God's plan for your life, you should study His Word and live by it. When you do, you will accumulate a storehouse of wisdom that will enrich your own life and the lives of your family members, your friends, and the world.

– Your Daily Journey Through Psalms –

Teach me to do Your will, for You are my God. May Your gracious Spirit lead me on level ground.

Psalm 143:10 HCSB

Choosing Wise Role Models

The one who walks with the wise will become wise, but a companion of fools will suffer harm.

Proverbs 13:20 HCSB

Here's a simple yet effective way to strengthen your faith: Choose role models whose faith in God is strong.

When you emulate godly people, you become a more godly person yourself. That's why you should seek out mentors who, by their words and their presence, make you a better person and a better Christian.

Today, as a gift to yourself, select, from your friends and family members, find a mentor whose judgement you trust. Then listen carefully to your mentor's advice and be willing to accept that advice, even if accepting it requires effort, or pain, or both. Consider your mentor to be God's gift to you. Thank God for that gift, and use it for the glory of His kingdom.

It takes a wise person to give good advice, but an even wiser person to take it.

Marie T. Freeman

– Your Daily Journey Through Psalms –
God is our refuge and strength, a helper who is always found in times of trouble.

Psalm 46:1 HCSB

His Open Arms

Draw near to God, and He will draw near to you.

A s you continue your journey on the road of life, you'll face many experiences: some good, and some not so good. When the sun is shining and all is well, it is easy to have faith. But, when life takes an unexpected turn for the worse, as it will from time to time, your faith will be tested. In times of trouble and doubt, God remains faithful to you. Will you remain faithful to Him?

The Lord is waiting for you with open arms. He seeks to bring you closer to Him, and He will use surprising methods to do so. Your task as a believer is to accept the Master's hug—and His everlasting love—in every circumstance and in every stage of life.

When once we are assured that God is good, then there can be nothing left to fear.

Hannah Whitall Smith

– Your Daily Journey Through Psalms –

But the mercy of the LORD is from everlasting to everlasting upon them that fear him, and his righteousness unto children's children . . . .

Psalm 103:17 KJV

Embraced by Him

In love He predestined us to be adopted through Jesus Christ for Himself, according to His favor and will.

Ephesians 1:4-5 HCSB

Every day of our lives—indeed, every moment of our lives   we are embraced by God. He is always with us, and His love for us is deeper and more profound than we can imagine.

Gloria Gaither observed, "Being loved by Him whose opinion matters most gives us the security to risk loving, too—even loving ourselves."

Lisa Whelchel had this advice: "Believing that you are loved will set you free to be who God created you to be. So rest in His love and just be yourself."

Let these words serve as a powerful reminder: you are a marvelous, glorious being, created by a loving God Who wants you to become—completely and without reservation—the woman He created you to be.

Life in God is a great big hug that lasts forever!

Barbara Johnson

– Your Daily Journey Through Psalms –

As for God, his way is perfect: the word of the LORD is tried: he is a buckler to all those that trust in him.

Psalm 18:30 KJV

Our Greatest Refuge

For you need endurance, so that after you have done God's will, you may receive what was promised.

Hebrews 10:36 HCSB

God is our greatest refuge. When every earthly support system fails, God remains steadfast, and His love remains unchanged. When we encounter life's inevitable disappointments and setbacks, God remains faithful. When we suffer loses that leave us breathless, God is always with us, always ready to respond to our prayers, always working in us and through us to turn tragedy into triumph.

Author and speaker Patsy Clairmont observed, "If you are walking toward Jesus to the best of your ability, He will see you through life's unpredictable waters—but you must risk launching the boat." And that's sound advice because even during life's most difficult days, God stands by us. Our job, of course, is to return the favor and stand by Him.

Whether our fear is absolutely realistic or out of proportion in our minds, our greatest refuge is Jesus Christ.

Luci Swindoll

– Your Daily Journey Through Psalms –

I was helpless, and He saved me.

Psalm 116:6 HCSB

The Rule for Christians

Therefore, whatever you want others to do for you, do also the same for them—this is the Law and the Prophets.

Matthew 7:12 HCSB

The words of Matthew 7:12 remind us that, as believers in Christ, we are commanded to treat others as we wish to be treated. This commandment is, indeed, the Golden Rule for Christians of every generation. When we weave the thread of kindness into the very fabric of our lives, we give glory to the One who gave His life for ours.

Because we are imperfect human beings, we are, on occasion, selfish, thoughtless, or cruel. But God commands us to behave otherwise. He teaches us to rise above our own imperfections and to treat others with unselfishness and love. When we observe God's Golden Rule, we help build His kingdom here on earth. And, when we share the love of Christ, we share a priceless gift; may we share it today and every day that we live.

It is one of the most beautiful compensations of life that no one can sincerely try to help another without helping herself.

Barbara Johnson

– Your Daily Journey Through Psalms –

The entirety of Your word is truth, and all Your righteous judgments endure forever.

Psalm 119:160 HCSB

Integrity Now

The one who lives with integrity is righteous; his children who come after him will be happy.

Proverbs 20:7 HCSB

Wise women understand that integrity is a crucial building block in the foundation of a well-lived life. Integrity is built slowly over a lifetime. It is the sum of every right decision, every honest word, every noble thought, and every heartfelt prayer. It is forged on the anvil of honorable work and polished by the twin virtues of generosity and humility. Integrity is a precious thing—difficult to build, but easy to tear down; godly women value it and protect it at all costs.

As believers in Christ, we must seek to live each day with discipline, honesty, and faith. When we do, at least two things happen: integrity becomes a habit, and God blesses us because of our obedience to Him.

Living a life of integrity isn't always the easiest way, but it is always the right way. And God clearly intends that it should be our way, too.

Often, our character is at greater risk in prosperity than in adversity.

Beth Moore

– Your Daily Journey Through Psalms –

Before I was afflicted I went astray, but now I keep Your word.

Psalm 119:67 HCSB

The Peace That Passes All Understanding

Peace, peace to you, and peace to him who helps you, for your God helps you.

1 Chronicles 12:18 HCSB

Through His Son, God offers a "peace that passes all understanding," but He does not force His peace upon us. God's peace is a blessing that we, as children of a loving Father, must claim for ourselves but sometimes we are slow to do so. Why? Because we are fallible human beings with limited understanding and limited faith.

Have you found the lasting peace that can be yours through Jesus, or are you still rushing after the illusion of "peace and happiness" that the world promises but cannot deliver?

Today, as a gift to yourself, to your family, and to your friends, claim the inner peace that is your spiritual birthright: the peace of Jesus Christ.

Where the soul is full of peace and joy, outward surroundings and circumstances are of comparatively little account.

Hannah Whitall Smiith

– Your Daily Journey Through Psalms –

Abundant peace belongs to those who love Your instruction; nothing makes them stumble.

Psalm 119:165 HCSB

Your Own Worst Critic?

But godliness with contentment is a great gain.

1 Timothy 6:6 HCSB

A re you your own worst critic? If so, it's time to become a little more understanding of the woman you see whenever you look into the mirror.

Millions of words have been written about various ways to improve self-image and increase self-esteem. Yet, maintaining a healthy self-image is, to a surprising extent, a matter of doing three things: 1. behaving ourselves 2. thinking healthy thoughts 3. finding a purpose for your life that pleases your Creator and yourself.

The Bible affirms the importance of self-acceptance by teaching Christians to love others as they love themselves (Matthew 22:37-40). God accepts us just as we are. And, if He accepts us—faults and all—then who are we to believe otherwise?

Being loved by Him whose opinion matters most gives us the security to risk loving, too—even loving ourselves.

Gloria Gaither

– Your Daily Journey Through Psalms –

For You formed my inward parts; You covered me in my mother's womb. I will praise You, for I am fearfully and wonderfully made; Marvelous are Your works.

Psalm 139:13-14 NKJV

Solving Problems

Blessed be the God and Father of our Lord Jesus Christ, the Father of mercies and the God of all comfort. He comforts us in all our affliction, so that we may be able to comfort those who are in any kind of affliction, through the comfort we ourselves receive from God.

2 Corinthians 1:3-4 HCSB

Life is an exercise in problem-solving. The question is not whether we will encounter problems; the real question is how we will choose to address them. When it comes to solving the problems of everyday living, we often know precisely what needs to be done, but we may be slow in doing it—especially if what needs to be done is difficult or uncomfortable for us. So we put off till tomorrow what should be done today.

The words of Psalm 34 remind us that the Lord solves problems for "people who do what is right." And usually, doing "what is right" means doing the uncomfortable work of confronting our problems sooner rather than later. So with no further ado, let the problem-solving begin . . . now.

– Your Daily Journey Through Psalms –

People who do what is right may have many problems, but the Lord will solve them all.

Psalm 34:19 NCV

Swamped by Your Possessions?

Your life should be free from the love of money. Be satisfied with what you have, for He Himself has said, I will never leave you or forsake you.

Hebrews 13:5 HCSB

D o you sometimes feel swamped by your possessions? Do you seem to be spending more and more time keeping track of the things you own while making mental notes of the things you intend to buy? If so, here's a word of warning: your fondness for material possessions is getting in the way of your relationships—your relationships with the people around you and your relationship with God.

Society teaches us to honor possessions . . . God teaches us to honor people. And if we seek to be worthy followers of Christ, we must never invest too much energy in the acquisition of "stuff." Earthly riches are here today and all too soon gone. Our real riches, of course, are in heaven, and that's where we should focus our thoughts and our energy.

– Your Daily Journey Through Psalms –

If riches increase, do not set your heart on them.

Psalm 62:10 NKJV

Taking Up His Cross

Then He said to them all, "If anyone desires to come after Me, let him deny himself, and take up his cross daily, and follow Me. For whoever desires to save his life will lose it, but whoever loses his life for My sake will save it."

Luke 9:23-24 NKJV

When Jesus addressed His disciples, He warned that each one must, "take up his cross and follow me." The disciples must have known exactly what the Master meant. In Jesus' day, prisoners were forced to carry their own crosses to the location where they would be put to death. Thus, Christ's message was clear: in order to follow Him, Christ's disciples must deny themselves and, instead, trust Him completely. Nothing has changed since then.

If we are to be dutiful disciples of the One from Galilee, we must trust Him and we must follow Him. Jesus never comes "next." He is always first. He shows us the path of life.

Do you seek to be a worthy disciple of Jesus? Then pick up His cross today and follow in His footsteps. When you do, you can walk with confidence: He will never lead you astray.

– Your Daily Journey Through Psalms –

You reveal the path of life to me; in Your presence is abundant joy; in Your right hand are eternal pleasures.

Psalm 16:11 HCSB

His Peace

But now in Christ Jesus you who once were far off have been brought near by the blood of Christ. For He Himself is our peace.

Ephesians 2:13-14 NKJV

For busy women, a moment's peace can be a scarce commodity. But no matter how numerous the interruptions and demands of the day, God is ever-present, always ready and willing to offer solace to those who seek "the peace that passes all understanding."

Have you found the genuine peace that can be yours through Jesus Christ? Or are you still rushing after the illusion of "peace and happiness" that the world promises but cannot deliver? Today, as a gift to yourself, to your family, and to your friends, claim the inner peace that is your spiritual birthright: the peace of Jesus Christ. It is offered freely; it has been paid for in full; it is yours for the asking. So ask. And then share.

In the center of a hurricane there is absolute quiet and peace. There is no safer place than in the center of the will of God.

Corrie ten Boom

– Your Daily Journey Through Psalms –
For He will give His angels orders concerning you, to protect you in all your ways.

Psalm 91:11 HCSB

Your Primary Obligation

For His divine power has given us everything required for life and godliness, through the knowledge of Him who called us by His own glory and goodness.

2 Peter 1:3 HCSB

When God created you, He equipped you with an assortment of talents and abilities that are uniquely yours. It's up to you to discover those talents and to use them, but the world may encourage you to do otherwise. At times, society will attempt to pigeonhole you, to standardize you, and to make you fit into a particular, preformed mold. Perhaps God has other plans.

At times, because you're an imperfect human being, you may become so wrapped up in meeting society's expectations that you fail to focus on God's expectations.

Who will you try to please today: God or society? Your primary obligation is not to please imperfect men and women. Your obligation is to strive diligently to meet the expectations of an all-knowing and perfect God. Period.

– Your Daily Journey Through Psalms –

You are the God who works wonders; You revealed Your strength among the peoples.

Psalm 77:14 HCSB

The Power of Prayer

Don't worry about anything, but in everything, through prayer and petition with thanksgiving, let your requests be made known to God.

Philippians 4:6 HCSB

"The power of prayer": these words are so familiar, yet sometimes we forget what they mean. Prayer is a powerful tool for communicating with our Creator; it is an opportunity to commune with the Giver of all things good. Prayer helps us find strength for today and hope for the future. Prayer is not a thing to be taken lightly or to be used infrequently.

Is prayer an integral part of your daily life, or is it a hit-or-miss habit? Do you "pray without ceasing," or is your prayer life an afterthought?

The quality of your spiritual life will be in direct proportion to the quality of your prayer life. Prayer changes things, and it changes you. Today, instead of worrying about your next decision, ask God to lead the way. Don't limit your prayers to meals or to bedtime. Pray constantly about things great and small. God is listening, and He wants to hear from you now.

– Your Daily Journey Through Psalms –

I call on You in the day of my distress, for You will answer me.

Psalm 86:7 HCSB

Sharing Your Testimony

And I say to you, anyone who acknowledges Me before men, the Son of Man will also acknowledge him before the angels of God.

Luke 12:8 HCSB

Our personal testimonies are extremely important, but sometimes, because of shyness or insecurities, we're afraid to share our experiences. And that's unfortunate.

In his second letter to Timothy, Paul shares a message to believers of every generation when he writes, "God has not given us a spirit of timidity" (1:7). Paul's meaning is clear: When sharing our beliefs, we, as Christians, must be courageous, forthright, and unashamed.

We live in a world that desperately needs the healing message of Christ Jesus. Every believer, each in his or her own way, bears responsibility for sharing the Good News of our Savior.

Billy Graham observed, "Our faith grows by expression. If we want to keep our faith, we must share it." If you are a follower of Christ, the time to express your belief in Him is now. You know how He has touched your heart; help Him do the same for others.

– Your Daily Journey Through Psalms –

From the rising of the sun to its going down the Lord's name is to be praised.

Psalm 113:3 NKJV

Accepting Christ

Yet we know that no one is justified by the works of the law but by faith in Jesus Christ. And we have believed in Christ Jesus, so that we might be justified by faith in Christ and not by the works of the law, because by the works of the law no human being will be justified.

Galatians 2:16 HCSB

God's love for you is deeper and more profound than you can imagine. God's love for you is so great that He sent His only Son to this earth to die for your sins and to offer you the priceless gift of eternal life. Now, you must decide whether or not to accept God's gift. Will you ignore it or embrace it? Will you return it or neglect it? Will you accept Christ, or will you turn from Him?

Your decision to accept Christ is the pivotal decision of your life. It is a decision that you cannot ignore. It is a decision that is yours and yours alone. It is a decision with profound consequences, both earthly and eternal. Accept God's gift: Accept Christ today.

Surrender to the Lord is not a tremendous sacrifice, not an agonizing performance. It is the most sensible thing you can do.

Corrie ten Boom

– Your Daily Journey Through Psalms –
But I call to God, and the Lord will save me.

Psalm 55:16 HCSB

Ask Him

Until now you have asked for nothing in My name. Ask and you will receive, that your joy may be complete.

John 16:24 HCSB

God gives the gifts; we, as believers, should accept them—but oftentimes, we don't. Why? Because we fail to trust our Heavenly Father completely, and because we are, at times, surprisingly stubborn. Luke 11 teaches us that God does not withhold spiritual gifts from those who ask. Our obligation, quite simply, is to ask for them.

Are you a woman who asks God to move mountains in your life, or are you expecting Him to stumble over molehills? Whatever the size of your challenges, God is big enough to handle them. Ask for His help today, with faith and with fervor, and then watch in amazement as your mountains begin to move.

God will help us become the people we are meant to be, if only we will ask Him.

Hannah Whitall Smith

— Your Daily Journey Through Psalms —

O praise the LORD, all ye nations: praise him, all ye people. For his merciful kindness is great toward us: and the truth of the LORD endureth for ever. Praise ye the LORD.

Psalm 117 KJV

Counting Your Blessings

The Lord bless you and keep you; The Lord make His face shine upon you, And be gracious to you.

Numbers 6:24-25 NKJV

Because you are a woman, you have been specially blessed by the Creator. God has given you blessings that are, in truth, simply too numerous to count. Your blessings include life, family, freedom, friends, talents, and possessions, for starters. But, your greatest blessing—a priceless treasure that is yours for the asking—is God's gift of salvation through Christ Jesus.

The gifts you receive from God are multiplied when you share them with others. Today, give thanks to God for your blessings and demonstrate your gratitude by sharing those blessings with your family, with your friends, and with the world.

Do we not continually pass by blessings innumerable without notice, and instead fix our eyes on what we feel to be our trials and our losses, and think and talk about these until our whole horizon is filled with them, and we almost begin to think we have no blessings at all?

Hannah Whitall Smith

– Your Daily Journey Through Psalms –

To You, O my Strength, I will sing praises; for God is my defense, my God of mercy.

Psalm 59:17 NKJV

When It's Hard to Be Cheerful

Finally, brothers, rejoice. Be restored, be encouraged, be of the same mind, be at peace, and the God of love and peace will be with you.

2 Corinthians 13:11 HCSB

On some days, as every woman knows, it's hard to be cheerful. Sometimes, as the demands of the world increase and our energy sags, we feel less like "cheering up" and more like "tearing up." But even in our darkest hours, we can turn to God, and He will give us comfort.

Few things in life are more sad, or, for that matter, more absurd, than a grumpy Christian. Christ promises us lives of abundance and joy, but He does not force His joy upon us. We must claim His joy for ourselves, and when we do, Jesus, in turn, fills our spirits with His power and His love.

When we earnestly commit ourselves to the Savior of mankind, when we place Jesus at the center of our lives and trust Him as our personal Savior, He will transform us, not just for today, but for all eternity. Then we, as God's children, can share Christ's joy and His message with a world that needs both.

— Your Daily Journey Through Psalms —
My lips will shout for joy when I sing praise to You.
Psalm 71:23 HCSB

Living Courageously

Do not fear, for I am with you; do not be afraid, for I am your God. I will strengthen you; I will help you; I will hold on to you with My righteous right hand.

Isaiah 41:10 HCSB

Christian women have every reason to live courageously. After all, the final battle has already been won on the cross at Calvary. But even dedicated followers of Christ may find their courage tested by the inevitable disappointments and fears that visit the lives of believers and non-believers alike.

When you find yourself worried about the challenges of today or the uncertainties of tomorrow, you must ask yourself whether or not you are ready to place your concerns and your life in God's all-powerful, all-knowing, all-loving hands. If the answer to that question is yes—as it should be—then you can draw courage today from the source of strength that never fails: your Heavenly Father.

There comes a time when we simply have to face the challenges in our lives and stop backing down.

John Eldredge

– Your Daily Journey Through Psalms –

Be of good courage, and he shall strengthen your heart, all ye that hope in the LORD.

Psalm 31:24 KJV

If You Become Discouraged

The Lord is the One who will go before you. He will be with you; He will not leave you or forsake you. Do not be afraid or discouraged.

Deuteronomy 31:8 HCSB

Even the most devout Christians can become discouraged, and you are no exception. After all, you live in a world where expectations can be high and demands can be even higher.

If you find yourself enduring difficult circumstances, don't lose hope. If you face uncertainties about the future, don't become anxious. And if you become discouraged with the direction of your day or your life, don't despair. Instead, lift your thoughts and prayers to your Heavenly Father. He is a God of possibility, not negativity. You can be sure that He will guide you through your difficulties and beyond them . . . far beyond.

The difference between winning and losing is how we choose to react to disappointment.

Barbara Johnson

– Your Daily Journey Through Psalms –
Help me, Lord my God; save me according to Your faithful love.

Psalm 109:26 HCSB

When We Must Wait for God

Wait on the Lord, and He will rescue you.

Proverbs 20:22 HCSB

L ife demands patience . . . and lots of it! We live in an imperfect world inhabited by imperfect people. Sometimes, we inherit troubles from others, and sometimes we create trouble for ourselves. In either case, what's required is patience.

Lamentations 3:25-26 reminds us that, "The Lord is wonderfully good to those who wait for him and seek him. So it is good to wait quietly for salvation from the Lord" (NIV). But, for most of us, waiting quietly for God is difficult. Why? Because we are fallible human beings, sometimes quick to anger and sometimes slow to forgive.

The next time you find your patience tested to the limit, remember that the world unfolds according to God's timetable, not ours, knowing that God's timing is always best.

Two signposts of faith: "Slow Down" and "Wait Here."

Charles Stanley

– Your Daily Journey Through Psalms –

Indeed, let no one who waits on You be ashamed; . . . For You are the God of my salvation; On You I wait all the day.

Psalm 25:3, 5 NKJV

Our Hopes and His Peace

And as they thus spake, Jesus himself stood in the midst of them, and saith unto them, Peace be unto you.

Luke 24:36 KJV

The beautiful words of John 14:27 give us hope: "Peace I leave with you, my peace I give unto you . . . ." Jesus offers us peace, not as the world gives, but as He alone gives. We, as believers, can accept His peace or ignore it.

When we accept the peace of Jesus Christ into our hearts, our lives are transformed. And then, because we possess the gift of peace, we can share that gift with fellow Christians, family members, friends, and associates. If, on the other hand, we choose to ignore the gift of peace—for whatever reason—we cannot share what we do not possess.

As every woman knows, peace can be a scarce commodity in our demanding world. How, then, can we find the peace that we so desperately desire? By turning our days and our lives over to God. Elisabeth Elliot writes, "If my life is surrendered to God, all is well. Let me not grab it back, as though it were in peril in His hand but would be safer in mine!" May we give our lives, our hopes, and our prayers to the Lord, and, by doing so, accept His will and His peace.

– Your Daily Journey Through Psalms –
Rest in the Lord, and wait patiently for Him.

Psalm 37:7 NKJV

Real Prosperity

Now godliness with contentment is great gain. For we brought nothing into this world, and it is certain we can carry nothing out. And having food and clothing, with these we shall be content.

1 Timothy 6:6-8 NKJV

We live in an era of prosperity, a time when many of us have been richly blessed with an assortment of material possessions that our forebears could have scarcely imagined. As believers living in these prosperous times, we must be cautious: we must keep prosperity in perspective.

The world stresses the importance of material possessions; God does not. The world offers the promise of happiness through wealth and public acclaim; God offers the promise of peace through His Son. When in doubt, we must distrust the world and trust God. The world often makes promises that it cannot keep, but when God makes a promise, He keeps it, not just for a day or a year or a lifetime, but for all eternity.

– Your Daily Journey Through Psalms –

For the Lord God is a sun and shield. The Lord gives grace and glory; He does not withhold the good from those who live with integrity. Lord of Hosts, happy is the person who trusts in You!

Psalm 84:11-12 HCSB

Purpose Day by Day

Yet Lord, You are our Father; we are the clay, and You are our potter; we all are the work of Your hands.

Isaiah 64:8 HCSB

Each morning, as the sun rises in the east, you welcome a new day, one that is filled to the brim with opportunities, with possibilities, and with God. As you contemplate God's blessings in your own life, you should prayerfully seek His guidance for the day ahead.

Discovering God's unfolding purpose for your life is a daily journey, a journey guided by the teachings of God's Holy Word. As you reflect upon God's promises and upon the meaning that those promises hold for you, ask God to lead you throughout the coming day. Let your Heavenly Father direct your steps; concentrate on what God wants you to do now, and leave the distant future in hands that are far more capable than your own: His hands.

In the very place where God has put us, whatever its limitations, whatever kind of work it may be, we may indeed serve the Lord Christ.

Elisabeth Elliot

– Your Daily Journey Through Psalms –

I will instruct you and show you the way to go; with My eye on you, I will give counsel.

Psalm 32:8 HCSB

Beyond the Comfort Zone

Be not afraid, only believe.

Mark 5:36 KJV

Risk is an inevitable fact of life. From the moment we arise in the morning until the moment we drift off to sleep at night, we face a wide array of risks, both great and small.

Some risks, of course, should be avoided at all costs—these include risky behaviors that drive us farther and farther away from God's will for our lives. Yet other risks—the kinds of risks that we must take in order to expand our horizons and expand our faith—should be accepted as the inevitable price we must pay for living full and productive lives.

Have you planted yourself firmly inside your own comfort zone? If so, it's time to reconsider the direction and scope of your activities. God has big plans for you, but those plans will most likely require you to expand your comfort zone—or leave it altogether.

With each new experience of letting God be in control, we gain courage and reinforcement for daring to do it again and again.

Gloria Gaither

– Your Daily Journey Through Psalms –

He restoreth my soul.

Psalm 23:3 KJV

The Importance of Words

No rotten talk should come from your mouth, but only what is good for the building up of someone in need, in order to give grace to those who hear.

Ephesians 4:29 HCSB

How important are the words we speak? More important than we may realize. Our words have echoes that extend beyond place or time. If our words are encouraging, we can lift others up; if our words are hurtful, we can hold others back.

Do you seek to be a source of encouragement to others? And, do you seek to be a worthy ambassador for Christ? If so, you must speak words that are worthy of your Savior. So avoid angry outbursts. Refrain from impulsive outpourings. Terminate tantrums. Instead, speak words of encouragement and hope to your family and friends, who, by the way, most certainly need all the hope and encouragement they can find.

The things that we feel most deeply we ought to learn to be silent about, at least until we have talked them over thoroughly with God.

Elisabeth Elliot

– Your Daily Journey Through Psalms –

Whoever of you loves life and desires to see many good days, keep your tongue from evil and your lips from speaking lies.

Psalm 34:12-13 NIV

What We Become

For it is God who is working among you both the willing and the working for His good purpose.

Philippians 2:13 HCSB

The old saying is both familiar and true: "What we are is God's gift to us; what we become is our gift to God." Each of us possesses special talents, gifted by God, that can be nurtured carefully or ignored totally. Our challenge, of course, is to use our abilities to the greatest extent possible and to use them in ways that honor our Savior.

Are you using your natural talents to make God's world a better place? If so, congratulations. But if you have gifts that you have not fully explored and developed, perhaps you need to have a chat with the One who gave you those gifts in the first place. Your talents are priceless treasures offered from your Heavenly Father. Use them. After all, an obvious way to say "thank You" to the Giver is to use the gifts He has given.

What we are is God's gift to us. What we become is our gift to God.

Anonymous

– Your Daily Journey Through Psalms –
In thee, O Lord, do I put my trust; let me never be put into confusion.

Psalm 71:1 KJV

He Cares for You

Trust in the Lord with all your heart, and do not rely on your own understanding; think about Him in all your ways, and He will guide you on the right paths.

Proverbs 3:5-6 HCSB

Open your Bible to its center, and you'll find the Book of Psalms. In it are some of the most beautiful words ever translated into the English language, with none more beautiful than the 23rd Psalm. David describes God as being like a shepherd who cares for His flock. No wonder these verses have provided comfort and hope for generations of believers.

On occasion, you will confront circumstances that trouble you to the very core of your soul. When you are afraid, trust in God. When you are worried, turn your concerns over to Him. When you are anxious, be still and listen for the quiet assurance of God's promises. And then, place your life in His hands. He is your Shepherd today and throughout eternity. Trust the Shepherd.

Sometimes the very essence of faith is trusting God in the midst of things He knows good and well, we cannot comprehend.

Beth Moore

– Your Daily Journey Through Psalms –

The LORD is my rock, and my fortress, and my deliverer; my God, my strength, in whom I will trust . . . .

Psalm 18:2 KJV

Out of Balance?

Happy is a man who finds wisdom and who acquires understanding.

Proverbs 3:13 HCSB

Sometimes, amid the concerns of everyday life, we lose perspective. Life seems out of balance as we confront an array of demands that sap our strength and cloud our thoughts. What's needed is a renewed faith, a fresh perspective, and God's wisdom.

Here in the 21st century, commentary is commonplace and information is everywhere. But the ultimate source of wisdom, the kind of timeless wisdom that God willingly shares with His children, is still available from a single unique source: the Holy Bible.

The wisdom of the world changes with the ever-shifting sands of public opinion. God's wisdom does not. His wisdom is eternal. It never changes. And it most certainly is the wisdom that you must use to plan your day, your life, and your eternal destiny.

He teaches us, not just to let us see ourselves correctly, but to help us see Him correctly.

Kathy Troccoli

– Your Daily Journey Through Psalms –

Whoever is wise will observe these things, and they will understand the lovingkindness of the Lord.

Psalm 107:43 NKJV

Don't Be Worried . . .
You Are Protected

But seek first the kingdom of God and His righteousness,
and all these things shall be added to you. Therefore do not
worry about tomorrow, for tomorrow will worry about its
own things. Sufficient for the day is its own trouble.

Matthew 6:33-34 NKJV

Because we are fallible human beings, we worry. Even though we, as Christians, have the assurance of salvation—even though we, as Christians, have the promise of God's love and protection—we find ourselves fretting over the countless details of everyday life.

If you are like most women, you may, on occasion, find yourself worrying about health, about finances, about safety, about relationships, about family, and about countless other challenges of life, some great and some small. Where is the best place to take your worries? Take them to God. Take your troubles to Him, and your fears, and your sorrows. And remember: God is trustworthy . . . and you are protected.

– Your Daily Journey Through Psalms –

Cast your burden on the Lord, and He will support you; He
will never allow the righteous to be shaken.

Psalm 55:22 HCSB

Accepting the Past

One thing I do, forgetting those things which are behind and reaching forward to those things which are ahead, I press toward the goal for the prize of the upward call of God in Christ Jesus.

Philippians 3:13-14 NKJV

When you find the courage to accept the past by forgiving all those who have injured you (including yourself), you can then look to the future with a sense of optimism and hope.

Because we are saved by a risen Christ, we can have hope for the future, no matter how troublesome our circumstances may seem. After all, God has promised that we are His throughout eternity. And, He has told us that we must place our hopes in Him.

Of course, we will face disappointments and failures while we are here on earth, but these are only temporary defeats. Of course, this world can be a place of trials and tribulations, but we are secure. God has promised us peace, joy, and eternal life. And God keeps His promises today, tomorrow, and forever.

– Your Daily Journey Through Psalms –

God—His way is perfect; the word of the Lord is pure. He is a shield to all who take refuge in Him.

Psalm 18:30 HCSB

His Healing Touch

The Lord says, "Peace, peace to the one who is far or near, and I will heal him."

Isaiah 57:19 HCSB

Are you concerned about your spiritual, physical, or emotional health? If so, there is a timeless source of comfort and assurance that is as near as your next breath. That source of comfort, of course, is God.

God is concerned about every aspect of your life, including your health. And, when you face concerns of any sort—including health-related challenges—God is with you. So trust your medical doctor to do his or her part, and turn to your family and friends for moral, physical, and spiritual support. But don't be afraid to place your ultimate trust in your benevolent Heavenly Father. His healing touch, like His love, endures forever.

Jesus Christ is the One by Whom, for Whom, through Whom everything was made. Therefore, He knows what's wrong in your life and how to fix it.

Anne Graham Lotz

– Your Daily Journey Through Psalms –

My soul, praise the Lord, and do not forget all His benefits. He forgives all your sin; He heals all your diseases. He redeems your life from the Pit; He crowns you with faithful love and compassion.

Psalm 103:2-4 HCSB

Accepting His Abundance

I am the vine, you are the branches. He who abides in Me, and I in him, bears much fruit; for without Me you can do nothing.

John 15:5 NKJV

Are you the kind of woman who accepts God's spiritual abundance without reservation? If so, you are availing yourself of the peace and the joy that He has promised. Do you sincerely seek the riches that our Savior offers to those who give themselves to Him? Then follow Him. When you do, you will receive the love and the abundance that Jesus offers to those who follow Him.

Seek first the salvation that is available through a personal, passionate relationship with Christ, and then claim the joy, the peace, and the spiritual abundance that the Shepherd offers His sheep.

If you want purpose and meaning and satisfaction and fulfillment and peace and hope and joy and abundant life that lasts forever, look to Jesus.

Anne Graham Lotz

– Your Daily Journey Through Psalms –
He who sacrifices thank offerings honors me, and he prepares the way so that I may show him the salvation of God.

Psalm 50:23 NIV

About Anger

Don't let the sun go down on your anger, and don't give the Devil an opportunity.

Ephesians 4:26-27 HCSB

Perhaps God gave each of us one mouth and two ears in order that we might listen twice as much as we speak. Unfortunately, many of us do otherwise, especially when we become angry.

Anger is a natural human emotion that is sometimes necessary and appropriate. Even Jesus Himself became angered when He confronted the moneychangers in the temple. But, more often than not, our frustrations are of the more mundane variety. When you are tempted to lose your temper over the minor inconveniences of life, don't. Turn away from anger, and turn instead to God.

Anger unresolved will only bring you woe.

Kay Arthur

Bitterness and anger, usually over trivial things, make havoc of homes, churches, and friendships.

Warren Wiersbe

– Your Daily Journey Through Psalms –
Refrain from anger and turn from wrath; do not fret—it leads only to evil.

Psalm 37:8 NIV

God's Roadmap

Every word of God is pure; He is a shield to those who put their trust in Him.

Proverbs 30:5 NKJV

The Bible is a roadmap for life here on earth and for life eternal. As Christians, we are called upon to study God's Holy Word, to trust its promises, to follow its commandments, and to share its Good News with the world.

As women who seek to follow in the footsteps of the One from Galilee, we must study the Bible and meditate upon its meaning for our lives. Otherwise, we deprive ourselves of a priceless gift from our Creator. God's Holy Word is, indeed, a transforming, life-changing, one-of-a-kind treasure. And, a passing acquaintance with the Good Book is insufficient for Christians who seek to obey God's Word and to understand His will.

The Reference Point for the Christian is the Bible. All values, judgments, and attitudes must be gauged in relationship to this Reference Point.

Ruth Bell Graham

– Your Daily Journey Through Psalms –

The words of the LORD are pure words: as silver tried in a furnace of earth.

Psalm 12:6 KJV

Integrity:
It's Always the Right Way

The one who lives with integrity lives securely, but whoever perverts his ways will be found out.

Proverbs 10:9 HCSB

Wise women know the importance of character. Character is built slowly over a lifetime. It is the sum of every right decision, every honest word, every noble thought, and every heartfelt prayer. It is forged on the anvil of honorable work and polished by the twin virtues of generosity and humility. Character is a precious thing difficult to build, but easy to tear down; godly women value it and protect it at all costs . . . and they encourage their children to do the same.

Sow an act, and you reap a habit. Sow a habit and you reap a character. Sow a character and you reap a destiny.

Anonymous

Integrity of heart is indispensable.

John Calvin

– Your Daily Journey Through Psalms –
I will set no wicked thing before mine eyes . . . .

Psalm 101:3 KJV

Trusting Your Conscience

*Let us draw near with a true heart in full assurance of faith,
our hearts sprinkled clean from an evil conscience and our
bodies washed in pure water.*

Hebrews 10:22 HCSB

It has been said that character is what we are when nobody is watching. How true. When we do things that we know aren't right, we try to hide them from our families and friends. But even then, God is watching.

Few things in life torment us more than a guilty conscience. And, few things in life provide more contentment than the knowledge that we are obeying the conscience that God has placed in our hearts.

If you sincerely want to create the best possible life for yourself and your loved ones, never forsake your conscience. And remember this: when you walk with God, your character will take care of itself . . . and you won't need to look over your shoulder to see who, besides God, is watching.

– Your Daily Journey Through Psalms –
*O righteous God, who searches minds and hearts, bring to an
end the violence of the wicked and make the righteous secure.*

Psalm 7:9 NIV

Difficult Decisions

Now if any of you lacks wisdom, he should ask God, who gives to all generously and without criticizing, and it will be given to him.

James 1:5 HCSB

Are you facing a difficult decision, a troubling circumstance, or a powerful temptation? If so, it's time to step back, to stop focusing on the world, and to focus, instead, on the will of your Father in heaven. The world will often lead you astray, but God will not. His counsel leads you to Himself, which, of course, is the path He has always intended for you to take.

Everyday living is an exercise in decision-making. Today and every day you must make choices: choices about what you will do, what you will worship, and how you will think. When in doubt, make choices that you sincerely believe will bring you to a closer relationship with God. And if you're uncertain of your next step, pray about it. When you do, answers will come. And you may rest assured that when God answers prayer, His answers are the right ones for you.

– Your Daily Journey Through Psalms –

How happy is everyone who fears the Lord, who walks in His ways!

Psalm 128:1 HCSB

Big Dreams

With God's power working in us, God can do much, much more than anything we can ask or imagine.

Ephesians 3:20 NCV

She was born in rural Mississippi and lived with her grandmother in a house that had no indoor plumbing. She made it to college in Nashville where she got her start in television. Over time, she moved to the top of her profession, and her show, "Oprah," was an unparalleled success.

When questioned about her journey to the top, Oprah said, "God can dream a bigger dream than we can dream for ourselves." She was right. So try Oprah's formula: increase the size of your dreams. Because the Good Lord's plan for each of us is big, very big. But it's up to us to accept the part, to step up on stage, and to perform.

The future lies all before us. Shall it only be a slight advance upon what we usually do? Ought it not to be a bound, a leap forward to altitudes of endeavor and success undreamed of before?

Annie Armstrong

– Your Daily Journey Through Psalms –
Those who are blessed by Him will inherit the land.

Psalm 37:22 HCSB

Faith and Wholeness

Now the just shall live by faith.

Hebrews 10:38 NKJV

A suffering woman sought healing in an unusual way: she simply touched the hem of Jesus' garment. When she did, Jesus turned and said, "Daughter, be of good comfort; thy faith hath made thee whole" (Matthew 9:22 KJV). We, too, can be made whole when we place our faith completely and unwaveringly in the person of Jesus Christ.

When you place your faith, your trust, indeed your life in the hands of Christ Jesus, you'll be amazed at the marvelous things He can do with you and through you. So strengthen your faith through praise, through worship, through Bible study, and through prayer. Then, trust God's plans. Your Heavenly Father is standing at the door of your heart. If you reach out to Him in faith, He will give you peace and heal your broken spirit. Be content to touch even the smallest fragment of the Master's garment, and He will make you whole.

– Your Daily Journey Through Psalms –

Yea, though I walk through the valley of the shadow of death, I will fear no evil: for thou art with me; thy rod and thy staff they comfort me.

Psalm 23:4 KJV

God's Forgiveness

But God, who is abundant in mercy, because of His great love that He had for us, made us alive with the Messiah even though we were dead in trespasses. By grace you are saved!
Ephesians 2:4-5 HCSB

God's power to forgive, like His love, is infinite. Despite your shortcomings, despite your sins, God offers you immediate forgiveness and eternal life when you accept Christ as your Savior.

As a believer who is the recipient of God's forgiveness, how should you behave towards others? Should you forgive them (just as God has forgiven you) or should you remain embittered and resentful? The answer, of course, is found in God's Word: you are instructed to forgive others. When you do, you not only obey God's command, you also free yourself from a prison of your own making.

When it comes to forgiveness, God doesn't play favorites and neither should you. You should forgive all those who have harmed you (not just the people who have asked for forgiveness or those who have made restitution). Complete forgiveness is God's way, and it should be your way, too. Anything less is an affront to Him and a burden to you.

– Your Daily Journey Through Psalms –
Help me, O Lord my God! Oh, save me according to Your mercy.

Psalm 109:26 NKJV

His Will and Ours

Blessed are those servants whom the master, when he comes, will find watching.

Luke 12:37 NKJV

God has will, and so do we. He gave us the power to make choices for ourselves, and He created a world in which those choices have consequences. The ultimate choice that we face, of course, is what to do about God. We can cast our lot with Him by choosing Jesus Christ as our personal Savior, or not. The choice is ours alone.

We also face thousands of small choices that make up the fabric of daily life. When we align those choices with God's commandments, and when we align our lives with God's will, we receive His abundance, His peace, and His joy. But when we struggle against God's will for our lives, we reap a bitter harvest indeed.

Today, you'll face thousands of small choices; as you do, use God's Word as your guide. And, as you face the ultimate choice, place God's Son and God's will and God's love at the center of your life. You'll discover that God's plan is far grander than any you could have imagined.

– Your Daily Journey Through Psalms –

Teach me to do Your will, for You are my God; Your Spirit is good. Lead me in the land of uprightness.

Psalm 143:10 NKJV

He Loves You

Humble yourselves therefore under the mighty hand of God, so that He may exalt you in due time, casting all your care upon Him, because He cares about you.

1 Peter 5:6-7 HCSB

When we worship God with faith and assurance, when we place Him at the absolute center of our lives, we invite His love into our hearts. In turn, we grow to love Him more deeply as we sense His love for us. St. Augustine wrote, "I love you, Lord, not doubtingly, but with absolute certainty. Your Word beat upon my heart until I fell in love with you, and now the universe and everything in it tells me to love you." Let us pray that we, too, will turn our hearts to our Heavenly Father, knowing with certainty that He loves us and that we love Him.

God is love and God's love is perfect. When we open ourselves to His perfect love, we are touched by the Creator's hand, and we are transformed, not just for a day, but for all eternity.

Today, as you carve out quiet moments of thanksgiving and praise for your Heavenly Father, open yourself to His presence and to His love. He is here, waiting. His love is here, always. Accept it—now—and be blessed.

– Your Daily Journey Through Psalms –

May Your faithful love rest on us, Lord, for we put our hope in You.

Psalm 33:22 HCSB

Protected by
the Hand of God

*For whatever is born of God overcomes the world. And this
is the victory that has overcome the world—our faith.*

1 John 5:4 NKJV

Have you ever faced challenges that seemed too big to handle? Have you ever faced big problems that, despite your best efforts, simply could not be solved? If so, you know how uncomfortable it is to feel helpless in the face of difficult circumstances. Thankfully, even when there's nowhere else to turn, you can turn your thoughts and prayers to God, and He will respond.

God's hand uplifts those who turn their hearts and prayers to Him. Count yourself among that number. When you do, you can live courageously and joyfully, knowing that "this too will pass"—but that God's love for you will not. And you can draw strength from the knowledge that you are a marvelous creation, loved, protected, and uplifted by the ever-present hand of God.

– Your Daily Journey Through Psalms –

*For the Lord watches over the way of the righteous, but the
way of the wicked leads to ruin.*

Psalm 1:6 HCSB

God's Gift to You

For everything created by God is good, and nothing should be rejected if it is received with thanksgiving.

1 Timothy 4:4 HCSB

Life is God's gift to you, and He intends that you celebrate His glorious gift. If you're a woman who treasures each day, you will be blessed by your Father in heaven.

For Christian believers, every day begins and ends with God and His Son. Christ came to this earth to give us abundant life and eternal salvation. Our task is to accept Christ's grace with joy in our hearts and praise on our lips. Believers who fashion their days around Jesus are transformed: They see the world differently, they act differently, and they feel differently about themselves and their neighbors.

So whatever this day holds for you, begin it and end it with God as your partner and Christ as your Savior. And throughout the day, give thanks to the One who created you and saved you. God's love for you is infinite. Accept it joyously and be thankful.

– Your Daily Journey Through Psalms –

You pulled me from the brink of death, my feet from the cliff-edge of doom. Now I stroll at leisure with God in the sunlit fields of life.

Psalm 56:13 MSG

The Wisdom to Be Humble

Who is wise and understanding among you? He should show his works by good conduct with wisdom's gentleness.

James 3:13 HCSB

Humility is not, in most cases, a naturally occurring human trait. Most of us, it seems, are more than willing to overestimate our own accomplishments. We are tempted to say, "Look how wonderful I am!" . . . hoping all the while that the world will agree with our own self-appraisals. But those of us who fall prey to the sin of pride should beware—God is definitely not impressed by our prideful proclamations.

God honors humility and He rewards those who humbly serve Him. So if you've acquired the wisdom to be humble, then you are to be congratulated. But if you've not yet overcome the tendency to overestimate your own accomplishments, then God still has some important (and perhaps painful) lessons to teach you—lessons about humility that you still need to learn.

Personal humility is a spiritual discipline and the hallmark of the service of Jesus.

Franklin Graham

– Your Daily Journey Through Psalms –

Though the Lord is great, he cares for the humble, but he keeps his distance from the proud.

Psalm 138:6 NLT

Laughing With Life

Laugh with your happy friends when they're happy . . . .
Romans 12:15 MSG

Barbara Johnson observes, "In our tense, uptight society where folks are rushing to make appointments they have already missed, a good laugh can be a refreshing as a cup of cold water in the desert." And she's right. Laughter is, indeed, God's gift, and He intends that we enjoy it. Yet sometimes, because of the inevitable stresses of everyday life, laughter seems only a distant memory.

As Christians, we have every reason to be cheerful and to be thankful. Our blessings from God are beyond measure, starting, of course, with a gift that is ours for the asking, God's gift of salvation through Christ Jesus.

Few things in life are more absurd than the sight of a grumpy Christian. So today, as you go about your daily activities, approach life with a grin and a chuckle. After all, God created laughter for a reason . . .

Laughter is nutrition for your soul, a tourniquet to stop the bleeding of a broken heart, an encouraging tonic for the discouraged.

Barbara Johnson

– Your Daily Journey Through Psalms –

Shout to the Lord, all the earth; be jubilant, shout for joy, and sing.

Psalm 98:4 HCSB

Sharing the Good News

I will also make you a light for the nations, to be My salvation to the ends of the earth.

Isaiah 49:6 HCSB

Whether you realize it or not, you are on a personal mission for God. As a Christian woman, that mission is straightforward: Honor God, accept Christ as your Savior, raise your family in a loving, Christ-centered home, and be a servant to those who cross your path.

Of course, you will encounter impediments as you attempt to discover the exact nature of God's purpose for your life, but you must never lose sight of the overriding purposes that God has established for all believers. You will encounter these overriding purposes again and again as you worship your Creator and study His Word.

Every day offers countless opportunities to serve God and to worship Him. When you do so, He will bless you in miraculous ways. May you continue to seek God's will, may you trust His Word, and may you place Him where He belongs: at the very center of your life.

– Your Daily Journey Through Psalms –
My heart is steadfast, O God, my heart is steadfast.

Psalm 57:7 NASB

Feeling Blue?

I have heard your prayer, I have seen your tears; surely I will heal you.

2 Kings 20:5 NKJV

The sadness that accompanies any significant loss is an inevitable fact of life. In time, sadness runs its course and gradually abates. Depression, on the other hand, is a physical and emotional condition that is highly treatable.

If you find yourself feeling "blue," perhaps it's a logical reaction to the ups and downs of daily life. But if you or someone close to you have become dangerously depressed, it's time to seek professional help.

Some days are light and happy, and some days are not. When we face the inevitable dark days of life, we must choose how we will respond. Will we allow ourselves to sink even more deeply into our own sadness, or will we do the difficult work of pulling ourselves out? We bring light to the dark days of life by turning first to God, and then to trusted family members, friends, and medical professionals. When we do, the clouds will eventually part, and the sun will shine once more upon our souls.

– Your Daily Journey Through Psalms –

For thou wilt light my candle: the LORD my God will enlighten my darkness.

Psalm 18:28 KJV

The Wisdom to Persevere

But as for you, be strong; don't be discouraged, for your work has a reward.

2 Chronicles 15:7 HCSB

The occasional disappointments and failures of life are inevitable. Such setbacks are simply the price that we must pay for our willingness to take risks as we follow our dreams. But even when we encounter setbacks, we must never lose faith.

The reassuring words of Hebrews 10:36 serve as a comforting reminder that perseverance indeed pays: "You have need of endurance, so that when you have done the will of God, you may receive what was promised" (NASB).

Are you willing to trust God's Word? And are you willing to keep "fighting the good fight," even when you've experienced unexpected difficulties? If so, you may soon be surprised at the creative ways that God finds to help determined people like you . . . people who possess the wisdom and the courage to persevere.

God never gives up on you, so don't you ever give up on Him.

Marie T. Freeman

– Your Daily Journey Through Psalms –

I have set the Lord always before me; because He is at my right hand I shall not be moved.

Psalm 16:8 NKJV

Your Potential

*Believe in the Lord your God, and you will be established;
believe in His prophets, and you will succeed.*

2 Chronicles 20:20 HCSB

D o you expect your future to be bright? Are you
willing to dream king-sized dreams . . . and are
you willing to work diligently to make those
dreams happen? Hopefully so—after all, God promises
that we can do "all things" through Him. Yet most of
us live far below our potential. We take half measures;
we dream small dreams; we waste precious time and energy on the distractions of the world. But God has other
plans for us.

You and your loved ones possess great potential, potential that you must use or forfeit. And the time to fulfill that potential is now.

If you want to reach your potential, you need to add a
strong work ethic to your talent.

John Maxwell

– Your Daily Journey Through Psalms –

*You pulled me from the brink of death, my feet from the cliff-
edge of doom. Now I stroll at leisure with God in the sunlit
fields of life.*

Psalm 56:13 MSG

Asking Him for Strength

Keep asking, and it will be given to you. Keep searching, and you will find. Keep knocking, and the door will be opened to you. For everyone who asks receives, and the one who searches finds, and to the one who knocks, the door will be opened.

Matthew 7:7-8 HCSB

Are you a woman in need of renewal? Ask God to strengthen you. Are you troubled? Take your concerns to Him in prayer. Are you discouraged? Seek the comfort of God's promises. Do you feel that you or your family members are living under a cloud of uncertainty? Ask God where He wants you to go, and then go there. In all matters, ask for God's guidance and avail yourself of God's power. You may be certain that He hears your prayers . . . and you may be certain that He will answer.

God uses our most stumbling, faltering faith-steps as the open door to His doing for us "more than we ask or think."

Catherine Marshall

– Your Daily Journey Through Psalms –

The LORD will give strength to His people; The LORD will bless His people with peace.

Psalm 29:11 NKJV

God's Guidebook

All Scripture is given by inspiration of God, and is profitable for doctrine, for reproof, for correction, for instruction in righteousness, that the man of God may be complete, thoroughly equipped for every good work.

2 Timothy 3:16-17 NKJV

God has given us a guidebook for righteous living called the Holy Bible. It contains thorough instructions which, if followed, lead to fulfillment, righteousness, and salvation. But, if we choose to ignore God's commandments, the results are as predictable as they are tragic.

God has given us the Bible for the purpose of knowing His promises, His power, His commandments, His wisdom, His love, and His Son. As we study God's teachings and apply them to our lives, we live by the Word that shall never pass away.

Today, let us follow God's commandments, and let us conduct our lives in such a way that we might be shining examples to our friends, to our families, and, most importantly, to those who have not yet found Christ.

– Your Daily Journey Through Psalms –

Show me thy ways, O LORD; teach me thy paths. Lead me in thy truth, and teach me: for thou art the God of my salvation; on thee do I wait all the day.

Psalm 25:4-5 KJV

How Character Is Built

We also rejoice in our afflictions, because we know that affliction produces endurance, endurance produces proven character, and proven character produces hope.

Romans 5:3-4 HCSB

Beth Moore correctly observed, "Those who walk in truth walk in liberty." As believers in Christ, we must seek to live each day with discipline, honesty, and faith. When we do, at least two things happen: integrity becomes a habit, and God blesses us because of our obedience to Him. Living a life of integrity isn't always the easiest way, but it is always the right way . . . and God intends that it should be our way, too.

Character isn't built overnight; it is built slowly over a lifetime. It is the sum of every sensible choice, every honorable decision, and every honest word. It is forged on the anvil of sincerity and polished by the virtue of fairness. Character is a precious thing—preserve yours at all costs.

– Your Daily Journey Through Psalms –

Blessed is the man who walks not in the counsel of the ungodly, nor stands in the path of sinners, nor sits in the seat of the scornful; but his delight is in the law of the Lord, and in His law he meditates day and night. He shall be like a tree planted by the rivers of water, that brings forth its fruit in its season, whose leaf also shall not wither; and whatever he does shall prosper.

Psalm 1:1-3 NKJV

Claiming Contentment in a Discontented World

But godliness with contentment is a great gain.
1 Timothy 6:6 HCSB

Everywhere we turn, or so it seems, the world promises us contentment and happiness. We are bombarded by messages offering us the "good life" if only we will purchase products and services that are designed to provide happiness, success, and contentment. But the contentment that the world offers is fleeting and incomplete. Thankfully, the contentment that God offers is all encompassing and everlasting.

Do you sincerely want to be a contented Christian? Then set your mind and your heart upon God's love and His grace. Seek first the salvation that is available through a personal relationship with Jesus Christ, and then claim the joy, the contentment, and the spiritual abundance that God offers His children.

– Your Daily Journey Through Psalms –
How priceless is your unfailing love! Both high and low among men find refuge in the shadow of your wings. They feast on the abundance of your house; you give them drink from your river of delights. For with you is the fountain of life; in your light we see light.

Psalm 36:7-9 NIV

Discipline Matters

I discipline my body and bring it under strict control, so that after preaching to others, I myself will not be disqualified.
1 Corinthians 9:27 HCSB

God's Word is clear: as believers, we are called to lead lives of discipline, diligence, moderation, and maturity. But the world often tempts us to behave otherwise. Everywhere we turn, or so it seems, we are faced with powerful temptations to behave in undisciplined, ungodly ways.

We live in a world in which leisure is glorified and misbehavior is glamorized. But God has other plans. He did not create us for lives of mischief or mediocrity; He created us for far greater things.

God rewards diligence and righteousness just as certainly as He punishes laziness and sin. As believers in a just God, we should behave accordingly.

If one examines the secret behind a championship football team, a magnificent orchestra, or a successful business, the principal ingredient is invariably discipline.
James Dobson

– Your Daily Journey Through Psalms –
Before I was afflicted I went astray, but now I keep Your word.

Psalm 119:67 HCSB

Words of Encouragement and Hope

The lips of the righteous feed many.

Proverbs 10:21 HCSB

The words that we speak have the power to do great good or great harm. If we speak words of encouragement and hope, we can lift others up. And that's exactly what God commands us to do!

Sometimes, when we feel uplifted and secure, it is easy to speak kind words. Other times, when we are discouraged or tired, we can scarcely summon the energy to uplift ourselves, much less anyone else. God intends that we speak words of kindness, wisdom, and truth, no matter our circumstances, no matter our emotions. When we do, we share a priceless gift with the world, and we give glory to the One who gave His life for us. As believers, we must do no less.

Words. Do you fully understand their power? Can any of us really grasp the mighty force behind the things we say? Do we stop and think before we speak, considering the potency of the words we utter?

Joni Eareckson Tada

– Your Daily Journey Through Psalms –

I will boast only in the Lord; let all who are discouraged take heart.

Psalm 34:2 NLT

The Attitude of Gratitude

*For everything created by God is good, and nothing should be
rejected if it is received with thanksgiving.*

1 Timothy 4:4 HCSB

For most of us, life is busy and complicated. As
women, we have countless responsibilities and
obligations. Amid the rush and crush of the daily
grind, it is easy to lose sight of God and His blessings.
But, when we forget to slow down and say "Thank You"
to our Maker, we rob ourselves of His presence, His
peace, and His joy.

Instead of ignoring God, we must praise Him many
times each day. Then, with gratitude in our hearts, we
can face the day's duties with the perspective and power
that only He can provide.

Think of the blessings we so easily take for granted: Life
itself; preservation from danger; every bit of health we
enjoy; every hour of liberty; the ability to see, to hear, to
speak, to think, and to imagine all this comes from the
hand of God.

Billy Graham

– Your Daily Journey Through Psalms –

*Surely the righteous shall give thanks to Your name; The
upright shall dwell in Your presence.*

Psalm 140:13 NKJV

Forgiveness and God's Plan

For if you forgive people their wrongdoing, your heavenly Father will forgive you as well. But if you don't forgive people, your Father will not forgive your wrongdoing.

Matthew 6:14-15 HCSB

God has big plans for you. Your challenge is straightforward: discern His path and follow it. But beware: bitterness can get in the way.

Bitterness is a roadblock on the path that God has planned for your life. If you allow yourself to become resentful, discouraged, envious, or embittered, you will become "spiritually stuck." But, if you obey God's Word and forgive those who have harmed you, you will experience God's peace as you follow His path.

If you seek to live in accordance with God's will for your life—and you should—then you will live in accordance with His commandments. And don't forget: for Christians, forgiving others is never optional; forgiveness is required.

God intends to use you in wonderful, unexpected ways if you let Him. The decision to seek God's plan and to follow it is yours and yours alone. Don't let bitterness, or any other sin, get in the way.

– Your Daily Journey Through Psalms –

Fret not thyself because of evildoers, neither be thou envious against the workers of iniquity. For they shall soon be cut down like the grass, and wither as the green herb.

Psalm 37:1-2 KJV

Your Spiritual Journey

Consider it a great joy, my brothers, whenever you experience various trials, knowing that the testing of your faith produces endurance. But endurance must do its complete work, so that you may be mature and complete, lacking nothing.

James 1:2-4 HCSB

The journey toward spiritual maturity lasts a lifetime. As Christians, we can and should continue to grow in the love and the knowledge of our Savior as long as we live. When we cease to grow, either emotionally or spiritually, we do ourselves a profound disservice. But, if we study God's Word, if we obey His commandments, and if we live in the center of His will, we will not be "stagnant" believers; we will, instead, be growing Christians . . . and that's exactly what God wants for our lives.

As I have continued to grow in my Christian maturity, I have discovered that the Holy Spirit does not let me get by with anything.

Anne Graham Lotz

– Your Daily Journey Through Psalms –

When I observe Your heavens, the work of Your fingers, the moon and the stars, which You set in place, what is man that You remember him?

Psalm 8:3-4 HCSB

God's Attentiveness

For the eyes of the Lord range throughout the earth to show Himself strong for those whose hearts are completely His.

2 Chronicles 16:9 HCSB

God is not distant, and He is not disinterested. To the contrary, your Heavenly Father is attentive to your needs. In fact, God knows precisely what you need and when you need it. But, He still wants to talk with you, and if you're a faithful believer, you should want to talk to Him, too.

Do you have questions that you simply can't answer? Ask for the guidance of your Creator. Do you sincerely seek the gift of everlasting love and eternal life? Accept the grace of God's only begotten Son. Whatever your need, no matter how great or small, pray about it. Instead of waiting for mealtimes or bedtimes, follow the instruction of your Savior: pray always and never lose heart.

Our future may look fearfully intimidating, yet we can look up to the Engineer of the Universe, confident that nothing escapes His attention or slips out of the control of those strong hands.

Elisabeth Elliot

– Your Daily Journey Through Psalms –

This is my comfort in my affliction, for Your word has given me life.

Psalm 119:50 NKJV

Smile

Jacob said, "For what a relief it is to see your friendly smile. It is like seeing the smile of God!"

Genesis 33:10 NLT

A smile is nourishment for the heart, and laughter is medicine for the soul—but sometimes, amid the stresses of the day, we forget to take our medicine. Instead of viewing our world with a mixture of optimism and humor, we allow worries and distractions to rob us of the joy that God intends for our lives.

So the next time you find yourself dwelling upon the negatives of life, refocus your attention to things positive. The next time you find yourself falling prey to the blight of pessimism, stop yourself and turn your thoughts around. With God as your protector and Christ as your Savior, you're blessed now and forever. So smile!

Laughter is like premium gasoline: It takes the knock out of living.

Anonymous

– Your Daily Journey Through Psalms –
Oh, clap your hands, all you peoples! Shout to God with the voice of triumph!

Psalm 47:1 NKJV

When Mistakes Become Lessons

The one who conceals his sins will not prosper, but whoever confesses and renounces them will find mercy.

Proverbs 28:13 HCSB

We are imperfect women living in an imperfect world; mistakes are simply part of the price we pay for being here. But, even though mistakes are an inevitable part of life's journey, repeated mistakes should not be. When we commit the inevitable blunders of life, we must correct them, learn from them, and pray to God for the wisdom not to repeat them. And then, if we are successful, our mistakes become lessons, and our lives become adventures in growth, not stagnation.

As you place yourself under the sovereign lordship of Jesus Christ, each mistake or failure can lead you right back to the throne.

Barbara Johnson

– Your Daily Journey Through Psalms –

How can a young man keep his way pure? By keeping Your word.

Psalm 119:9 HCSB

Full Confidence

Now may the God of hope fill you with all joy and peace in believing, so that you may overflow with hope by the power of the Holy Spirit.

Romans 15:13 HCSB

Sometimes, peace can be a scarce commodity in a demanding, 21st-century world. How, then, can we find the peace that we so desperately desire? By slowing down, by keeping problems in perspective, by counting our blessings, and by trusting God.

Dorothy Harrison Pentecost writes, "Peace is full confidence that God is Who He say He is and that He will keep every promise in His Word."

And Beth Moore advises, "Prayer guards hearts and minds and causes God to bring peace out of chaos."

So today, as you journey out into the chaos of the world, bring God's peace with you. And remember: the chaos is temporary, but God's peace is not.

To know God as He really is—in His essential nature and character—is to arrive at a citadel of peace that circumstances may storm, but can never capture.

Catherine Marshall

– Your Daily Journey Through Psalms –

Return unto thy rest, O my soul; for the LORD hath dealt bountifully with thee.

Psalm 116:7 KJV

Perseverance and Purpose

So we must not get tired of doing good, for we will reap at the proper time if we don't give up.

Galatians 6:9 HCSB

As you continue to seek God's purpose for your life, you will undoubtedly experience your fair share of disappointments, detours, false starts, and failures. When you do, don't become discouraged: God's not finished with you yet.

The old saying is as true today as it was when it was first spoken: "Life is a marathon, not a sprint." That's why wise travelers select a traveling companion who never tires and never falters. That partner, of course, is your Heavenly Father.

Are you tired? Ask God for strength. Are you discouraged? Believe in His promises. Are you defeated? Pray as if everything depended upon God, and work as if everything depended upon you. And finally, have faith that you play important role in God's great plan for mankind—because you do.

– Your Daily Journey Through Psalms –

Sustain me as You promised, and I will live; do not let me be ashamed of my hope.

Psalm 119:116 HCSB

It Pays to Praise

Therefore, through Him let us continually offer up to God a sacrifice of praise, that is, the fruit of our lips that confess His name.

Hebrews 13:15 HCSB

The Bible makes it clear: it pays to praise God. But sometimes, we allow ourselves to become so preoccupied with the demands of everyday life that we forget to say "Thank You" to the Giver of all good gifts.

Worship and praise should be a part of everything we do. Otherwise, we quickly lose perspective as we fall prey to the demands of the moment.

Do you sincerely desire to be a worthy servant of the One who has given you eternal love and eternal life? Then praise Him for who He is and for what He has done for you. And don't just praise Him on Sunday morning. Praise Him all day long, every day, for as long as you live . . . and then for all eternity.

I am to praise God for all things, regardless of where they seem to originate. Doing this is the key to receiving the blessings of God. Praise will wash away my resentments.

Catherine Marshall

– Your Daily Journey Through Psalms –

I am always praising you; all day long I honor you.

Psalm 71:8 NCV

First Things First

But whoever listens to me will live securely and be free from the fear of danger.

Proverbs 1:33 HCSB

"First things first." These words are easy to speak but hard to put into practice. For busy women living in a demanding world, placing first things first can be difficult indeed. Why? Because so many people are expecting so many things from us!

If you're having trouble prioritizing your day, perhaps you've been trying to organize your life according to your own plans, not God's. A better strategy, of course, is to take your daily obligations and place them in the hands of the One who created you. To do so, you must prioritize your day according to God's commandments, and you must seek His will and His wisdom in all matters. Then, you can face the day with the assurance that the same God who created our universe out of nothingness will help you place first things first in your own life.

Do you feel overwhelmed or confused? Turn the concerns of this day over to God—prayerfully, earnestly, and often. Then listen for His answer . . . and trust the answer He gives.

– Your Daily Journey Through Psalms –
My heart is steadfast, O God, my heart is steadfast.

Psalm 57:7 NASB

His Answer to Our Guilt

If My people who are called by My name will humble themselves, and pray and seek My face, and turn from their wicked ways, then I will hear from heaven, and will forgive their sin and heal their land.

2 Chronicles 7:14 NKJV

All of us have sinned. Sometimes our sins result from our own stubborn rebellion against God's commandments. And sometimes, we are swept up in events that are beyond our abilities to control. Under either set of circumstances, we may experience intense feelings of guilt. But God has an answer for the guilt that we feel. That answer, of course, is His forgiveness. When we confess our wrongdoings and repent from them, we are forgiven by the One who created us.

Are you troubled by feelings of guilt or regret? If so, you must repent from your misdeeds, and you must ask your Heavenly Father for His forgiveness. When you do so, He will forgive you completely and without reservation. Then, you must forgive yourself just as God has forgiven you: thoroughly and unconditionally.

– Your Daily Journey Through Psalms –

The sacrifices of God are a broken spirit; a broken and contrite hear, O God, you will not despise.

Psalm 51:17 NIV

Priorities for Marriage and Family

Never let loyalty and faithfulness leave you. Tie them around your neck; write them on the tablet of your heart. Then you will find favor and high regard in the sight of God and man.

Proverbs 3:3-4 HCSB

I t takes time to build a strong marriage . . . lots of time. Yet we live in a world where time seems to be an ever-shrinking commodity as we rush from place to place with seldom a moment to spare.

If you are a wife, has the busy pace of life robbed you of sufficient time with your husband? If so, it's time to adjust your priorities. And God can help.

When you allow God to help you organize your day, you'll soon discover that there is ample time for your spouse and your family . . . but there may not be enough time to do everything else. When choosing between family priorities and "everything else," choose family.

There is nothing wrong with a marriage that sacrifice wouldn't heal.

Elisabeth Elliot

– Your Daily Journey Through Psalms –
I have sought You with all my heart; don't let me wander from Your commands.

Psalm 119:10 HCSB

Community Life

About brotherly love: you don't need me to write you because you yourselves are taught by God to love one another.

1 Thessalonians 4:9 HCSB

As we travel along life's road, we build lifelong relationships with a small, dear circle of family and friends. And how best do we build and maintain these relationships? By following the Word of God. Healthy relationships are built upon honesty, compassion, responsible behavior, trust, and optimism. Healthy relationships are built upon the Golden Rule. Healthy relationships are built upon sharing and caring. All of these principles are found time and time again in God's Holy Word. When we read God's Word and follow His commandments, we enrich our own lives and the lives of those who are closest to us.

Love is an attribute of God. To love others is evidence of a genuine faith.

Kay Arthur

– Your Daily Journey Through Psalms –
How good and pleasant it is when brothers can live together!
Psalm 133:1 HCSB

Keep Thanking Him

And whatever you do, in word or in deed, do everything in the name of the Lord Jesus, giving thanks to God the Father through Him.

Colossians 3:17 HCSB

The words of 1 Thessalonians 5:18 remind us to give thanks in every circumstance of life. But sometimes, when our hearts are troubled and our lives seem to be spinning out of control, we don't feel much like celebrating. Yet God's Word is clear: In all circumstances, our Father offers us His love, His strength, and His Grace. And, in all circumstances, we must thank Him.

Have you thanked God today for blessings that are too numerous to count? Have you offered Him your heartfelt prayers and your wholehearted praise? If not, it's time slow down and offer a prayer of thanksgiving to the One who has given you life on earth and life eternal.

If you are a thoughtful Christian, you will be a thankful Christian. No matter your circumstances, you owe God so much more than you can ever repay, and you owe Him your heartfelt thanks. So thank Him . . . and keep thanking Him, today, tomorrow and forever.

– Your Daily Journey Through Psalms –

Give thanks to the Lord, for He is good; His faithful love endures forever.

Psalm 106:1 HCSB

A God of Infinite Possibilities

We are troubled on every side, yet not distressed; we are perplexed, but not in despair . . . .

2 Corinthians 4:8 KJV

As we travel the roads of life, all of us are confronted with streets that seem to be dead ends. When we do, we may become discouraged. After all, we live in a society where expectations can be high and demands even higher.

If you find yourself enduring difficult circumstances, remember that God remains in His heaven. If you become discouraged with the direction of your day or your life, turn your thoughts and prayers to Him. He is a God of possibility, not negativity. He will guide you through your difficulties and beyond them. And then, with a renewed spirit of optimism and hope, you can thank the Giver of all things good for gifts that are simply too profound to fully understand and for treasures that are too numerous to count.

When we face an impossible situation, all self-reliance and self-confidence must melt away; we must be totally dependent on Him for the resources.

Anne Graham Lotz

– Your Daily Journey Through Psalms –

This is my comfort in my affliction, for Your word has given me life.

Psalm 119:50 NKJV

New Beginnings

Do not remember the former things, nor consider the things of old. Behold, I will do a new thing.

Isaiah 43:18-19 NKJV

Each new day offers countless opportunities to serve God, to seek His will, and to obey His teachings. But each day also offers countless opportunities to stray from God's commandments and to wander far from His path.

Sometimes, we wander aimlessly in a wilderness of our own making, but God has better plans for us. And, whenever we ask Him to renew our strength and guide our steps, He does so.

Consider this day a new beginning. Consider it a fresh start, a renewed opportunity to serve your Creator with willing hands and a loving heart. Ask God to renew your sense of purpose as He guides your steps. Today is a glorious opportunity to serve God. Seize that opportunity while you can; tomorrow may indeed be too late.

The amazing thing about Jesus is that He doesn't just patch up our lives, He gives us a brand new sheet, a clean slate to start over, all new.

Gloria Gaither

– Your Daily Journey Through Psalms –
God, create a clean heart for me and renew a steadfast spirit within me.

Psalm 51:10 HCSB

In Focus

Let your eyes look forward; fix your gaze straight ahead.
Proverbs 4:25 HCSB

What is your focus today? Are you willing to focus your thoughts and energies on God's blessings and upon His will for your life? Or will you turn your thoughts to other things? This day—and every day hereafter—is a chance to celebrate the life that God has given you. It's also a chance to give thanks to the One who has offered you more blessings than you can possibly count.

Today, why not focus your thoughts on the joy that is rightfully yours in Christ? Why not take time to celebrate God's glorious creation? Why not trust your hopes instead of your fears? When you do, you will think optimistically about yourself and your world . . . and you can then share your optimism with others. They'll be better for it, and so will you. But not necessarily in that order.

Whatever we focus on determines what we become.
E. Stanley Jones

– Your Daily Journey Through Psalms –
The heavens declare the glory of God, and the sky proclaims the work of His hands.

Psalm 19:1 HCSB

Rest and Recharge Your Batteries

Come unto me, all ye that labor and are heavy laden, and I will give you rest.

Matthew 11:28 KJV

E ven the most inspired Christians can, from time to time, find themselves running on empty. The demands of daily life can drain us of our strength and rob us of the joy that is rightfully ours in Christ. When we find ourselves tired, discouraged, or worse, there is a source from which we can draw the power needed to recharge our spiritual batteries. That source is God.

God expects us to work hard, but He also intends for us to rest. When we fail to take the rest that we need, we do a disservice to ourselves and to our families.

Is your spiritual battery running low? Is your energy on the wane? Are your emotions frayed? If so, it's time to turn your thoughts and your prayers to God. And when you're finished, it's time to rest.

Life is strenuous. See that your clock does not run down.

Mrs. Charles E. Cowman

– Your Daily Journey Through Psalms –
Rest in God alone, my soul, for my hope comes from Him.

Psalm 62:5 HCSB

The Heart of a Servant

A generous person will be enriched.

Proverbs 11:25 HCSB

You are a wondrous creation treasured by God . . . how will you respond? Will you consider each day a glorious opportunity to celebrate life and improve your little corner of the world? Hopefully so because your corner of the world, like so many other corners of the world, can use all the help it can get.

Nicole Johnson observed, "We only live once, and if we do it well, once is enough." Her words apply to you. You can make a difference, a big difference in the quality of your own life and lives of your neighbors, your family, and your friends.

You make the world a better place whenever you find a need and fill it. And in these difficult days, the needs are great—but so are your abilities to meet those needs.

In the very place where God has put us, whatever its limitations, whatever kind of work it may be, we may indeed serve the Lord Christ.

Elisabeth Elliot

– Your Daily Journey Through Psalms –

Delight yourself also in the Lord, and He shall give you the desires of your heart.

Psalm 37:4 NKJV

Depending Upon God

Come to Me, all you who are weary and burdened, and I will give you rest. Take My yoke upon you and learn from Me, because I am gentle and humble in heart, and you will find rest for your souls. For My yoke is easy and My burden is light.

Matthew 11:28-30 HCSB

God's love and support never changes. From the cradle to the grave, God has promised to give you the strength to meet any challenge. God has promised to lift you up and guide your steps if you let Him. God has promised that when you entrust your life to Him completely and without reservation, He will give you the courage to face any trial and the wisdom to live in His righteousness.

God's hand uplifts those who turn their hearts and prayers to Him. Will you count yourself among that number? Will you accept God's peace and wear God's armor against the temptations and distractions of our dangerous world? If you do, you can live courageously and optimistically, knowing that you have been forever touched by the loving, unfailing, uplifting hand of God.

– Your Daily Journey Through Psalms –

Search for the Lord and for His strength; seek His face always. Remember the wonderful works He has done.

Psalm 105:4-5 HCSB

Busy with Our Thoughts

People's thoughts can be like a deep well, but someone with understanding can find the wisdom there.

Proverbs 20:5 NCV

Because we are human, we are always busy with our thoughts. We simply can't help ourselves. Our brains never shut off, and even while we're sleeping, we mull things over in our minds. The question is not if we will think; the question is how will we think and what will we think about.

Today, focus your thoughts on God and His will. And if you've been plagued by pessimism and doubt, stop thinking like that! Place your faith in God and give thanks for His blessings. Think optimistically about your world and your life. It's the wise way to use your mind. And besides, since you will always be busy with your thoughts, you might as well make those thoughts pleasing (to God) and helpful (to you and yours).

No matter how little we can change about our circumstances, we always have a choice about our attitude toward the situation.

Vonette Bright

– Your Daily Journey Through Psalms –

Let the words of my mouth, and the meditation of my heart, be acceptable in thy sight, O Lord, my strength and my redeemer.

Psalm 19:14 KJV

Embracing Every Stage of Life

The glory of young men is their strength, and the splendor of old men is gray hair.

Proverbs 20:29 HCSB

We live in a society that glorifies youth. The messages that we receive from the media are unrelenting: We are told that we must do everything within our power to retain youthful values and a youthful appearance. The goal, we are told, is to remain "forever young"—yet this goal is not only unrealistic, it is also unworthy of women who understand what genuine beauty is, and what it isn't. When it comes to "health and beauty" . . . you should focus more on health than on beauty. In fact, when you take care of your physical, spiritual, and mental health, your appearance will tend to take care of itself. And remember: God loves you during every stage of life—so embrace the aging process for what it is: an opportunity to grow closer to your loved ones and to your Creator.

Youth and age touch only the surface of our lives.

C. S. Lewis

– Your Daily Journey Through Psalms –

Don't discard me in my old age: as my strength fails, do not abandon me.

Psalm 71:9 HCSB

The Balancing Act

Come to Me, all you who labor and are heavy laden, and I will give you rest. Take My yoke upon you and learn from Me, for I am gentle and lowly in heart, and you will find rest for your souls. For My yoke is easy and My burden is light.
Matthew 11:28-30 NKJV

Face facts: life is a delicate balancing act, a tight-rope walk with over-commitment on one side and under-commitment on the other. And it's up to each of us to walk carefully on that rope, not falling prey to pride (which causes us to attempt too much) or to fear (which causes us to attempt too little).

God's Word promises us the possibility of abundance (John 10:10). And we are far more likely to experience that abundance when we lead balanced lives.

Are you doing too much—or too little? If so, it's time to have a little chat with God. And if you listen carefully to His instructions, you strive to achieve a more balanced life, a life that's right for you and your loved ones. When you do, everybody wins.

I came that they may have life, and have it abundantly.
John 10:10 NASB

– Your Daily Journey Through Psalms –
You are my hope, O Lord God; You are my trust from my youth.

Psalm 71:5 NKJV

The Best Day to Celebrate

Rejoice in the Lord always. I will say it again: Rejoice!
Philippians 4:4 HCSB

What is the best day to celebrate life? This one! Today and every day should be a day of prayer and celebration as we consider the Good News of God's free gift: salvation through Jesus Christ.

What do you expect from the day ahead? Are you expecting God to do wonderful things, or are you living beneath a cloud of apprehension and doubt? The familiar words of Psalm 118:24 remind us of a profound yet simple truth: "This is the day which the LORD hath made" (KJV). Our duty, as believers, is to rejoice in God's marvelous creation. Now.

Our God is the sovereign Creator of the universe! He loves us as His own children and has provided every good thing we have; He is worthy of our praise every moment.

Shirley Dobson

– Your Daily Journey Through Psalms –
This is the day the LORD has made; we will rejoice and be glad in it.

Psalm 118:24 NKJV

Worshipping the Christ Child

For there is born to you this day in the city of David a Savior, who is Christ the Lord. And this will be the sign to you: You will find a Babe wrapped in swaddling cloths, lying in a manger.

Luke 2:11-12 NKJV

God sent His Son to transform the world and to save it. The Christ Child was born in the most humble of circumstances: in a nondescript village, to parents of simple means, far from the seats of earthly power.

God sent His Son, not as a conqueror or a king, but as an innocent babe. Jesus came, not to be served, but to serve. Jesus did not preach a message of retribution or revenge; He spoke words of compassion and forgiveness. We must do our best to imitate Him.

In the second chapter of Luke, we read about shepherds who were tending their flocks on the night Christ was born. May we, like those shepherds of old, leave our fields—wherever they may be—and pause to worship God's priceless gift: His only begotten Son.

– Your Daily Journey Through Psalms –

I rejoiced with those who said to me, "Let us go to the house of the Lord."

Psalm 122:1 HCSB

Considering the Cross

For Christ did not send me to baptize, but to preach the gospel—not with clever words, so that the cross of Christ will not be emptied of its effect.

1 Corinthians 1:17 HCSB

A s we consider Christ's sacrifice on the cross, we should be profoundly humbled and profoundly grateful. And today, as we come to Christ in prayer, we should do so in a spirit of quiet, heartfelt devotion to the One who gave His life so that we might have life eternal.

He was the Son of God, but He wore a crown of thorns. He was the Savior of mankind, yet He was put to death on a roughhewn cross made of wood. He offered His healing touch to an unsaved world, and yet the same hands that had healed the sick and raised the dead were pierced with nails.

Christ humbled Himself on a cross—for you. He shed His blood—for you. He has offered to walk with you through this life and throughout all eternity. As you approach Him today in prayer, think about His sacrifice and His grace. And be humble.

– Your Daily Journey Through Psalms –

I was helpless, and He saved me.

Psalm 116:6 HCSB

A Glorious Opportunity

Don't work only while being watched, in order to please men, but as slaves of Christ, do God's will from your heart. Render service with a good attitude, as to the Lord and not to men.
Ephesians 6:6-7 HCSB

Can you honestly say that you are an enthusiastic believer? Are you passionate about your faith and excited about your path? Hopefully so. But if your zest for life has waned, it is now time to redirect your efforts and recharge your spiritual batteries. And that means refocusing your priorities by putting God first.

Nothing is more important than your wholehearted commitment to your Creator and to His only begotten Son. Your faith must never be an afterthought; it must be your ultimate priority, your ultimate possession, and your ultimate passion.

You are the recipient of Christ's sacrificial love. Accept it enthusiastically and share it passionately. Jesus deserves your enthusiasm; the world deserves it; and you deserve the experience of sharing it.

– Your Daily Journey Through Psalms –
Because you've always stood up for me, I'm free to run and play.

Psalm 63:7 MSG

Your Eternal Journey

For God so loved the world that He gave His only begotten Son, that whoever believes in Him should not perish but have everlasting life.

John 3:16 NKJV

Eternal life is not an event that begins when you die. Eternal life begins when you invite Jesus into your heart right here on earth. So it's important to remember that God's plans for you are not limited to the ups and downs of everyday life. If you've allowed Jesus to reign over your heart, you've already begun your eternal journey.

As mere mortals, our vision for the future, like our lives here on earth, is limited. God's vision is not burdened by such limitations: His plans extend throughout all eternity.

Let us praise the Creator for His priceless gift, and let us share the Good News with all who cross our paths. We return our Father's love by accepting His grace and by sharing His message and His love. When we do, we are blessed here on earth and throughout all eternity.

– Your Daily Journey Through Psalms –
You will show me the path of life; in Your presence is fullness of joy; at Your right hand are pleasures forevermore.

Psalm 16:11 NKJV

Following Christ

But whoever keeps His word, truly in him the love of God is perfected. This is how we know we are in Him: the one who says he remains in Him should walk just as He walked.

1 John 2:5-6 HCSB

Each day, as we awaken from sleep, we are confronted with countless opportunities to serve God and to follow in the footsteps of His Son. When we do, our Heavenly Father guides our steps and blesses our endeavors.

As citizens of a fast-changing world, we face challenges that sometimes leave us feeling overworked, overcommitted, and overwhelmed. But God has different plans for us. He intends that we slow down long enough to praise Him and to glorify His Son. When we do, He lifts our spirits and enriches our lives.

Today provides a glorious opportunity to place yourself in the service of the One who is the Giver of all blessings. May you seek His will, may you trust His Word, and may you walk in the footsteps of His Son.

– Your Daily Journey Through Psalms –

I will thank you, Lord, in front of all the people. I will sing your praises among the nations. For your unfailing love is higher than the heavens. Your faithfulness reaches to the clouds.

Psalm 108:3-4 NLT

Cheerful Generosity

So let each one give as he purposes in his heart, not grudgingly or of necessity; for God loves a cheerful giver.

2 Corinthians 9:7 NKJV

Are you a cheerful giver? If you intend to obey God's commandments, you must be. When you give, God looks not only at the quality of your gift, but also at the condition of your heart. If you give generously, joyfully, and without complaint, you obey God's Word. But, if you make your gifts grudgingly, or if the motivation for your gift is selfish, you disobey your Creator, even if you have tithed in accordance with Biblical principles.

Today, take God's commandments to heart and make this pledge: Be a cheerful, generous, courageous giver. The world needs your help, and you need the spiritual rewards that will be yours when you give faithfully, prayerfully, and cheerfully.

When somebody needs a helping hand, he doesn't need it tomorrow or the next day. He needs it now, and that's exactly when you should offer to help. Good deeds, if they are really good, happen sooner rather than later.

Marie T. Freeman

– Your Daily Journey Through Psalms –

Blessed is he that considereth the poor: the LORD will deliver him in time of trouble.

Psalm 41:1 KJV

God's Faithfulness

God is faithful, by whom you were called into the fellowship of His Son, Jesus Christ our Lord.

1 Corinthians 1:9 NKJV

God is faithful to us even when we are not faithful to Him. God keeps His promises to us even when we stray far from His path. God offers us countless blessings, but He does not force His blessings upon us. If we are to experience His love and His grace, we must claim them for ourselves.

God is with you. Listen prayerfully to the quiet voice of your Heavenly Father. Talk with God often; seek His guidance; watch for His signs; listen to the wisdom that He shares through the reliable voice of your own conscience.

God loves you, and you deserve all the best that God has to offer. You can claim His blessings today by being faithful to Him.

It is a joy that God never abandons His children. He guides faithfully all who listen to His directions.

Corrie ten Boom

– Your Daily Journey Through Psalms –

Blessed is he whose help is the God of Jacob, whose hope is in the LORD his God, the Maker of heaven and earth, the sea, and everything in them—the LORD, who remains faithful forever.

Psalm 146:5-6 NIV

Our Merciful Father

See, we count as blessed those who have endured. You have heard of Job's endurance and have seen the outcome from the Lord: the Lord is very compassionate and merciful.

James 5:11 HCSB

God's hand offers forgiveness and salvation. God's mercy, like His love, is infinite and everlasting—it knows no boundaries. As a demonstration of His mercy, God sent His only Son to die for our sins, and we must praise our Creator for that priceless gift.

Romans 3:23 reminds us of a universal truth: "All have sinned, and come short of the glory of God" (KJV). All of us, even the most righteous among us, are sinners. But despite our imperfections, our merciful Father in heaven offers us salvation through the person of His Son.

As Christians, we have been blessed by a merciful, loving God. May we accept His mercy. And may we, in turn, show love and mercy to our friends, to our families, and to all whom He chooses to place along our paths.

– Your Daily Journey Through Psalms –

Have mercy upon me, O God, according to thy lovingkindness: according unto the multitude of thy tender mercies blot out my transgressions. Wash me thoroughly from mine iniquity, and cleanse me from my sin.

Psalm 51:1-2 KJV

When Grief Visits

But God, who comforts the humble, comforted us . . . .
2 Corinthians 7:6 HCSB

Grief visits all of us who live long and love deeply. When we lose a loved one, or when we experience any other profound loss, darkness overwhelms us for a while, and it seems as if we cannot summon the strength to face another day—but, with God's help, we can.

Thankfully, God promises that He is "close to the brokenhearted" (Psalm 34:18 NIV). In times of intense sadness, we can turn to Him, and we can turn to close friends and family. When we do, we can be comforted . . . and in time we will be healed.

Concentration camp survivor Corrie ten Boom noted, "There is no pit so deep that God's love is not deeper still." Let is remember those words and live by them . . . especially when the days seem dark.

Suffering may be someone's fault or it may not be anyone's fault. But if given to God, our suffering becomes an opportunity to experience the power of God at work in our lives and to give glory to Him.

Anne Graham Lotz

– Your Daily Journey Through Psalms –
The Lord is for me; I will not be afraid. What can man do to me?

Psalm 118:6 HCSB

Look for the Joy

I am come that they might have life, and that they might have it more abundantly.

John 10:10 KJV

Barbara Johnson says, "You have to look for the joy. Look for the light of God that is hitting your life, and you will find sparkles you didn't know were there."

Have you experienced that kind of joy? Hopefully so, because it's not enough to hear someone else talk about being joyful—you must actually experience that kind of joy in order to understand it.

Should you expect to be a joy-filled woman 24 hours a day, seven days a week, from this moment on? No. But you can (and should) experience pockets of joy frequently—that's the kind of joy-filled life that a woman like you deserves to live.

You have to look for the joy. Look for the light of God that is hitting your life, and you will find sparkles you didn't know were there.

Barbara Johnson

– Your Daily Journey Through Psalms –

You will show me the path of life; in Your presence is fullness of joy; at Your right hand are pleasures forevermore.

Psalm 16:11 NKJV

Listening to God

The one who is from God listens to God's words. This is why you don't listen, because you are not from God.

John 8:47 HCSB

Sometimes God speaks loudly and clearly. More often, He speaks in a quiet voice—and if you are wise, you will be listening carefully when He does. To do so, you must carve out quiet moments each day to study His Word and sense His direction.

Can you quiet yourself long enough to listen to your conscience? Are you attuned to the subtle guidance of your intuition? Are you willing to pray sincerely and then to wait quietly for God's response? Hopefully so. Usually God refrains from sending His messages on stone tablets or city billboards. More often, He communicates in subtler ways. If you sincerely desire to hear His voice, you must listen carefully, and you must do so in the silent corners of your quiet, willing heart.

When we come to Jesus stripped of pretensions, with a needy spirit, ready to listen, He meets us at the point of need.

Catherine Marshall

– Your Daily Journey Through Psalms –

Blessed is the man whose strength is in You, whose heart is set on pilgrimage.

Psalm 84:5 NKJV

Picking and Choosing

You must follow the Lord your God and fear Him. You must keep His commands and listen to His voice; you must worship Him and remain faithful to Him.

Deuteronomy 13:4 HCSB

We are sorely tempted to pick and choose which of God's commandments we will obey and which of His commandments we will discard. But the Bible clearly instructs us to do otherwise.

God's Word commands us to obey all of His laws, not just the ones that are easy or convenient. When we do, we are blessed by a loving Heavenly Father.

John Calvin had this advice to believers of every generation: "Let us remember therefore this lesson: That to worship our God sincerely we must evermore begin by hearkening to His voice, and by giving ear to what He commands us. For if every person goes after his own way, we shall wander. We may well run, but we shall never be a whit nearer to the right way, but rather farther away from it." Enough said!

– Your Daily Journey Through Psalms –

The entirety of Your word is truth, and all Your righteous judgments endure forever.

Psalm 119:160 HCSB

Planning (and Working) for the Future

The plans of the diligent certainly lead to profit, but anyone who is reckless only becomes poor.

Proverbs 21:5 HCSB

Are you willing to plan for the future—and are you willing to work diligently to accomplish the plans that you've made? The Book of Proverbs teaches that the plans of hardworking people (like you) are rewarded.

If you desire to reap a bountiful harvest from life, you must plan for the future while entrusting the final outcome to God. Then, you must do your part to make the future better (by working dutifully), while acknowledging the sovereignty of God's hands over all affairs, including your own.

Are you in a hurry for success to arrive at your doorstep? Don't be. Instead, work carefully, plan thoughtfully, and wait patiently. Remember that you're not the only one working on your behalf: God, too, is at work. And with Him as your partner, your ultimate success is guaranteed.

– Your Daily Journey Through Psalms –
If the Lord delights in a man's way, he makes his steps firm.

Psalm 37:23 NIV

Worship Him

But an hour is coming, and is now here, when the true worshipers will worship the Father in spirit and truth. Yes, the Father wants such people to worship Him. God is Spirit, and those who worship Him must worship in spirit and truth.

John 4:23-24 HCSB

Where do we worship? In our hearts or in our church? The answer is both. As Christians who have been saved by a loving, compassionate Creator, we are compelled not only to worship the Creator in our hearts but also to worship Him in the presence of fellow believers.

We live in a world that is teeming with temptations and distractions—a world where good and evil struggle in a constant battle to win our hearts and souls. Our challenge, of course, is to ensure that we cast our lot on the side of God. One way to ensure that we do so is by the practice of regular, purposeful worship with our families. When we worship God faithfully and fervently, we are blessed.

In the sanctuary, we discover beauty: the beauty of His presence.

Kay Arthur

– Your Daily Journey Through Psalms –
Serve the Lord with gladness.

Psalm 100:2 HCSB

Passion for Life

Do not lack diligence; be fervent in spirit; serve the Lord.
Romans 12:11 HCSB

Are you passionate about your life, your loved ones, your work, and your faith? As a believer who has been saved by a risen Christ, you should be.

As a Christian woman, you have every reason to be enthusiastic about life, but sometimes the struggles of everyday living may cause you to feel decidedly unenthusiastic. If you feel that your zest for life is slowly fading away, it's time to slow down, to rest, to count your blessings, and to pray. When you feel worried or weary, you must pray fervently for God to renew your sense of wonderment and excitement.

Life with God is a glorious adventure; revel in it. When you do, God will most certainly smile upon your work and your life.

One can never consent to creep when one feels an impulse to soar.

Helen Keller

– Your Daily Journey Through Psalms –
Abundant peace belongs to those who love Your instruction; nothing makes them stumble.

Psalm 119:165 HCSB

Heaven Is Home

Let not your heart be troubled: ye believe in God, believe also in me. In my Father's house are many mansions: if it were not so, I would have told you. I go to prepare a place for you. And if I go and prepare a place for you, I will come again, and receive you unto myself; that where I am, there ye may be also.

John 14:1-3 KJV

Sometimes the troubles of this old world are easier to tolerate when we remind ourselves that heaven is our true home. An old hymn contains the words, "This world is not my home; I'm just passing through." Thank goodness!

This crazy world can be a place of trouble and danger. Thankfully, God has offered you a permanent home in heaven, a place of unimaginable glory, a place that your Heavenly Father has already prepared for you.

In John 16:33, Jesus tells us He has overcome the troubles of this world. We should trust Him, and we should obey His commandments. When we do, we can withstand any problem, knowing that our troubles are temporary, but that heaven is not.

– Your Daily Journey Through Psalms –

Thy kingdom is an everlasting kingdom, and thy dominion endureth throughout all generations.

Psalm 145:13 KJV

His Abundance

I have come that they may have life, and that they may have it more abundantly.

John 10:10 NKJV

The Bible gives us hope—as Christians we can enjoy lives filled with abundance.

But what, exactly, did Jesus mean when, in John 10:10, He promised "life . . . more abundantly"? Was He referring to material possessions or financial wealth? Hardly. Jesus offers a different kind of abundance: a spiritual richness that extends beyond the temporal boundaries of this world.

Is material abundance part of God's plan for our lives? Perhaps. But in every circumstance of life, during times of wealth or times of want, God will provide us what we need if we trust Him (Matthew 6). May we, as believers, claim the riches of Christ Jesus every day that we live, and may we share His blessings with all who cross our path.

It would be wrong to have a "poverty complex," for to think ourselves paupers is to deny either the King's riches or to deny our being His children.

Catherine Marshall

– Your Daily Journey Through Psalms –
Those who are blessed by Him will inherit the land.

Psalm 37:22 HCSB

Your Priceless Treasures

Then He took a child, had him stand among them, and taking him in His arms, He said to them, "Whoever welcomes one little child such as this in My name welcomes Me. And whoever welcomes Me does not welcome Me, but Him who sent Me."

Mark 9:36-37 HCSB

Think, for a moment, about the children in your life and the children in your world. Every child is a priceless gift from the Creator. And, with the Father's gift comes immense responsibility.

As parents, friends of parents, aunts, and grandmothers, we should understand the critical importance of raising our children with care, with love, and with God.

As Christians, we are commanded to care for our children . . . all of them. So let us care for our children here at home and pray for all children around the world. Every child is God's child. May we, as concerned adults, behave—and pray—accordingly.

Our faithfulness, or lack of it, will have an overwhelming impact on the heritage of our children.

Beth Moore

– Your Daily Journey Through Psalms –
Children are a gift from the LORD; they are a reward from him.

Psalm 127:4 NLT

Love With No Limits

For I am persuaded that neither death nor life, nor angels nor principalities nor powers, nor things present nor things to come, nor height nor depth, nor any other created thing, shall be able to separate us from the love of God which is in Christ Jesus our Lord.

Romans 8:38-39 NKJV

Even though we are imperfect, fallible human beings, even though we have fallen far short of God's commandments, Christ loves us still. His love is perfect; it does not waver—it does not change. Our task, as believers, is to accept Christ's love and to encourage others to do likewise.

In today's troubled world, we all need the love and the peace that is found through the Son of God. Thankfully, Christ's love has no limits. We, in turn, should love Him with no limits, beginning now and ending never.

Behold, behold the wondrous love, That ever flows from God above / Through Christ His only Son, Who gave / His precious blood our souls to save.

Fanny Crosby

– Your Daily Journey Through Psalms –

The Lord is near to all who call upon Him, to all who call upon Him in truth. He will fulfill the desire of those who fear Him; He also will hear their cry and save them. The Lord preserves all who love Him.

Psalm 145:18-20 NKJV

Your Daily Journey

Then He said to them all, "If anyone wants to come with Me, he must deny himself, take up his cross daily, and follow Me."

Luke 9:23 HCSB

Even the most inspired women can, from time to time, find themselves running on empty. Why? Because the inevitable demands of daily life can drain us of our strength and rob us of the joy that is rightfully ours in Christ. Thankfully, God stands ready to renew our spirits, even on the darkest of days. God's Word is clear: When we genuinely lift our hearts and prayers to Him, He renews our strength.

Are you almost too weary to lift your head? Then bow it—in prayer. Offer your concerns and your needs to your Father in Heaven. He is always at your side, offering His love and His strength.

Your search to discover God's purpose for your life is not a destination; it is a journey that unfolds day by day. And, that's exactly how often you should seek direction from your Creator: one day at a time, each day followed by the next, without exception.

– Your Daily Journey Through Psalms –

The fear of the Lord is the beginning of wisdom; all who follow His instructions have good insight.

Psalm 111:10 HCSB

Beyond Doubt

Now if any of you lacks wisdom, he should ask God, who gives to all generously and without criticizing, and it will be given to him. But let him ask in faith without doubting. For the doubter is like the surging sea, driven and tossed by the wind.

James 1:5-6 HCSB

If you've never had any doubts about your faith, then you can stop reading this page now and skip to the next. But if you've ever been plagued by doubts about your faith or your God, keep reading.

Even some of the most faithful Christians are, at times, beset by occasional bouts of discouragement and doubt. But even when we feel far removed from God, God is never far removed from us. He is always with us, always willing to calm the storms of life—always willing to replace our doubts with comfort and assurance.

Whenever you're plagued by doubts, that's precisely the moment you should seek God's presence by genuinely seeking to establish a deeper, more meaningful relationship with His Son. Then you may rest assured that in time, God will calm your fears, answer your prayers, and restore your confidence.

– Your Daily Journey Through Psalms –
Be still, and know that I am God.

Psalm 46:10 NKJV

Never Compromise

Love must be without hypocrisy. Detest evil; cling to what is good. Show family affection to one another with brotherly love. Outdo one another in showing honor.

Romans 12:9-10 HCSB

This world is God's creation, and it contains the wonderful fruits of His handiwork. But, it also contains countless opportunities to stray from God's will. Temptations are everywhere, and the devil, it seems, never takes a day off. Our task, as caring Christians, is to do all that we can to protect our families, our friends, and ourselves from the evils of the world.

We must recognize evil and fight it. When we observe life objectively, and when we do so with eyes and hearts that are attuned to God's Holy Word, we can no longer be neutral believers. And when we are no longer neutral, God rejoices while the devil despairs.

Don't condone what God condemns.

Anonymous

If you try to be everything to everybody, you will end up being nothing to anybody.

Vance Havner

– Your Daily Journey Through Psalms –
Don't get angry. Don't be upset; it only leads to trouble.

Psalm 37:8 NCV

The Commandment to Forgive

Be merciful, just as your Father also is merciful.
Luke 6:36 HCSB

Life would be much simpler if you could forgive people "once and for all" and be done with it. Yet forgiveness is seldom that easy. Usually, the decision to forgive is straightforward, but the process of forgiving is more difficult. Forgiveness is a journey that requires effort, time, perseverance, and prayer.

God instructs you to treat other people exactly as you wish to be treated. And since you want to be forgiven for the mistakes that you make, you must be willing to extend forgiveness to other people for the mistakes that they have made. If you can't seem to forgive someone, you should keep asking God to help you until you do. And you can be sure of this: if you keep asking for God's help, He will give it.

We will never comprehend what it cost our Lord in physical agony to offer His forgiveness to everyone—no exceptions.

Anne Graham Lotz

– Your Daily Journey Through Psalms –
My flesh and my heart may fail, but God is the strength of my heart . . . .

Psalm 73:26 HCSB

He Taught Us to Be Generous

I have shown you in every way, by laboring like this, that you must support the weak. And remember the words of the Lord Jesus, that He said, "It is more blessed to give than to receive."

Acts 20:35 NKJV

The thread of generosity is woven—completely and inextricably—into the very fabric of Christ's teachings. As He sent His disciples out to heal the sick and spread God's message of salvation, Jesus offered this guiding principle: Freely you have received, freely give (Matthew 10:8 NIV). The principle still applies. If we are to be disciples of Christ, we must give freely of our time, our possessions, and our love. All of us have been blessed, and all of us are called to share those blessings without reservation.

Today, make this pledge and keep it: Be a cheerful, generous, courageous giver. The world needs your help, and you need the spiritual rewards that will be yours when you share your possessions, your talents, and your time.

– Your Daily Journey Through Psalms –

Blessed is he that considereth the poor: the LORD will deliver him in time of trouble.

Psalm 41:1 KJV

The Ultimate Gift

Thanks be to God for His indescribable gift.
2 Corinthians 9:15 HCSB

Christ died on the cross so that we might have eternal life. This gift, freely given from God's only Son, is the priceless possession of everyone who accepts Him as Lord and Savior.

Thankfully, God's grace is not an earthly reward for righteous behavior; it is, instead, a blessed spiritual gift. When we accept Christ into our hearts, we are saved by His grace. The familiar words from the book of Ephesians make God's promise perfectly clear: "For it is by grace you have been saved, through faith—and this not from yourselves, it is the gift of God—not by works, so that no one can boast" (2:8-9 NIV).

God's grace is the ultimate gift, and we owe Him our eternal gratitude. Our Heavenly Father is waiting patiently for each of us to accept His Son and receive His grace. Let us accept that gift today so that we might enjoy God's presence now and throughout all eternity.

– Your Daily Journey Through Psalms –
O praise the LORD, all ye nations: praise him, all ye people. For his merciful kindness is great toward us: and the truth of the LORD endureth for ever. Praise ye the LORD.
Psalm 117 KJV

He Has a Plan for You

Now may the God of peace, who brought up from the dead our Lord Jesus—the great Shepherd of the sheep—with the blood of the everlasting covenant, equip you with all that is good to do His will . . . .

Hebrews 13:20-21 HCSB

God has a plan for your life. He understands that plan as thoroughly and completely as He knows you. And, if you seek God's will earnestly and prayerfully, He will make His plans known to you in His own time and in His own way.

If you sincerely seek to live in accordance with God's will for your life, you will live in accordance with His commandments. You will study God's Word, and you will be watchful for His signs.

Sometimes, God's plans seem unmistakably clear to you. But other times, He may lead you through the wilderness before He directs you to the Promised Land. So be patient and keep seeking His will for your life. When you do, you'll be amazed at the marvelous things that an all-powerful, all-knowing God can do.

– Your Daily Journey Through Psalms –

You will show me the path of life; in Your presence is fullness of joy; at Your right hand are pleasures forevermore.

Psalm 16:11 NKJV

Beyond Guilt

Blessed is the man who does not condemn himself.
Romans 14:22 HCSB

All of us have made mistakes. Sometimes our failures result from our own shortsightedness. On other occasions, we are swept up in events that are beyond our abilities to control. Under either set of circumstances, we may experience intense feelings of guilt. But God has an answer for the guilt that we feel. That answer, of course, is His forgiveness.

When we ask our Heavenly Father for His forgiveness, He forgives us completely and without reservation. Then, we must do the difficult work of forgiving ourselves in the same way that God has forgiven us: thoroughly and unconditionally.

If you're feeling guilty, then it's time for a special kind of housecleaning—a housecleaning of your mind and your heart . . . beginning NOW!

If God has forgiven you, why can't you forgive yourself?
Marie T. Freeman

– Your Daily Journey Through Psalms –
How can I know all the sins lurking in my heart? Cleanse me from these hidden faults. Keep me from deliberate sins! Don't let them control me. Then I will be free of guilt and innocent of great sin.

Psalm 19:12-13 NLT

The Joy He Has Promised

Now I am coming to You, and I speak these things in the world so that they may have My joy completed in them.
John 17:13 HCSB

Christ intends that we should share His joy. Yet sometimes, amid the inevitable hustle and bustle of life-here-on-earth, we can forfeit—albeit temporarily—the joy of Christ as we wrestle with the challenges of daily living.

Corrie ten Boom correctly observed, "Jesus did not promise to change the circumstances around us. He promised great peace and pure joy to those who would learn to believe that God actually controls all things." So here's a prescription for better spiritual health: Learn to trust God, and open the door of your soul to Christ. When you do, He will most certainly give you the peace and pure joy He has promised.

Jesus did not promise to change the circumstances around us. He promised great peace and pure joy to those who would learn to believe that God actually controls all things.

Corrie ten Boom

– Your Daily Journey Through Psalms –
Weeping may spend the night, but there is joy in the morning.
Psalm 30:5 HCSB

Pleasing God

Therefore, whether we are at home or away, we make it our aim to be pleasing to Him.

2 Corinthians 5:9 HCSB

Sometimes, because you're an imperfect human being, you may become so wrapped up in meeting society's expectations that you fail to focus on God's expectations. To do so is a mistake of major proportions—don't make it. Instead, seek God's guidance as you focus your energies on becoming the best "you" that you can possibly be. And, when it comes to matters of conscience, seek approval not from your peers, but from your Creator.

Who will you try to please today: God or man? Your primary obligation is not to please imperfect men and women. Your obligation is to strive diligently to meet the expectations of an all-knowing and perfect God. Trust Him always. Love Him always. Praise Him always. And seek to please Him. Always.

Get ready for God to show you not only His pleasure, but His approval.

Joni Eareckson Tada

– Your Daily Journey Through Psalms –
You are the God who does wonders; You have declared Your strength among the peoples.

Psalm 77:14 NKJV

God Responds

Therefore I say to you, whatever things you ask when you pray, believe that you receive them, and you will have them.

Mark 11:24 NKJV

When we petition God, He responds. God's hand is not absent, and it is not distant. It is responsive.

On his second missionary journey, Paul started a small church in Thessalonica. A short time later, he penned a letter that was intended to encourage the new believers at that church. Today, almost 2,000 years later, 1 Thessalonians remains a powerful, practical guide for Christian living.

In his letter, Paul advises members of the new church to "pray without ceasing." His advice applies to Christians of every generation. When we weave the habit of prayer into the very fabric of our days, we invite God to become a partner in every aspect of our lives. When we consult God on an hourly basis, we avail ourselves of His wisdom, His strength, and His love.

Today, allow the responsive hand of God to guide you and help you. Pray without ceasing, and then rest assured: God is listening . . . and responding!

– Your Daily Journey Through Psalms –

I sought the LORD, and he heard me, and delivered me from all my fears.

Psalm 34:4 KJV

God's Lessons

Listen to counsel and receive instruction so that you may be wise in later life.

Proverbs 19:20 HCSB

When it comes to learning life's lessons, we can either do things the easy way or the hard way. The easy way can be summed up as follows: when God teaches us a lesson, we learn it . . . the first time! Unfortunately, too many of us learn much more slowly than that.

When we resist God's instruction, He continues to teach, whether we like it or not. Our challenge, then, is to discern God's lessons from the experiences of everyday life. Hopefully, we learn those lessons sooner rather than later because the sooner we do, the sooner He can move on to the next lesson and the next, and next . . . .

God is able to take mistakes, when they are committed to Him, and make of them something for our good and for His glory.

Ruth Bell Graham

– Your Daily Journey Through Psalms –

Lord, tell me when the end will come and how long I will live. Let me know how long I have. You have given me only a short life . . . . Everyone's life is only a breath.

Psalm 39:4-5 NCV

Seeking God

You will seek Me and find Me when you search for Me with all your heart.

Jeremiah 29:13 HCSB

The familiar words of Matthew 6 remind us that, as believers, we must seek God and His kingdom. And when we seek Him with our hearts open and our prayers lifted, we need not look far: God is with us always.

Sometimes, however, in the crush of our daily duties, God may seem far away, but He is not. God is everywhere we have ever been and everywhere we will ever go. He is with us night and day; He knows our thoughts and our prayers. And, when we earnestly seek Him, we will find Him because He is here, waiting patiently for us to reach out to Him.

Today, let us reach out to the Giver of all blessings. Let us turn to Him for guidance and for strength. Today, may we, who have been given so much, seek God and invite Him into every aspect of our lives. And, let us remember that no matter our circumstances, God never leaves us; He is here . . . always right here.

– Your Daily Journey Through Psalms –
My soul thirsts for God, for the living God.

Psalm 42:2 NKJV

Living Righteously

But, as the One who called you is holy, you also are to be holy in all your conduct; for it is written, Be holy, because I am holy.

1 Peter 1:15-16 HCSB

When we seek righteousness in our own lives—and when we seek the companionship of those who do likewise—we reap the spiritual rewards that God intends for us to enjoy. When we behave ourselves as godly women, we honor God. When we live righteously and according to God's commandments, He blesses us in ways that we cannot fully understand.

Today, as you fulfill your responsibilities, hold fast to that which is good, and associate yourself with believers who behave themselves in like fashion. When you do, your good works will serve as a powerful example for others and as a worthy offering to your Creator.

Do nothing that you would not like to be doing when Jesus comes. Go no place where you would not like to be found when He returns.

Corrie ten Boom

– Your Daily Journey Through Psalms –

The righteous shall flourish like the palm tree: he shall grow like a cedar in Lebanon.

Psalm 92:12 KJV

His Path

We encouraged, comforted, and implored each one of you to walk worthy of God, who calls you into His own kingdom and glory.

1 Thessalonians 2:12 HCSB

How will you respond to Christ's sacrifice? Will you take up His cross and follow Him (Luke 9:23) or will you choose another path? When you place your hopes squarely at the foot of the cross, when you place Jesus squarely at the center of your life, you will be blessed.

The 19th-century writer Hannah Whitall Smith observed, "The crucial question for each of us is this: What do you think of Jesus, and do you yet have a personal acquaintance with Him?" Indeed, the answer to that question determines the quality, the course, and the direction of our lives today and for all eternity.

Experience has taught me that the Shepherd is far more willing to show His sheep the path than the sheep are to follow. He is endlessly merciful, patient, tender, and loving. If we, His stupid and wayward sheep, really want to be led, we will without fail be led. Of that I am sure.

Elisabeth Elliot

– Your Daily Journey Through Psalms –

I will instruct you and teach you in the way you should go; I will guide you with My eye.

Psalm 32:8 NKJV

Whom Do You Trust?

The one who understands a matter finds success, and the one who trusts in the Lord will be happy.

Proverbs 16:20 HCSB

Where will you place your trust today? Will you trust in the ways of the world, or will you trust in the Word and the will of your Creator? If you aspire to do great things for God's kingdom, you will trust Him completely.

Trusting God means trusting Him in every aspect of your life. You must trust Him with your relationships. You must trust Him with your finances. You must follow His commandments and pray for His guidance. Then, you can wait patiently for God's revelations and for His blessings.

When you trust your Heavenly Father without reservation, you can rest assured: in His own fashion and in His own time, God will bless you in ways that you never could have imagined. So trust Him, and then prepare yourself for the abundance and joy that will most certainly be yours through Him.

– Your Daily Journey Through Psalms –

As for God, His way is perfect; the word of the Lord is proven; He is a shield to all who trust in Him.

Psalm 18:30 NKJV

Beyond the World's Wisdom

No one should deceive himself. If anyone among you thinks he is wise in this age, he must become foolish so that he can become wise. For the wisdom of this world is foolishness with God, since it is written: He catches the wise in their craftiness.

1 Corinthians 3:18-19 HCSB

The world has it's own brand of wisdom, a brand of wisdom that is often wrong and sometimes dangerous. God, on the other hand, has a different brand of wisdom, a wisdom that will never lead you astray. Where will you place your trust today? Will you trust in the wisdom of fallible men and women, or will you place your faith in God's perfect wisdom? The answer to this question will determine the direction of your day and the quality of your decisions.

Are you tired? Discouraged? Fearful? Be comforted and trust God. Are you worried or anxious? Be confident in God's power. Are you confused? Listen to the quiet voice of your Heavenly Father—He is not a God of confusion. Talk with Him; listen to Him; trust Him. His wisdom, unlike the "wisdom" of the world, will never let you down.

– Your Daily Journey Through Psalms –

The fear of the Lord is the beginning of wisdom: a good understanding have all they that do his commandments: his praise endureth for ever.

Psalm 111:10 KJV

The Great Commission

Go, therefore, and make disciples of all nations, baptizing them in the name of the Father and of the Son and of the Holy Spirit, teaching them to observe everything I have commanded you. And remember, I am with you always, to the end of the age.

Matthew 28:19-20 HCSB

Are you a bashful Christian, one who is afraid to speak up for your Savior? Do you leave it up to others to share their testimonies while you stand on the sidelines, reluctant to share yours? Too many of us are slow to obey the last commandment of the risen Christ; we don't do our best to "make disciples of all the nations."

Christ's Great Commission applies to Christians of every generation, including our own. As believers, we are commanded to share the Good News with our families, with our neighbors, and with the world. Jesus invited His disciples to become fishers of men. We, too, must accept the Savior's invitation, and we must do so today. Tomorrow may indeed be too late.

– Your Daily Journey Through Psalms –

Teach me Your way, Lord, and I will live by Your truth. Give me an undivided mind to fear Your name.

Psalm 86:11 HCSB

And the Greatest of These

Love is patient; love is kind. Love does not envy; is not boastful; is not conceited; does not act improperly; is not selfish; is not provoked; does not keep a record of wrongs; finds no joy in unrighteousness, but rejoices in the truth; bears all things, believes all things, hopes all things, endures all things.

1 Corinthians 13:4-7 HCSB

The beautiful words of 1st Corinthians 13 remind us that love is God's commandment: "But now abide faith, hope, love, these three; but the greatest of these is love" (v. 13, NASB). Faith is important, of course. So, too, is hope. But, love is more important still. Christ showed His love for us on the cross, and, as Christians, we are called upon to return Christ's love by sharing it. Today, let us spread Christ's love to families, friends, and strangers by word and by deed.

You can be sure you are abiding in Christ if you are able to have a Christlike love toward the people that irritate you the most.

Vonette Bright

– Your Daily Journey Through Psalms –
The earth and everything in it, the world and its inhabitants, belong to the Lord.

Psalm 24:1 HCSB

Faith-filled Christianity

Commit your works to the Lord, and your thoughts will be established.

Proverbs 16:3 NKJV

A s you take the next step in your life's journey, you should do so with feelings of hope and anticipation. After all, as a Christian, you have every reason to be optimistic about life. As John Calvin observed, "There is not one blade of grass, there is no color in this world that is not intended to make us rejoice." But, sometimes, rejoicing may be the last thing on your mind. Sometimes, you may fall prey to worry, frustration, anxiety, or sheer exhaustion. What's needed is plenty of rest, a large dose of perspective, and God's healing touch, but not necessarily in that order.

A. W. Tozer writes, "Attitude is all-important. Let the soul take a quiet attitude of faith and love toward God, and from there on, the responsibility is God's. He will make good on His commitments." These words remind us that even when the challenges of the day seem daunting, God remains steadfast. And, so must we.

– Your Daily Journey Through Psalms –

My cup runs over. Surely goodness and mercy shall follow me all the days of my life; and I will dwell in the house of the Lord forever.

Psalm 23:5-6 NKJV

My Notes and Favorite Psalms

My Notes and Favorite Psalms

My Notes and Favorite Psalms

My Notes and Favorite Psalms

My Notes and Favorite Psalms

My Notes and Favorite Psalms

My Notes and Favorite Psalms